LIFE

AND

CONSCIENCE

A Hierarchical Perspective

MIGUEL OCHOA

iUniverse, Inc.
Bloomington

Life and Conscience
A hierarchical perspective

iUniverse books may be ordered through booksellers or by contacting:

iUniverse
1663 Liberty Drive
Bloomington, IN 47403
www.iuniverse.com
1-800-Authors (1-800-288-4677)

Because of the dynamic nature of the Internet, any web addresses or links contained in this book may have changed since publication and may no longer be valid. The views expressed in this work are solely those of the author and do not necessarily reflect the views of the publisher, and the publisher hereby disclaims any responsibility for them.

Any people depicted in stock imagery provided by Thinkstock are models, and such images are being used for illustrative purposes only.

Certain stock imagery © Thinkstock.

ISBN: 978-1-4759-6822-4 (sc)
ISBN: 978-1-4759-6823-1 (e)

Printed in the United States of America

iUniverse rev. date: 12/31/2012

INTRODUCTION

To any child who barely commences to open his eyes to the mysteries of the Cosmo surrounding him something appears obvious immediately, not only as a result of his studies but, even more, from the raw observation of Nature and the kaleidoscopic bombardment of sense data cluttering his youthful curiosity: a hierarchical stratification of events encompassing the entire spectrum of the physical world. Remote and vaguely conceived subatomic particles, he is told by the school teachers, come together to form a whole family of 'corpuscles' called atoms which themselves, their eager professors will emphasize, gather to form the chemical compounds defining the categories of 'substances' directly perceived by the senses and evolved in their complex associations into the manifolds of life.

But everything surrounding Man in his immediate environment, his enthusiastic lecturer will then explain, is constitutive part of the 'Earth', a round ball of 'matter' clustering with, at least, eight other similar objects in a planetary system centered by a large accumulation of flaming gases called 'The Sun', which we learn to identify with the blindingly bright hot spot appearing every clear morning from the East dissipating the darkness of the night.

But wait, our good teacher will add, don't lose track of the night because darkness will bring even more dazzling perspectives of the Heavens. Many of the bright spots twinkling cool and remote are nothing but myriads of 'suns' representing parts of a large cluster called 'The Milky Way' by the ancient Greeks. This cluster holds more than one hundred billions stars which, unfortunately, the modern gift of pollution brought down on us by 'progress' and industrialization has rendered for most of us practically impossible to behold in its serene and majestic beauty. And beware, he finally will add triumphantly, this enormous 'Milky Way' is nothing but a miserable speck in an ocean of receding galaxies which for lack of a better term we call 'The Universe', and according to present scientific fashion we conceive as 'exploding'.

Even in the organization of 'matter' around us there appears to be hierarchies. Biological compounds form unicellular organisms (like virus, bacteria and other protozoa), or specialized cellular units that join in complex aggregations (metazoan organisms) constituting the variety of animals and plants populating our immediate surroundings, which in their turn also coalesce into groups of animals or plants constituting herds, schools, packs, forests, anthills and in the case of Man, human societies.

What about the 'forces' providing for the cohesion of this cosmic integration? Modern Physics claims that four forces hold together the Universe: the strong and weak forces, which hold the atoms and subatomic particles together in harmonious more or less stable conformations (and of which we do not have direct sensory experience), electromagnetism, a force we have mastered in many ways and finally gravitation, the one more familiar to us but not because of that better understood.

Yet, even these forces would have not been sufficient to keep biological beings together. Structural boundaries, like the cell membrane, are needed to provide confinement and demarcation to the living organism, an interface capable of impeding cellular dissolution but requiring expenditure of substantial amount of energy, provided by chemical processes, to maintain. Finally intercellular cohesion keeps tissues in one piece permitting the existence and proliferation of metazoan organisms. Yet, the realization of these complex associations has not come easy to Man. Many of the facts were until recently not directly observable or obvious. We live at one end of a long scientific tradition which strongly influence our thoughts, believes and behavior. Large numbers of the facts above enumerated were until very recently, and some still are, controversial to a degree, mostly because they are removed from direct sensory experience.

For the ancient Greek philosophers the 'stuff' of the divine was entirely different to that of worldly things. Plato's icosahedrons and Aristotle's quintessence are only expressions of that notion. The pristine heavens could not be composed of the same corruptible and sordid substances from which we and all material bodies surrounding us are. Not even the atomists pretended that all atoms were equal. Those conclusions, of course, followed naturally from sense experience. Things on Earth were subjected to visible decay while the celestial bodies were eternal and immutable, an obvious sign of their superior and separate

Nature. Life itself was conceived as resulting from the penetration of a divine element into base matter, an essence or 'anima' which imbued earthly creatures with the gift of independent motion, a temporary state that like anything worldly eventually was bound to disappear or transform into something else.

It is a remarkable fact that not until the XIX Century, with the Theory of Evolution in Biology and the XX Century with the rise of Modern Physics, the essential unity and common origin of all that exists in the Cosmo was accepted. Everything we know, finally was realized, is composed of the same elemental units and building blocks (proton, neutrons electrons etc.), perceptible variations only resulting from the ways these elements associate with each other, both quantitatively and qualitatively. The manifolds of Nature, the apparently disparage and multifarious Forms of the material world are, we now know, the results of these fundamental arrangements. Ultimately all universal events are basically equally constituted. Even energy and matter, until relatively recent two totally independent dimensions of Reality, had today been revealed as different aspects of the same basic substratum of what 'exist'.

Modern Science also has exposed the fabric of universal events at our cosmic level of activity, a concatenation allowing the formulation of predictive relational laws that accounts for the immense success of our present technology. Although microcosmic events possess certain degree of inherent uncertainty they are, nevertheless, quantified and only some discrete 'configurations 'are permitted. Celestial mechanics, on the other hand, is amenable to exact description and prediction despite of the fact that no 'explanation' for the 'nature' of gravitation and motion has been found.

According to modern theories, Life, a unique conformation of matter on Earth, appears to have originated from the inanimate world some three billion years ago in the primitive pre-Cambrian seas (if we assume the first living organisms as reaching our planet from outer space riding on the back of meteorites or by any other unconventional means, we are only pushing the problem one step further) from non-living chemical compounds, and since then the process of hierarchical stratification has accelerated, a process in which we participate, whether willingly or reluctantly, by being beyond our power to control. Tellhard de Chardin was the first, in his cosmology, to attribute to all living forms a Consciousness whose complexity paralleled their position in the evolutionary scale.

The fate of Man, like that of any other social animal, depends fundamentally of the group; in the human case a vast array of cultural connotations including religious, linguistic, social, political and economic factors constitutive parts of our cultural heritage, imprints of 'civilized life'. This 'civilization' however is continuously evolving and human values steadily transformed with it, dragging mankind at an accelerating pace toward an unknown destination in the more or less distant future.

Organic theories of society are not new. The pre-Socratic philosopher Anaximenes is credited with the first written comparison of Man and Nature when in one of his fragments preserved by Stobaeus he states that "Just as our soul which is air holds us together so it is breath and air that encompasses the whole world". Ever since Plato's first attempt to compare Man with the State, in the Republic, there has been numerous efforts, not only in antiquity but even up to relatively recent times, to search for similarities between the human individual and the communities he forms. Philo of Alexandria with his theories of Man as a 'brachycosm' in his syncretistic works tried to harmonize Hebrew Religion with Greek Philosophy, and more recently John of Salisbury, Hobbes and Rousseau, among many others, pointed to some analogies between Man and society, more or less in a symbolic manner, as illustrations to graphically express their philosophical ideas. With the biological advances of the XVIII and XIX centuries, however, particularly with the firm establishment of the Cell Theory in Biology, organic views of human society gained in importance and became a vogue, at the beginning being used still metaphorically to make some points like was the case with Spencer, but later on were exposed in their own merits, 'literally' for what they represented, as was the case with the works of Lilienfeld, Worms and Novikow.

Organic theories, like their relatives microcosmic theories of Man, had fallen in disrepute since the XX Century because of logical and metaphysical objections (which I do not believe to be as formidable as they are purported to be), as well as the 'absence of practical consequences'. The real culprits, I think, are scientific 'atomism' and 'incertitude', on one hand, and on the other the impugnations of the existentialist doctrine with its denial of historical 'meaning' and the glorification of 'freedom' as the only valid attribute of the human 'Soul'. The notion of 'regularities' and 'order' in human affairs, from where predictions could be drawn and lessons learned from historical analysis, had been criticized, down played, and ridiculed by many as sterile 'scientification' of the humanities. History, it is claimed, has no 'plot' and Man has no 'Destiny'.

I believe these notions are mistaken on two counts. Firstly, recent findings in Bio-neurology cast serious doubts about our cherished conception of personal freedom. It appears that genetic and environmental factors influence the quality and specificity of neuronal associations, in other words, the physiology and morphology of these brain cells. If human behavior depends precisely on these associations, it would, by derivation, relate also to inherited and environmental conditions beyond our control at the present time. Freedom becomes nothing but a beautiful illusion, a myth difficult to dispel because of the lack of perceptual hindrances to our volitions (in view of the internal, non-sensorial character of these restrictions). Man, in reality, CANNOT BE EMANCIPATED FROM HIS HEREDITY AND ENVIRONMENTAL EXPERIENCES INCLUDING CULTURE OF WHICH HE IS A PRODUCT AND A PRISONER.

Secondly, I believe that although perhaps there is no discernible 'Plot' or 'Grand Design ' in history, there exist general trends we would all agreed upon: Namely the cumulative nature of 'technology' and the progressive increase complexity of human society with the coalescence of socio-political units into ever larger groups.

Contrary to other opinions, I think that from historic and cultural analysis TESTABLE HYPOTHESIS could be design with useful lessons for posterity. The inquire into history, as a manifestation of human evolution, could make possible predictions otherwise impossible. I also believe that Biology offers a clue to understand the cultural and historical vicissitudes of mankind, a model to investigate social dynamics.

CONTENTS

CHAPTER I

What is Life? What can we conclusively state to be the common denominator of everything we claim to be alive? The answer appears obvious even to any high school student growing during this most surprising 'biological revolution' of present times. Any self-replicating system underlined by a material substratum with some internal organization (the replicating unit) could be conceived as 'alive'. Implicit in this definition is the concept that the 'substratum' is made up of complex organic molecules with a backbone or skeleton of carbon, and few other (remarkable few) elements which fill and hook to the carbonic frame. If we now ask which is the smallest collection of these elements capable of fulfilling such requirements, the answer is also readymade and almost automatic: The nucleic acids RNA and DNA.

This answer, however, leaves us with some degree of dissatisfaction and confusion; there is something still evading us, something not for being subtle less important. If Life is represented and defined as auto-reproducing Form, there are basic structures in Nature also composed of complex molecular aggregates and, again, capable of growth and multiplication in a seemingly self-perpetuating process (assuming some basic requirements are met), but that are not fundamentally constituted of carbon: Crystals.

Crystals consist of repetitive units (the lattice) with specific and periodic arrangements of their constitutive elements which, under optimal environmental conditions, are capable of self-replication also. Our broad definition, therefore, includes then not only carbon based compounds but any other combination of elemental building blocks satisfying the preconditions above mentioned. In fact, there are scientists who believe that the original biological units were created of clays and other crystals rather than carbon compounds, which slowly 'usurped' their place in the biological machinery. However, these clay lattices lack one fundamental characteristic we associate with true Life; that is, an 'urge' to survive and reproduce its Form.

PERPETUATION AND PROGRESSIVE TRANSFORMATION OF A MORPHOLOGICAL BLUE PRINT, that is what seems to be the universal manifestation and characteristic of Life, from the most humble and rudimentary creature to the highly complex multi-cellular organisms. It almost appears as if this simple model acting as a template for evolution accounts as a single justification for the living world and its plurality, of which the most basic instincts of preservation and reproduction are but clear revelations.

Being so conceived Life immediately displays a unique feature, a structural property serving as a sharp dividing line from the inanimate or 'inorganic' world: A genuine sense of intelligible purpose. Purpose is the distinguishing property of Life, what makes it different to a piece of rock or the gyrations of celestial bodies, something that we can appreciate as an 'objective' specific goal: A deliberate directional activity.

But what does it means, we might ask, to possess such a sense of purpose? Doesn't it entail some precondition? We don't see any meaning in fire converting wood into ashes, no ascertainable 'reason to be' is apparent in the activity of inorganic or inanimate matter, nothing we can discover to have an 'aim'. In order to possess an 'aim' events need, at least for humans who are the 'inventors' of that notion, this presence of a directional recognizable activity. If none is discernible events for us lack the essential characteristics of what we call "Life".

But for something to be imbued with a goal isn't necessary for it to be repository of something else? Who chooses the goal? Could anything which is unaware of itself be capable of having it? Nothing lifeless could be conceived as animated of volitional urges which are a requirement for purposive activity. Furthermore, volition, as we all know, is a fundamental part, a basic constitutive element of a mysterious entity: CONSCIENCE.

Some critics might contend that in the complex molecules of what we had accepted are simple units of Life (DNA and RNA) to talk of a 'conscience' is a farfetched assumption, and that entirely mechanical or physico-chemical forces give the processes their apparent goal oriented attributes. Seemingly self aware purposeful activity in these elemental units of life, they would add, is only a mirage.

I believe that such argument becomes lost in the semantic connotations of terms and concepts with considerable religious derivations in human languages. After all, it can be argued that even our actions can be viewed as the end result of extraordinarily complex concatenated biological phenomena. No identifiable essential qualitative difference needs to be present between the behavioral responses of a bacteria and a human other that in the former they are simpler. This conclusion will appear as absurd to many but if there is 'something else' in the case of Man there is no reason to think it is less 'logical' in a bacteria.

What this 'something else' could be? If Life everywhere appears animated by this characteristic goal oriented activity, why is there a necessity to postulate we are differently constituted that any other living form? The root of this conception appears to be in the animistic thought of our ancestors, who in order to explain purpose concluded that there has to be 'something' coming from 'outside', a metaphysical entity of a sort, an 'Anima' which was the center of awareness, a 'Soul' source of all our acts and the abode of the intangible Conscience.

If biological phenomena scientifically do not need of any 'genie in the black box' conception, if the field of physical sciences has advanced sufficiently as to see the irrelevancy of such scheme, why should we persist in maintaining the notion that we enjoy an special kind of volition? The reason, of course, is unknown but it does not matter to our discussion. WHATEVER THE NATURE OF CONSCIENCE IS THERE SHOULD NOT BE ANY FUNDAMENTAL DIFFERENCE BETWEEN THAT OF HUMANS AND THE MOST RUDIMENTARY LIVING ORGANISM.

This is not to say that there is not, or should not be, dissimilarities between these consciences. The degree of awareness obviously has to be radically different in rudimentary creatures when compared to superior forms of Life; in fact, an entire spectrum is clearly perceived among them. In the Zoological Kingdom, at least, the lower echelons in the evolutionary tree possess, when compared to the upper branches, a more primitive conscience as judged by objective criteria at our disposal: Like the magnitude and variety of their purposeful behavior, the rapidity and richness of their responses to environmental stimuli of every kind, and their capability to cope and adapt themselves to threats and dangers to their survival. PARALLELED TO THE ASCENDING TREE OF BIOLOGICAL COMPLEXITY THERE IS A HIERARCHY OF INCREASING COMPLEXITY OF CONSCIENCE.

At the lower end of the Life spectrum primitive conscience

in rudimentary organisms is very limited in their survival options. Survival in these cases depend on remarkable adaptations to environmental conditions, perhaps partially the consequence of their rapid reproductive capacity, but still their functions are restricted to biochemical mechanisms lacking the ability to rapid decision making, which is the prerogative of higher stages in the biological hierarchy. Yet, perhaps resulting from their prodigious reproduction, mutational rate, and transfer of genetic material among organisms (at least in bacteria and viruses), these creatures are capable of remarkable survival capacity; as could be appreciated in the "resistance" many bacteria have developed to many antibiotics, provoking a therapeutic nightmare for the Health Profession.

At the opposite end of the spectrum we find the highly complex Human Conscience capable of the reflective act of self-awareness, the conscience of the Cartesian Cogito, the 'I think' rather than 'there are thoughts', the 'I see' rather than 'there are sights', the 'I hear' rather than 'there are sounds'. Man's Conscience is different because it recognizes its individuality, its separate existence. In order to build society Man had, to certain extent, to harness his instincts and their environment rather than to blend with it. This split at the root of Being is the source of his sense of responsibility and the realization of his own finitude, the fear we try to align with religion and the hope for 'salvation'.

This, more than anything else, is what distinguishes Man from other animals, the notion that the World is his House, the abode of his endeavors and the shrine of his expectations, because humans live with and by this hope for bettering their sojourn here on Earth and the attainment of a putative after-life, a feeling so deeply rooted in our psyche that we can see prove of it in the archeological evidence, even in the ancient remains of Homo Neanderthal. But the vanishing of innocence, the severance of the umbilical cord with Mother Earth which threw him into the World as a resented guest, HIS ORIGINAL SIN, was not Man's sexual temptation but rather his REFLECTIVE ACT, his repudiation of a sense of communion and identification with that Nature which had nurtured him through eons with love and care to live a vegetative existence. The reflective conscience of Man cost him the Earth Paradise but freed his soul from the trappings of a parasitic

4

existence, allowing the 'conquering' of his environs. He paid dearly for this sin by feeling alone and repudiated, exiled from the grace of God.

Conscience which arose as an instillation of purpose into matter reached a turning point in Man with the self realization of this purpose; with a self-awareness permitting 'civilization' but that otherwise severed his ties with Nature. The eating of the apple by Adam was an act of self-assertion and disobedience rather than an abject surrender to base instinctual drives. Man lost his Paradise but won the Earth.

If primitive living units, like cells, bacteria and viruses, possess a conscience, how it relates to those of their metazoan counterparts? Certainly the conscience of a multi-cellular organism cannot be considered an aggregation of those of his individual cells. Although all these cells still can be properly assumed to have a purpose of their own, this purpose is subservient to that of the multi-cellular organism to which they belong, the organism which appropriate and orchestrate their activities.

If that higher conscience is not a summation of the others, what else is it? It has to be something different, something 'new' that grew from the aggregation of more elemental units. We can with confidence state that A METAZOAN ORGANISM IS NOT AWARE OF THE LOWER STRATA OF CONSCIOUSNESS STIRRING WITHIN HIM. We can make such assertion because we personally ignore how our constitutive cells 'feel'. The interests, challenges, fears and pleasures of a multi-cellular Being are not the same as those of his constitutive cells. While the latter are concerned with physical and chemical stimuli corresponding to their immediate surroundings, a higher organism is unaware of them and instead is 'adapted' to confront and resolve a different set of environmental challenges. That doesn't mean the metazoan would not attempt to tackle by way of its more elemental units (the cells) those problems and challenges, it only means that it is not 'conscious' of those activities. A NEW LAYER OF CONSCIOUSNESS FORMED WHEN TWO CELLS HOLD TOGETHER FOR THE FIRST TIME.

There was need to surrender part of their individuality when cells bounded to each other in a permanent way; they had to consolidate their actions and goals FOR THE COMMON GOOD, in other words, their fates became inextricably associated. But their behavior demanded more than a mere covenant of wills. Moved by a different set of stimulus the new 'creature' began to act independently of its composing parts which were 'dragged along' by something superior, incomprehensible to them but forced to be 'shared' by the new higher conscience.

In fact, there are in Nature rudimentary organisms (the social amebas) which during most of their life cycles act as independent autonomous collections of unicellular entities only to, at a given moment and still for obscured reasons, coalesce into a sort of metazoan, a worm-like creature with sexual organs that burrows in the ground apparently for reproductive purposes. How this miracle comes about? How the aggregation of free living soil amebas could, by concerted effort, suddenly 'decide' to trespass a threshold of a sort, climb one step in the hierarchy and become a new thing? How this 'mass decision' takes place?

It is difficult to escape the conclusion that there has to be some kind of communication among the individual elements, otherwise such collective behavior is incomprehensible. The amebas, it was eventually found, interrelate by way of what has been defined biologically as a 'second messenger': cyclic AMP. This substance, known by biochemists to be in many animals the last intracellular link in hormonal and neural cascades of physiological commands, is found in colonies of amebas to be dissolved in the milieu where they grow and thrive. This means that here AMP acts as a 'transmitter' of information among the unicellular organisms, as first rather than second messenger, extra-cellularly rather than intra-cellularly.

In social amebas we see, paralleled to the proto-metazoan transformation, a morphologic specialization of the individual amebas for the specific functions each one is to carry out in the new organism, a metamorphosis of a sort, a predecessor to the elaborate tissue and organ specialization of more advanced groups, whether plants or animals. The process of hierarchical stratification which took a first giant leap when self-replicating molecules, like DNA, were superseded and integrated into prokaryotes (where the genetic material became embedded in a supporting protoplasm, and where phenotype became firstly separated from genotype), took a second leap with the first appearance on Earth of metazoan organisms in whom 'individual cellular freedom' became subordinated, also for the first time, to the tyranny of 'the group'.

This subordination took the form of total and abject surrender of their independence. The more specialized the cell the more difficult it is for her to survive in isolation. Other than in artificial man-provided environments none of these metazoan cells could manage to live an independent separated existence. How long would a liver cell or neuron survive in conditions where free-living protozoa thrive? Not for too long, of course. For one thing, they lack the capacity to digest many food products. Their nourishment has to be pre-processed for them by other cells.

But the metazoans, when compared to their more primitive cousins, have greater capability for locomotion and feeding, as well as, for selectively adapting to an immense variety of environmental conditions. Yet, it is a remarkable fact of evolution that while large numbers of unicellular species, both prokaryotes and eukaryotes, still live today little changed from their Precambrian ancestors, an immense number of more advanced species, both from the animal and botanic kingdoms, have already vanished. Even entire phyla, since the Cambrian radiation, had completely disappeared with no trace.

It is a widely held view among biological scientists that 'evolution' is a story of 'progressive improvement' or 'betterment', that the more complex the living organism the higher the degree of perfection is attained. This, of course, will depend much of what is understood by 'betterment 'or 'perfecting'. If by such we mean the number of behavioral options, or the rapidity and range of responses and adaptations to the variety of circumstances a creature faces, then the term clearly would apply. However, if we measures 'betterment' as the capacity for survival, then, as we had already seen, many unicellular organisms are more successful than other more advanced forms of life. Bacteria, one of the most primitive living groups, had been around for well over 3 billion years, and with relatively little modifications are still thriving in our days. Remarkably, even anaerobes manage to live in our modern oxidative atmosphere!

What can be conclusively affirm about Life on Earth is that it has expanded the magnitude and scale of its activities, that its options had multiplied in parallel to the increase in awareness, at least in the animal kingdom. From the primitive viruses and prions (little more than drifting molecule of DNA or RNA) which basic reproductive function in a primordial sea depended on the possibility of encountering in its surrounding milieu, and enlisting for the purpose of survival, the ingredients necessary to its reproduction and growth, to the multiplicity of tasks capable of being performed by a mammal, and the capacity to manipulate the environment reached by Man, there is a great chasm and the complexities of their consciences are also vastly apart. Yet in prokaryotes and many eukaryotes living today the fundamental tasks are still the orchestration of metabolic functions permitting growth and reproduction. Their only difference to more elemental or primitive self-replicating units, like the nucleotides mentioned above, is in many cases LIMITED LOCOMOTION AND TAXIS, the capacity to transport themselves toward desired objects or away from potentially injurious conditions in their immediate environment.

In higher animals, although the fundamental purpose of their activities is still the same (growth and reproduction), THE COMPLEXITY OF ENVIRONMENTAL CHALLENGES HAS CLIMBED TO A NEW HIERARCHY OF EVENTS. Their locomotion, for instance, is directed to larger objects, whether animated or not, and the time frame of their reactions is shorter, that is, more RAPID. Because of the development of sense perception, the range of stimuli capable of eliciting a 'reaction' also has expanded and the nervous system provides for elaborated sets of responses, consisting of the concatenation of simpler ones, which is integrated first as 'reflexes' and later in complex neurological associations called 'instincts'. But the further development of the nervous system has permitted higher animals also the capacity for rapid adaptation to novel situations by way of improvisations and 'learned behavior'. Whereas in rudimentary organisms (unicellular or multi-cellular types) new behavioral modes were only possible through genetic mutations or rearrangements (therefore mostly resorting to fast reproduction for adaptations), more advanced organisms in the biological tree are capable of learning new 'tricks' in relatively short time, even during the span of ONE GENERATION.

What we can then confidently state up to now is that THE DIVERSITY AND MAGNITUD OF CHOICES HAS EXPANDED IN THE BIOLOGICAL SPHERE, what we have chosen to call 'the scale'. Very often we are not 'conscious', for example, of what specific deleterious agents (like chemicals or infectious organisms) are at one time or another attempting to injure our bodies; we might feel "sick" but ignore the reasons why. Such 'awareness' has become the providence of our 'defense mechanisms' and 'immune system'. OUR LEVEL OF CONSCIOUSNESS HAS TRASCENDED THAT 'MICROSCOPIC LEVEL', NOT BECAUSE IT IS NOT IMPORTANT, LIKE EPIDEMICS SUFFICIENTLY PROVE, BUT BECAUSE OUR AWARENESS HAS CLIMBED IN HIERARCHY. We had relegated to a lower order of existence those purely biological tasks: The order of the 'vegetative functions'.

Three different planes or strata (each animated by a Conscience of its own) of unfolding activity we then have seen so far in the spectrum of Life in our planet: The level of the molecule (RNA and DNA), which are collections of atoms; the level of unicellularity (bacteria, protozoa etc.), constituting collections of molecules; and finally the level of multicellularity (all plants and animals), which represents collections of cells. Each of these planes, we had proposed, is animated by a conscience of its own: in charge of the orchestration of chemical processes in the molecules, the harnessing and organization of metabolic functions in cells, and with ways of unfolding life in our physical environment demanding adjustments to frequently changing conditions occasionally subjected to sudden variations, in multi-cellular animals. Each of these hierarchical levels unfolds their biological activities in different spatial dimensions: a drifting one-dimensional realm in the case of the molecules, a two dimensional world in the case of unicellular organisms (protozoans) animated occasionally of directional motions (taxis), and a three dimensional universe in those creatures (metazoans) possessing eye sight and a nervous system. (It has to be clarified that the wandering of unicellular organisms in their aquatic environment does not indicate an instinctual element in behavior which will require the possession of a nervous system. Their motions are related to chemical clues for feeding and reproduction.)

In the Botanic Kingdom the hierarchical stratification appears to end at the metabolic level, as is the case also among some animals, like the invertebrates. Plants, as with many primitive zoological species, are biologically self-sufficient and no sharing of tasks among members of the group, as happens with social animals, takes place. (This is not to deny that collections of plants of all kind do have an influence in the environment, but that is not a purposeful activity as far as we can tell). Even so, the ultimate goals of vegetative life (to survive and reproduce) are superbly represented among plants of every kind. The adaptations are so exquisite as to surprise and marvel the unaware. Reproduction is so well geared to utilize, in many cases, insects and birds as vehicles of germ cells that often the flowers adopt the shape and colors, even the smells, of one of the sexes (usually the female) of the insect vector with such a remarkable accuracy as to render suspect the theory of evolution by 'random mutations'.

Yet, plants, like the unicellular organisms, do not possess a nervous system, in other words, a centralized information processing center capable of providing for integration of bodily functions. THE CONSCIENCE OF A PLANT CANNOT, THEREFORE, BE DESCRIBED AS INSTINCTUAL (WHICH DO NOT EXCLUDE THE FUNDAMENTAL DRIVES TO SURVIVE AND REPRODUCE THEIR KIND) BUT SIMPLY AS STILL METABOLIC, ALTHOUGH AT A HIGHER LEVEL OF complexity than A SIMPLE CELL. The cells of plants, like in any other multi-cellular organism, differentiate morphologically according to their functional roles in systems of organs and tissues but, as it is well known, differ from most animals by the lack of a relational apparatus capable of coordinating locomotion and other biological functions.

That doesn't mean that plants escape the need for struggling to survive, but their adaptations to the environment are more subtle, in some cases resorting to mimicry to reproduce (we had already mentioned the example of some flowers which resemble butterflies, and others which ooze sexual stimulants or pheromones to attract insects) and defend themselves (spines and the synthesis of chemicals like phenols and tannins to fend off insect attacks), also at times resorting to morphologic variations to adapt to different environmental conditions(like cactus in desert regions and pines in high latitudes with cold climates and short daylight). Even it is claimed that plants can warn neighbors, by means of volatile substances, about the presence of dangerous insects, and on the other hand it is also well known that some arboreal specimens trap insects in sticky secretions. In fact, some researches even claim that plants can smell and hear, although, as far as I know, no identifiable sense organs for such functions had ever been detected.

But plants lack locomotion and then cannot individually defend themselves against threats demanding rapid response. A tree cannot escape the ax of a lumberjack or to be destroyed by a forest fire. As it was said, plant conscience still unfolds at a metabolic hierarchical level. The same could be said of many primitive metazoans in the Zoological Kingdom, like corals, anemones and sponges among others, which for most of their lives remained attached to solid places in their underwater realms and, intriguingly, frequently live in symbiotic associations with unicellular alga.

Prolific reproduction, mimicry, capability to synthesize their own foodstuff, chemical defenses against enemies, these are the tools and weapons used by plants, which are remarkable similar to those of many invertebrates and, therefore, seem to be very primitive; among the first resources used by Life on Earth. Such resources, no matter how elaborated and sophisticated they are, still belong to the vegetative or metabolic level of complexity.

But we have to be careful not to confuse this state of affairs in plant evolution with the fallacy of surmising that plants have no conscience. As it was said before, they lack the animal instinctual or human reflective conscience but, like unicellular organisms, possess a metabolic type, a kind nevertheless which transcend the unicellular realm to climb into a multi-cellular world of their own. This, of course, does not means that the plant 'knows', feels or is aware in any way of its constituting cells; it only signifies that in the Botanic Kingdom there is an arrest in the evolutionary tree at the level of metabolic conscience.

CHAPTER II

We should now ask ourselves if there is somewhere in the evolution of Life any indication of AN STILL HIGHER LEVEL OF BIOLOGICAL ORGANIZATION. I think there is; in fact it is all around us, so much so that we cannot escape to notice it: A society of animals (an aggregation of metazoans) which would add to MORE than just a simple sum of its elemental components. The prototype of these societies is the anthill and the beehive.

In social insect species we find many intriguing parallels between the organization of their communal groups and the structural and functional characteristics of multi-cellular organisms. Among bees the drones, queens, workers and fecundating males display different body shape according to the 'roles' they play in the community, in the same manner as a cell morphological specification vary according to the physiologic tasks each is destined to accomplish in the metazoan to which it belongs. In both cases we can confidently claim that INDIVIDUAL DESTINY IS INGRAINED IN MORPHOLOGY. Likewise, just like hormones and peptides are vehicles of communication between cells, smells (pheromones) and tactile clues provide for the transmission of information among social insects.

But perhaps the most intriguing similarity between a beehive and a metazoan organism is that invariably, in one case as in the other, the biological system undergoes a similar life cycle. In both cases the aggregates of simpler units experience a 'birth' in time, a phase of growth during which the 'number' of units (cells or bees) increase, followed by a period of stability or 'maturity' and finally of decline and ultimately 'death', when the animal experience the stoppage of all biological functions or the beehive is ultimately abandoned and the bees disperse.

During the life-cycle just described, the biological system in question,('animal' or 'beehive'), whether a congregation of cells or bees, will be preoccupied, like at any other hierarchical level of existence, with the fundamental tasks of nutrition and reproduction indispensable to the survival of the species. The big difference is the absence in a beehive of a discernible center for processing information and transmitting commands, that is to say, comparable to a nervous system. Yet, as it was said before, many primitive animals also lack a central nervous system, only exhibiting rudimentary neuronal associations with limited capabilities. The highly complex instinctual behavior of bees might partially replace for this deficiency. Humoral and tactile clues, among others, could also serve as vehicles of intercommunication among members of the group. Yet, the possibility of some collective decision-making mechanism escaping our comprehension could not be ruled out only based on the absence of any 'identifiable' candidate.

Bearing in mind these differences still remain a large body of similarities between a beehive, which is constituted by a congregation of bees, and a metazoan organism which represents a collection of cells, to suggest the possibility that the former had achieved a higher level of conscience than the individual bee, in the same way that an animal conscience is higher to that of its forming cells, although in both cases we still find the same general 'aims' of Life: An ultimate purpose to survive and perpetuate its own 'kind'.

I maintain that the morphologic and functional specifications of the members of a beehive (judging by our own individual experience in reference to our constitutive cells) is good evidence for the existence of some kind of collective consciousness transcending that of the individual bee. Some other animal groups, of course, appear deprived of this peculiar condition. For example, a herd of zebras, a pack of wolves, or a school of fishes, although gathering together perhaps for mutual protection, seem to lack the anatomical and social organization, manifested in the division of communal tasks, characteristic of the insect societies we had mentioned.

There are some mammalian groups, however, where a semblance of societal assignation of tasks begins to be noticeable. For instance, in a group of elephants some older females appear to be assigned with the chore of caring for the rest of the herd, guiding and protecting the group while the others wander, graze, bath and plow their way in the wilderness. In higher apes also a rudimentary segregation of chores following sexual lines is, again, manifested. In these species extended families form, with the mature males protecting and leading the groups, while the females care for the offspring (motherly instinct, common to all mammals, many birds, and even some fishes, is perhaps the first expression of selective social specialization, but being solely designed to ensure the survival of the newborn can only, in the more broad definitional sense, be accepted as a revelation of 'social consciousness').

Yet, in mammalian species, other than genital differences common to heterosexual animals and occasional plants, there are not, as is the case with social insects, any morphologic difference which would translate into specific 'social roles' within the animal community. Group consciousness in them, on the contrary, develops slowly, gradually reaching higher degree of perfection in the upper regions of the evolutionary branches. In human society, of course, is where the sheer variety and complexity of task assignment displayed by the social group reach such an unprecedented level as to even surpass the diversity of tissue and cellular classes found in advanced metazoan.

In Man alone the goals and aims of Life itself are expanded to include, not only survival and reproduction, feeding and sexuality, but actually a mastering of his world that goes beyond the above mentioned necessary objectives. This drive to 'conquer' and to 'control' results in considerable manipulation of the environment where He conducts his daily activities. (Many mammals like the beavers, and other vertebrates engage in limited manipulation of their habitat but it is instinctual, in no way representing a deliberate purpose to conquer it.)

This expansion of potentialities, this new 'mastery' of Nature Man was to undertake, required a new and powerful way to codify, store and transmit information, both horizontally (to others of the same generation) and vertically (to the following generations). Man, the animal, preserves his biological heritage in molecular 'codes' of DNA and RNA. Society preserves its culture in a novel and truly unprecedented code: LANGUAGE, a system of phonetic symbols that when translated into scripture, another system of symbols, allows the transmission of human thoughts and experiences among other members of the group and to future generations.

In fact, this mode of communication (language and scripture) has propitiated and enormously facilitated to Man the accumulation of information about his environment or 'knowledge', thus permitting the rapid adaptation to new challenges which otherwise would have taken much longer to be accomplished. Man survived the glacial cold not because, like the woolly rhinoceros and Proboscidiae, he developed a protective hairy coat, but on account of his appropriation of the skin of other animals for self protection. Humans with their language and intelligence were able to succeed in a relatively short period of time in what took other species much longer to achieve. The long and tedious, sometimes unreliable, genetic route has been bypassed, allowing, for the first time on Earth, a non-biological way of adaptation and evolution.

By developing language and scripture Man escaped THE TYRANNY OF MOLECULES and opened a new cosmic dimension with his achievements: the level of CULTURE. Humans therefore invented a new form of relating to and compiling information about his environment, a new form of recording and retrieving what has been learned and therefore of transmitting to his descendants this "acquired wisdom". On account of that Man has flown higher than any bird, dived deeper than many fishes, transported himself on Earth faster than any land animal, and even visited other planets. He has done this in the amazingly short time span of several million years (if we include Man's precursors in the evolutionary tree), achieving in his short presence in Planet Earth what takes zoological kingdoms entire geological eras to develop. THIS NOVEL WAY OF COMMUNICATION AMONG MEN SERVE IN SOCIETY THE SAME ROLE THAT CHEMICAL AND NERVOUS CLUES SERVE AMONG CELLS IN MULTICELLULAR ORGANISMS, OR GENES DO IN INTERGENERATIONAL TRANSMISSION OF INFORMATION IN ANIMAL AND BOTANIC SPECIES. MAN, THE MOST ADVANCED METAZOAN, HAS CREATED THE MEANS OF ACCESING A HIGHER HIERARCHICAL LEVEL OF INTEGRATION, THE HUMAN SOCIETY, WHICH INSTEAD OF BEING PREORDAINED BY GENES IS DETERMINED BY A PRODUCT OF THE HUMAN INTELLECT: LANGUAGE.

Language is also one of the most enduring cultural traits. Long after many other signs of vitality vanish in a human civilized group it could still linger proudly, and even after ceasing to be commonly spoken takes refuge in ceremonial events and traditional ritual performances, many of them 'approved' or sanctioned by custom or law.

A case in point is demotic scripture in Egypt, which was used for official acts and documents as well as for literary work up to the Christian era, to be slowly replaced by the more elaborated Coptic. If we consider

Coptic a product of Ptolemaic Egypt and, therefore, strange to the original 'spirit' of the Egyptian Culture, we will have to conclude that demotic was the last genuine Egyptian tongue spoken in this area, a tongue that was still used, although mainly in religious rituals, up to the end of the Ptolemaic dynasties roughly 500 years after the cessation of other original Egyptian cultural manifestation in the geographic locus of this ancient civilization.

Another case in point is Roman Culture and Latin. Cultural activity in the geographic locus of the Western Empire terminated, for all practical purposes, with the arrival of the Dark Ages and the lost of a centralized government. Vernacular Italian appears to have evolved as early as the VI Century AD and began to be written about the X Century, but legal, ecclesiastic, scientific and literary writings exclusively utilized Latin up to the XVI Century AD. Even more surprising is the fact that outside the frontiers of modern Italy, in other European countries, Latin was still used in numerous important occasions up to the XVIII Century, and after that in religious ceremonies, up to present times, all over the World.

What this situation amounts to is that Latin was used in the western world, in many different type of tasks, for more than a thousand years after the end of Roman Civilization and the cessation of any other expression of this great culture! The most extraordinary thing is that many great literary, philosophical and scientific masterpieces by non-Italians had also been written in this language, a phenomenon without precedent in history as far as I know. Such a fact clearly indicates the danger of viewing usage of a language as a measure of the vitality of a Culture.

The division of labor and specialization of roles in human society did not result, as it was already said, from morphologic and functional specifications as in the bees. On the contrary, other than the universal sexual organic differences between men and women and racial differences, humans, anatomically and physiologically, are fairly similar to each other. On the other hand, there are dramatic differences in talents, skills, and intellectual resources among individuals, which explain the unpredictability, plasticity and capacity to adapt of our species.

By the 'shape' of a bee, as we had seen, her behavior could be surmised. A worker would never comport like a queen or a drone. Their destiny is stereotyped forever in the phenotype. With Man, however, POTENTIALITIES CANNOT BE SURMISE AT FROM HIS HABITUS OR EVEN APPEARENCE. We might suspect, for example, that a person is a mugger or a saint by his dress, demeanor, etc., but we could never be completely certain; an element of doubt will always remain. In fact, WE CAN ONLY JUDGE MAN BY HIS ACTIONS, this is the only permissible way to discover what an individual person 'is like'. Contrary to the case of ants and bees no degree of knowledge in human anatomy or physiology will ever be able to provide for a conclusive prediction of a man behavior or potentialities. They cannot be guessed from his appearance.

It is only logical to assume that a being with such a complex society as Man, a mammal with the enormous power to create culture and civilization, the discoverer of methods for perfecting an awesome technology, one who has expanded the 'mastery' of his surroundings to the point of enabling him to transport himself to other celestial bodies and to tame many diseases, will also possess a different type of consciousness: That is, the reflective consciousness we already mentioned, the one that cost Him 'The Earth Paradise'.

But what about the society he has created? The first thing we can immediately notice is that there has been considerable change in the integration of human groups, from the primitive 'tribe' to the 'nations' which today form the political units of our species. We will take later on the subject of cultural classification of human communities, but it will be appropriate now to mention some of their intriguing sociological features. The first is the evidence of this evolution in the human group, this increasing complexity of social roles, a proliferation of tasks which mirrors the biological counterpart of cells in a metazoan. The second is the existence of idiosyncrasies, peculiarities in the collective deportment of human groups entirely comparable to the 'personality traits' exhibited by individuals.

The English Nation is thought to be phlegmatic and practical; they set in motion the Industrial Revolution and conquered a world empire in search for sources of raw materials and markets for their products.

Germans are reputed to be militaristic and regimented, as recent history fully documents. The Italians are perceived to be fun loving and artistically inclined, and the Spaniards dreamers and passionate, etc. These 'clichés', of course, are only manifestations of the collective Ethos of modern nations reaching to us through recent history, characteristics which (I do not pretend to be all-inclusive) had developed slowly during a formative period dating back in Europe, at least to the Renaissance. For more ancient civilizations only by what remains of the historical record or the achievements of their 'civilizations' is that we can, in a fragmentary manner, surmise their "personalities". The Egyptians, we know for instance, were adept to grandiose schemes expressions of their religious believes in life after death, as attested by the massive pyramids, the Sphinx etc. The Chinese, by their literature, art and philosophy are known to have endorsed the view of a harmonious blend of Man and Nature. The ancient Greeks, on the other hand, discovered 'Reason' and were the first to set themselves asunder as conquerors of this very Nature.

How could, if not for the development of a collective 'mind-set', be understood the 'sense of destiny' of the French revolutionaries, of the Greeks at Marathon and Plataea, of the Carthaginians in the crossing of the Alps, of the Spaniards in the conquest of a 'New World', of the Macedonians in 'Hellenizing' the Near East and North Africa with the conviction that they were 'divine emissaries', or the feverish determination and fanatical zeal of the Bolsheviks revolutionaries who thought themselves as the vanguard of a new human Era?

We all have felt on occasions that events, in an individual and historical sense, have 'escaped' our control, that in a very 'real' way we become the prisoners of our own destiny. No wander the ancients glorified Fate and in fact deified it. The guillotine during the French Revolution, for a while, appeared to had converted from an instrument of punishment into a terrorizing, cruel and sadistic God demanding his onerous share of human sacrifices, a modern Huitzilopochtli, before the revolutionary fervor was cleverly harnessed by a man named Napoleon who was able to turned the fratricidal struggle from internal self-destruction to external exploits.

This self destructive madness of the French revolutionaries is certainly reminiscent of the inordinate conduct of suicidal people.

Even a very human attribute, like insanity, appears sometimes to afflict societies and even nations. We only have to remember the 'collective madness' of Nazi Germany. Could in any other way be defined the genocidal obsession of the regime, or the conviction that they could subjugate the entire World? Even in fashions and fads there appears to be times when an idea, a theme or gimmick seems to capture the imagination of an entire generation. (A case in point is the present infatuation with communication gadgets, the compulsion for talking and 'texting' even in the most awkward of circumstances to the point of imperiling human life)

The psychology of the masses, their often uncontrollable and voluble moods, their 'irrationality', is a subject which had been talked, written and commented upon so frequently by social scientists, political philosophers and assortments of behaviorist psychologists, to need any special emphasis here. Suffice is to accept what appears to be an incontrovertible fact to all those who had dedicated time and effort to this field, namely, that 'the mood of the crowd' is a contagious phenomena, an almost irresistible current difficult to understand but capable of enlisting and dragging even sensible and intelligent individuals.

Politicians with 'charisma' know this and often play very effectively with cleverly selected symbols which serve well the ultimate purpose of gaining power, and channeling the public energies to the achievement of any specific goal they have in mind. The demagogue is capable of sensing immediately the 'pulse' of the 'masses', and of raising the people to a pitch of hysteria by intelligent manipulation of public emotions and sensitivities for their own personal gratification.

Irrational impulses of every kind are well known to be lurking beneath a sizable proportion of human acts, to the point of being exceptional the person who does not remember, at one time or another, having done something without knowing 'why'. Could this feeling be manifestation of a collective unconscious related to the existence of a supra-personal conscience?

In order to answer this question we have to take a hypothetical example which might parallel the situation. Gastric parietal cells secrete hydrochloric acid, a chemical needed for the proper digestion of food. The secretory activity of these cells is commanded by stimuli arising from the action of a hormone called Gastrin, produced by other cells in the Stomach, and also by messages from the parasympathetic nervous system. If we momentarily assume these cells to be animated by a reflective conscience like Man, then A FEELING OF IMPOTENCE TO UNDERSTAND THEIR OWN BEHAVIOR (secretion upon being stimulated) would be natural. The cells would have the impression of being acting without an explanation of why they act in the way they do. The realization of being required to elaborate something and, upon specific requests, to release it into the lumen of the Stomach, would not help them to comprehend the 'reason' and ultimate purpose of why they do so, which ultimately is the digestion of food. In fact, the cells would not have even the faintest idea that their activity promotes the absorption of nourishment necessary to sustain the life of the organism to which they belong, including their own survival. But, of course, to the gastric cells such a 'realization' is unthinkable because THEIR LIFE EVOLVES AT AN ENTIRELY DIFFERENT HIERARCHICAL ORDER, one from which their limited metabolic conscience is not allowed to transcend.

Before proceeding I would like to clarify what it means for a gastric cell to be in a different hierarchical order than the organism to which it belongs. The 'awareness' of a cell is not a SELF awareness, its conscience is not a 'reflective' conscience and therefore it is incapable of formulating questions which simply cannot be put through. The behavior of a cell, like that of an animal, is mediated by physiological systems of highly structured and complex mechanisms; it appears that probably Man alone is capable of advancing questions referable to 'final causes'. What I am claiming, however, is that there is, in principle, no reason why the gap between a unicellular and metazoan (therefore multi-cellular) animal consciousness has to be narrower than that from Man to a suppositional social-communal one of a higher order.

Granted that the range of 'activities' of a man are much broader than the stereotyped functions of a cell (or even of an ant in the anthill) but, nevertheless, if there were such a thing as a societal supra-conscience carrying its activity at a higher hierarchical order than Man, its ultimate purpose would be as unimaginable to us as it is for a cell the goals and strivings of a multi-cellular organism or, for that matter, of a gastric cell in the case of Man. This sense of futility, impotence and of 'being dragged by events' which so many of us sometimes feel and, in fact, could be conceived as 'the malady' of modern times, would then be understood.

Man history on Earth compares intriguingly with the life cycle of the social amebas we alluded to before. His beginnings, to be sure, were quite inauspicious as a free standing, self-sufficient, unimpressive small-game predator who roamed the globe in ever increasing hordes and, after a relatively long period of time, rather suddenly (in geological terms), formed a complex society where individuals specialized in different tasks serving the common need for survival. This transformation, certainly, implied considerable amount of sacrifice, of surrendering personal freedom for the benefits of organized society; the same type of obsequiousness displayed by the social ameba when, by joining forces with their sisters and acquiring functional specialization, converts temporarily into a metazoan organism for purposes of reproduction.

Man, the free roaming food-gatherer and hunter, sometimes approximately 5000 years ago, after the 'domestication' of some plants and animals, develops civilization and a written language, gives up his freedom, learns an occupation needed by others members of the human community where he belongs, and sacrifice for the security and stability of this new life his previous independence, commanded by a code of rules he promises to obey. In fact, it can be argued that he became 'a slave' of his own creation.

The fact of the matter is that MAN HAS DOMESTICATED HIMSELF. Here is the relevance of the example about social amebas. Man achievements as a group are the greatest in our known Universe, yet, we had paid dearly for it. Our personal freedoms are constrained with the development of complex sets of customs and social taboos. We have to hide our sexuality behind elaborate physical and psychological 'dresses' and to undergo a very prolonged period of training and education to conform to civilized life. Civilized man has been so used to eat processed food, his stomach is so trained to them, that if he does otherwise will become sick. Man has also to accept and abide to a whole array of conventionalisms to avoid been repudiated by others; restrains which impose a great burden to our emotional and instinctual make up. Finally, we have to pay our government taxes to help perpetuate the benefits for which procurement we had traded off our animal freedoms.

Both, Man and ameba have to give up something precious (their freedom) for the benefit of the group: THEY UNDERGO A PROCESS OF SELECTIVE COMMITMENT TO AN END. If so is the case, does the life of social amebas convey any messages for us? Could the evolution of civilization hold some ulterior and unheralded meaning incomprehensible to its constitutive human elements? I believe it does and a 'dimensional' example might further help to clarify the matter. Let us assume there are such things as tetra- dimensional Beings. It will be very difficult for us, tridimensional creatures, to conceive such monstrosities, but it would help in this regard to imagine the relations of a putative two dimensional being to us. Our third spatial dimension would be TIME for this two dimensional dwellers, a fact which should give us an insight as to what our time represents to a four dimensional being: another spatial dimension. By this approach we can try to search for some insight as to what kind of supra-organism human society resembles, and if possible, attempt to discern the teleological implication of 'civilized life' (perhaps a goal in the fifth dimension), by comparing it with the life cycle of social amebas.

No 'civilized' man, regardless of how versatile, could survive for too long unaided in any natural wilderness. Diseases, malnutrition, or accidents of many kinds will dispose of him in a relative short time. So vulnerable and dependent on his web of social support has he become that from being the most powerful creature on Earth in the company of his own kind, turns into the most weak and destitute of creatures when alone.

But how could humans had surrendered willingly their beastly liberties for the benefit of group support? How could they have become so dependent? Again, it is one of the biggest ironies of Life that Man is the species WHICH IS MORE POWERFUL AS A GROUP AND MORE VULNERABLE AS A SINGLE INDIVIDUAL. It is equally true that although one free-living ameba is no less adapted to her environment than any other protozoan, when she join forces with others of her own species to become a metazoan and specialize for reproductive purposes, THEY CLIMB UP TO A HIGHER ORDER IN THE EVOLUTIONARY SCALE. Even more, ANY humble protozoon is then better adjusted to survival in our planet than the individual ameba which has lost her freedom by this specialization. Now, it does not follows as necessarily obvious that living organisms will form groups because of any immanent realization that 'in togetherness there is strength'. In fact, many evolutionarily successful animals (both protozoan and metazoan) live their lives in a free, independent and even solitary state.

In what, then, do we pretend to be 'stronger' by keeping together? The answer appears simple but it is not. It can be argue that by staying in a group we are able to fend off better our enemies and increase our 'control' of our world and destiny. This response, of course, implies some hidden misconceptions, or at least presuppositions, as to what is the 'aim ' of Life and, therefore, of evolution. Yes, we live longer and healthier than our ancestors, but can we assert with certitude that Life 'Grand Design' is to subjugate and 'conquer' Nature? Is the equation of 'success' with 'strength' valid? Such a conviction will be nothing more than a plausible hypothesis. If we are part of Nature, some will contend, to 'conquer' It will be tantamount of conquering oneself; the classic tale of the lion chasing its own tail.

Another way to construe the goals of Life is to measure success by the time span a species, genus, or family of organisms had subsisted since its origins. Judged by this kind of yardstick, many of the most humble organisms, like photosynthetic bacteria, had the longest track record of continuous habitation in our planet, as the pre-Cambrian stromatolites indicate. 'Power', therefore, is only a relative criterion for evolutionary success and the Earth record is full with the fossils of many long gone evolutionary 'successes'.

We have to conclude, therefore, that nothing 'normal' or 'rational' urges animals to keep the company of their own kind. Any justification for our gregariousness is only excuses for instinctual tendencies, because MAN IS A SOCIAL ANIMAL and that is all. In this we resemble other social beings. We instinctively associate with members of our own species, but modern Man has invented 'Reason' and feels compelled to offer 'explanations' for the ways He acts. In what Man differs from other animals, however, is in the fact that his dependency to the group, if anything, has ostensibly increased as time has elapsed. There is no secret about it, MAN TODAY IS MORE DEPENDENT IN THE SUPPORT OF OTHERS THAN CAVE MAN WAS 40000 YEARS AGO. As already mentioned, we also differ from many social creatures in the absence of task-related morphologic differentiations and, instead, had relied in our 'technology' for survival; a fact that has increasingly removed us from contact with Nature and magnified our dependent condition.

The inescapable conclusion is, therefore, that Man gregarious proclivities are deeply rooted in his biological make-up and as such cannot be understood FROM INSIDE OUR DIMENSIONS OF ACTIVITY. In order to clarify what is meant by 'dimensions of activity', we have to return to a comparison similar to the one we alluded to when attempting to understand the fourth dimension by imagining a two dimensional being comprehension of the third dimension.

Man struggles to conduct his life at a level of REFLECTIVE CONSCIOUSNESS. This, it has already been said, is known to us because we are men and experience the truth of our individuality. We are aware of our physiological and psychological necessities because they are sensed in our own capacity as separated individual entities from other members of the human race. Now, Man, perhaps because of the quality of his consciousness (of his reflective capacity), vaguely seems to sense the existence of something still superior, something 'above' himself which different religions give different interpretations, but in general is conceived as a 'transcending power', an omnipotent and omniscient essence which rules the World and is called by us God, or gods, depending on whether we deal with a monotheistic or polytheistic religion denomination. The possibility that this feeling is rooted in the existence of a communal conscience (in this case supra-human) which conduct its life at a higher domain or strata of existence should be a valid working hypothesis. Jung used to talk about the universal symbols of the human mind, of why he defined as the 'collective unconscious'. There is no way we could, even remotely, ascertain what kind of goals this putative supra-conscience is trying to achieve. OUR SITUATION IS NO LESS INCOMPREHENSIBLE TO US THAN IT WOULD BE FOR THE METABOLIC CONSCIENCE OF A CELL TO UNDERSTAND THE COMPLEX YEARNINGS OF A METAZOAN ORGANISM. This is why the comparison to the ameba is relevant. How could the poor social ameba understand the urge compelling her to merge and join forces with her sisters for the purpose of procreation, an activity which takes place at a higher order of biological complexity and, therefore, of whose meaning she is permanently barred by being removed from her sensorial domain? Her plight would be as incomprehensible to her as, let us say, the reasons for a command to 'contract' would be to a muscle fiber in the leg of a gazelle being chase down by a leopard in an African savanna. Likewise, the urge of Man to form complex societies could be conditioned at a higher order of Life and cannot be rationalized by us at our cosmic level of activity. Like in the case of a social ameba it might represent THE UNFOLDING OF A GOAL DRIVEN URGE ARISING AT A HIGHER ORDER OF LIFE, AND THEREFORE INCOMPREHENSIBLE TO OUR LIMITED, LOWER PERSPECTIVE.

The situation is no different at the opposite end of the biological spectrum. There has to be an unbridgeable gap between the putative biochemical consciousness of an intracellular enzyme or organelle, dedicated to catalyze certain specific chemical reaction, and the metabolic one of a protozoan. The searching for basic nutrients or the reproduction urges by the latter should not even remotely be conceived by the enzyme, so used to be provided readily with the 'substratum' for its function. THE ACTIVITY OF EACH HIERARCHICAL LEVEL HAS TO BE TOTALLY UNKNOWN TO THE LOWER STRATA, WHICH NEVERTHELESS WOULD BE AFFECTED BY IT AND PERCIEVED AS STRANGE COMMANDS OR CONSTRAINS IN THE CONDUCT OF THEIR EXISTANCES.

Although each hierarchy of cosmic life encompasses those inferior to it, their consciences would not be able to intercommunicate; they will remain completely isolated from each other. Only with our reflective type is that we can conceive, from the goal directed nature of human strivings, the existence of these more rudimentary consciences (because, as stated before, the presence of goals in these lower realms of existence presupposes a more or less developed degree of awareness).THE RELATIONSHIP OF THE CHEMICAL CONSCIENCE OF AN ENZYME TO THE METABOLIC CONSCIENCE OF A CELL AND THAT OF THE LATTER TO THE INSTINCTUAL CONSCIENCE OF A METAZOA, SHOULD BE SIMILAR TO THE RELATIONSHIP OF THE POSTULATED ONE DIMENSIONAL BEING TO A TWO DIMENSIONAL AND OF THIS TO A THREE DIMENSIONAL ONE. Although each hierarchical level includes the lower types, any suppositional Being living in one of them would not be aware of how the others at lower or higher levels 'feel' like, or even if there is such a 'feel'; only Man, as we already said, with his reflective conscience can surmise that. We can imagine, for example, that for a two dimensional creature in a plane, like for instance a piece of paper, a corkscrew piercing thru this paper will appear as a point rotating in the plane. THE SHAPE OF THIS CORKSCREW WILL FOREVER BE FORBIDDEN TO THIS 'FLAT CREATURE'. THE THIRD SPACIAL DIMENSION WILL BE PERCIEVED AS MOTION AND THEREFORE IDENTIFIED WITH THEIR TIME. By analogy, we can then imagine the existence of a forth spatial dimension which would then be OUR TIME. We cannot transcend our reality but we can conceive the possibility of its existence.

For these reasons, then, the possibility of a supra-conscience superseding our realm of activity and whose physical locus is not a biological organism, as we know them, but a SUPRAORGANISM representing the whole of a community and of which, because of the explanations already given, we know nothing except by using the eye of our imagination, could in principle be postulated.

This comparison, of course, will appear as fantastic to many. How, they would ask, could such a parallel be established? How a concrete physical entity, like a living organism, with clear-cut physical boundaries and a definite 'shape' formed by the 'cohesiveness' of their cells, be confused with a 'shapeless' aggregation of free standing and independently acting units who come together at will and whose mutual convenience is their only 'glue'? In the case of humans, to many, this conglomerate of individuals would have even less attributes of a supra-organism than an anthill or a beehive because, at least, the latter, we already saw, are made up of insects, which differ from each other morphologically according to their roles in the insect communities, and their functional complementarities permits the survival of ALL.

In order to answer this objection we have to return to the previous dimensional example. FOR A FLAT TWO DIMENSIONAL CREATURE ENTITIES BELONGING TO A TRIDIMENSIONAL ORGANISM WILL BE CONCEIVED NOT AS PARTS OF ONE, BUT AS INDEPENDENT ENTITIES. The classical example of what we have just said is the branches of a tree. For a flat two dimensional being living in a 'plane' (cross section of a tree through the foliage), the branches will seem independent and 'separate' things, with no mutual anatomic continuity in a two dimensional world. It is only when the third dimension is taken into consideration that we are able to perceive this continuity and therefore behold the tree for what it is. To those creatures privileged with the perception of a third dimension is that the physical unity of something we call A TREE is revealed, in other words, that the converging branching pattern is recognizable. THE POSSIBILITY, THEN, THAT HUMANS REPRESENT UNITS OF A TETRA-DIMENSIONAL BEING WHO FIND THEIR CONTINUITY IN A PUTATIVE FORTH DIMENSIONAL SPACE COULD NOT BE RULED OUT ON THEORETICAL GROUNDS.

But how our activities UNKNOWINGLY to us could be serving an ulterior inscrutable purpose of a higher order? How can we be 'acting' precisely to satisfy those unimaginable designs without being, even remotely, aware of what is going on? Biology will help us in this regard also. One of the greatest organic wanders is the complex organization of the relational apparatus. The brain of Man, for example, is composed of approximately 100 billion neurons or 'thinking units', as many elements as there are stars in the Milky Way galaxy. How can this congregation of cells work so harmoniously as to seem animated by a single purpose? Our decisions appear to be the result of the integration of their activity, but which cells give the orders? Science has, so far, not yet penetrated into the secrets of neuronal circuitry, but somewhere in the maze of their intricate inter-communications our volition is 'produced'. Yet, if we consider neurons individually, their properties are very similar: the cell 'transmit' action potentials which crossing the synapses enter other cells or receive stimuli from other neurons. No anatomical or functional difference has as yet being discovered among these cells. Neuronal 'roles', seemed to depend, in great measure, from the 'position' they occupy in the constellation of the brain neuronal apparatus, but the goals and purpose of the 'whole' will remain unknown to the individual neuron.

In primitive animals, even vertebrates, the reaction to identical set of stimuli is rather uniform. Reflect acts and the more complex instinctual behavior are pretty much stereotyped but, as it is well known notably in higher mammals, larger 'menus' of options are available in the latter and account for the rudimentary 'personalities' we sometimes detect among them. In Man, however, the potential responses to identical stimuli are so numerous as to render human behavior frequently unpredictable.

For one thing, the range of 'problems', not immediately related to survival, confronted by human society demands a more diverse set of responses than a simple 'fight or flight' decision. Now, if as revealed from studies in Neuroanatomy and Neurophysiology, there are progressive integration of neuronal circuits in the brain, at some point in the maze of interconnected neurons a group of them have to be in charge of the decision making process and therefore of behavior. AT THIS POINT, WE HAVE TO ASSUME, THE METABOLIC CONSCIENCE OF CELLS IS TRANSFORMED INTO THE METAZOAN ONE OF MAN. (It has to be emphasized that although in higher vertebrates the menu of behavioral options at the disposal of the animal is also very broad, well beyond the reflect act and the instinctual action, only in Man, and perhaps in some other higher mammals, is that metazoan conscience becomes also REFLECTIVE in the sense that it is aware of the self)

Be as it may, however, volition does not appear to depend on ONE single cell (neuron), but rather results from the orchestrated efforts of the elite group. The individual elements only 'react' to received stimuli in ways that relate to poorly understood facilitating or inhibitory mechanisms, which might change according to the functional state at the synapses and on the 'mapping' or 'wiring' of these neuronal interconnections (which now are also known to vary with time by learning, training, and modulations by targeting chemical stimulus etc.).

Still, we have to emphasize that because neurons are cells, individual neuronal consciousness CONTINUES TO BE METABOLIC. The 'grand design' of the multi-cellular organism to which they belong still remains incomprehensible to the individual neuron, because it is unfolding at a HIGHER HIERARCHY, the commands being relayed in a 'code' of action potentials that constitute the only 'reality' in the neuronal microcosm. Even when the behavior of a metazoan results from the function of a SINGLE NEURON, like it is the case in some invertebrates with the motor neurons of simple reflex arch's, THE CELL IS ONLY RESPONDING TO NEUROPHYSIOLOGICAL COMMANDS RELATED THROUGH THESE ARCH'S. The vital need and purpose of her actions, the teleological ends to which she is subservient, escape its metabolic comprehension and understanding BECAUSE THE MEANING OF THE FUNCTION SHE IS RESPONDING TO IS WIRED IN THE ARCH ITSELF.

This analysis and conclusion equally could apply at a higher hierarchical level to the case of Man in relation to his society. The 'ruler', or ruling elites, are merely responding to SITUATIONS (the equivalent of stimuli to neurons) in the social 'milieu' where human conscience conduct its activity, and the response, or responses, are going to depend on previous CONDITIONING (by training, experience etc.) to them. THE ULTERIOR PURPOSE OF MAN ACTIONS, THOSE BEYOND HIS ACCESSIBLE REALITY, IS THEREFORE GOING TO REMAIN UNSCRUTABLE TO THE INDIVIDUAL HUMAN, BECAUSE THIS PURPOSE RESIDES ON A HIGHER SUPRA-LIMINAL HIERARCHICAL DOMAIN.

If we now analyze the way that human society is structured (and even that of some animal species) we will find always 'leaders' who either by force, age, experience, or by means of an elective process, take power and give commands for the conduct of affairs in the social group. Debates, surely, will occasionally take place within the ruling circles, yet, when a collective decision is made, it will be obeyed by the group. But doesn't a man, also, frequently hesitate before arriving at an individual decision? Doesn't this represents the end result of personal, emotional, and rational factors ultimately the consequence of different neuronal stimuli struggling for control of the "command center", that is, the efferent neurophysiologic pathway determining behavior? Hesitation, in the individual scale, can be reasonably equated to 'debate' in the social context; there are conflicting tendencies that should be reconciled before final collective action is instituted. When it does take place THE REFLECTIVE METAZOAN CONSCIENCE OF MAN IS TRANFORMED INTO THE TRASCENDING CONSCIENCE OF THE SOCIAL SUPRA-ORGANISM. We think that we know why we make a decision, or why we do things in the way we do, but as psychology sufficiently shows, frequently our acts are based in irrational urges difficult to define and understand, which could be serving an incomprehensible purpose at a higher hierarchical domain. Our personal situation is similar to the efferent neuron that doesn't understand the reason for the command she is giving a muscle to contract.

CHAPTER III

The resemblance of the phenomena of 'Life' to 'Culture' is an intriguing one. Biological Beings possess a general bodily blueprint or plan characteristic of the species and even of the family and genus. The Chordate, for example, display a vertebral column where the spinal cord resides and from where nerves issue to innervate the various organs. Locomotion in these animals consists of fins in fishes and legs in land animals, or a mixture of legs and wings in birds (except in the order ophidian which lost their limbs during evolution). Also, in view of the common ancestors, all these creatures are provided with similar digestive and excretory systems as well as organs for sensory reception. Comparative Anatomy teaches us that, in fact, biological organizational master plans reach out even into the tissue and cellular levels. There are, of course, variations in size, shape, degree of development, and functional characteristics of organ systems among many species, which are wider the farther apart their evolutionary lines are in the genealogical tree (like, the disappearance of their ancestor's gills and development of lungs in reptiles). These changes, however, take place by way of modifications to the general body plan, with no radical departures from it, confined to the restrictions imposed by biological rules of morphogenesis as old as metazoan themselves. (In this regard it is interesting to point out to a remarkable 'recapitulation' that takes place during embryogenesis. There is an ephemeral appearance during this period of organs which had vanished during evolution, like embryonic branchial pouches in mammals which are vestiges of the gills of fishes.)

Likewise, putative cultural supra-organisms exhibit general structural blueprints, specific ways of cultural unfolding which also appear to obey some sort of master plan no matter where on Earth the given culture is growing and evolving. There is, precluding an arrest, an early stage of mastering of fire and the creation of stone implements of increasing sophistication, used for defense, hunting or miscellaneous tasks. Some sorts of garments are eventually fashioned to cover and protect the body parts, followed by the manufacture of domestic utensils and the use of pottery. Ways of cultivating the fields and gathering the harvests eventually evolve with the advent of agriculture, and with it the means to measure, weigh and apportion land and goods, as well as, of erecting permanent settlements. A system of scripture and recording information is frequently invented and a socio-political organization takes form within the human community.

Now, it can be adduced that many of the typical patterns of cultural evolution result from the PRACTICAL NECESSITIES OF TECHNOLOGICAL DEVELOPMENT and that there are only a limited number of solutions to the problems posed by communal needs. Stone implements (cutting instruments for example) can be fashioned in only few possible ways (they all need a cutting edge and a handle).The same thing can be claimed of plows, houses, bowls, etc.

Another cultural characteristic that unquestionably promoted survival advantage to the social groups, and discloses a typical evolutionary blueprint, is the development of weapons. From Paleolithic times Man ingenuity had produce a formidable array of weapons. The early ones were rude implements, like the coarse flint stones with sharp edges (also of course used to cut a variety of other things), mazes, slings, bows and arrows, lances, buckles, shields for defense etc. These weapons were refined by more advanced cultures and new ones added to the repertory, like siege engines and catapults, many of which attained renowned celebrity by wining battles and in a sense changing the course of history. We need only to remember the siege engines of the Romans, the English long bows in Crecy and Agincourt, or the long pikes of the Swiss mercenaries so much sought after during the Renaissance. After the Chinese discovered gun powder whole catalog of new weapons revolutionized warfare. Suffice is to mention the role of cannons in the fall of Constantinople by the Turks and in European conflicts since the early Renaissance. The explosive radiation and perfecting of instruments of war had become, ever since, of paramount importance to world power.

According to the thesis of 'practical necessities', developmental patterns produce cases of evolutionary convergence, in other words, of similar ways to tackle the same existential problem. This is a well known phenomenon in the biological field. Wings, for example, are found in disparate group of animals far apart in the genealogical field, like insects, mammals and birds, as a way to penetrate some ecological niches. Fins too are exhibited by fishes, mammals and ancient reptiles. By analogy, in the social realm, it is then possible that the invention of bowls, arrows and plows represent cases of cultural convergence among different human communities.

However, the fact that many technical innovations simply did not have to occur is indicated by what happened with the wheel, a marvelous technical advance perfected very early by the Sumerians. Although its use became ubiquitous throughout the Mediterranean basin, and later in Europe and the Far East, no similar devise, as far as is known, was ever discovered in Bronze Age American cultures (although recently small wheeled artifacts, probably toys, had been found in Mesoamerican excavations) who, nevertheless, were able to build massive pyramids, fortifications and temples without them.

Other manifestations of culture, namely the spiritual, certainly are idiosyncratic and obviously unnecessary for the material survival of a human group. What urges Man to express himself in the visual arts, literature or music? Even more, why did they ORIGINATED AT ALL? Yet, these cultural exploits also display a general evolutionary sequence and appear to follow a common master plan. Visual arts and music, for instance, had gone through a general evolutionary blue-print of, firstly rough imitation of natural forms and sounds, later on of strivings to perfect shape, color and melody, and finally to a condition of abstraction when 'pure' color or sound are seek avidly. Again, not all cultures neatly manifest every stage of artistic or musical evolution, but the evolutionary guidelines we had just outlined are, in general, valid.

Likewise, religious development, also a fundamental aspect of culture, appears to contradict the conception of 'practical necessities'. The belief in the existence of deities which exert a beneficent, or malevolent, influence upon men is as ancient as Man himself. These beliefs had also generally gone through progressive animistic, polytheistic and monotheistic phases which, however, might be arrested at any point of the process without having reached the last, or even the intermediate stage. In general, these different phases roughly parallel the degree of sophistication attained by a given culture. Animistic cults, for instance, are usually associated with 'primitive' human societies, while polytheistic and monotheistic religions are more common in higher orbits of cultural attainment, with the latter universally considered the loftiest level of spiritual refinement.

If we assume that monotheism is the highest stage of religion evolution, it can be argued that the religious practices of many advanced civilizations (Greeks and Romans among others) do not seem as perfect as they should have been, given their achieved cultural level when compared to other contemporaneous nations (like the Jews). Nevertheless, it has never happened that a human community would attain a polytheistic level of belief without previously experiencing an animistic phase or embrace a monotheistic religion without previously endorsing the worship of a polytheistic pantheon of 'pagan' divinities.

To be sure, some cultural manifestations, as we will see later on in more detail, had been arrested in many societies, whether on a temporary or permanent basis, associated or not to a decadent state of the human group. Some literary and musical genres, for example, are in frank decline in Western nations (like poetry), particularly because they seem to interest a progressively more reduced circle of adepts, and because no new schools, styles, or even masterpieces had appeared now for several decades, while other genres, like movies, TV and musical performances, with the help of modern technology, had found wide acceptance. Whether this stagnation represents a temporary or permanent feature of Western cultural evolution is still to be seen.

Notwithstanding these fluctuations of cultural expressivity and tastes it can, nonetheless, be emphasized that, roughly speaking, cultural evolution everywhere in the world follows a predictable path centered on characteristics roughly comparable to the biological evolution of morphologic traits in the plant and animal kingdoms. The claim that such evolution is explained by practical necessities is negated, as it was said before, by developments in fields like art, music, literature and religion; a strange universality of forms difficult to reconcile with notions of utilitarian needs or technical demands. What changes often from one culture to another are the texture, design, styles and materials used in the elaboration of their universal survival necessities and cultural expressivity, that is, what serve as clues to determine the cultural line of descent of a given human community.

The conception of a human society as a supra-organism is reinforced by the pernicious biologism expressed in the 'evolutionary cycles' both Man and his societies are known to undergo. A youthful period of contagious enthusiasm, hope, ambition and optimism , both of a human group or an individual, eventually transform into a phase of 'maturity' when the early potentialities gives way to fulfillments and its natural urge for stability, the avoidance of undue risk, and a yearning for a fruitful enjoyment of whatever material and spiritual attainment had been achieved. Finally, a phase of decline sets in, an 'old age' when energies are sapped, the enthusiasm drained, a profound apathy or reluctance to 'change' becomes paramount, sometimes associated to doubts and paralysis of the Will. The general inertia ultimately leads to loss of ingenuity and originality, both materially and spiritually, which only possible outcome is 'passing away'.

I contend that there has never existed a single biological creature or human society that has escaped this perverse fate. The process might momentarily be arrested, or even reversed, only to invariably recur and inevitably continue its unrelenting course regardless of what measures are taken to avoid such an outcome. In the case of societies, toward the terminal stages, moral collapse frequently supervenes precipitating, with its spiritual bankruptcy, the inevitable 'demise' of the human group as an identifiable socio-cultural historic entity or supra-organism.

Why is it so? Why society as a plurality has to undergo a change so similar to each of its constitutive elements? The mysteries of the process of senescence have not been unraveled yet. Theories such as 'genetic exhaustion', progressive accumulation of waste products, and more recently, the glycosilation of tissue proteins, are still far from been proved by any modern means. The same can be claimed for the aging of a human community. Again, in this field, no theory has been sufficiently plausible to convince the majority of authorities. In one case, like in the other, Life is known to be competing against entropy, the executor of the most important of biological laws: the law of Finitude in Time. No historical group had ever challenged successfully this Second Law of Thermodynamics and there is no indication it ever will be subverted. No 'fountain of youth' had ever been found for Man the individual and no similar expedient had, so far, been discovered for human socio-political entities.

The view of a society as a meta-human supra-organism, therefore, will help us to understand the dynamics of societal changes by comparing its evolution to their biological counterpart: the metazoan. A human community is the 'product' of Man activity, who, with his culture, controls and influences the fate of the whole. Likewise, an animal or plant is the product of its constitutive cells, which through physiology, a product of cell activity, controls the life and well-being of the organism to which they belong and depends for survival. Each of these cells, like each man in the human community, has a role to play. In fact, without the coordinating activity of all of them life itself would not be possible.

Civilizations, like metazoan creatures, can live through periods of stability and instability or 'crisis', epochs of violent commotions, danger and perils, or of happiness and prosperity. Organisms could be disturbed by infections or cancers and societies by their equivalents: wars and internal upheavals. Nations can indulge in orgies of genocidal furor or attempts to subjugate their neighbors, like countless empire builders had done in the past. Individuals, in their turn, can commit suicide or, again, dominate and manipulate other people for lucrative or other purposes.

If the evolution, or 'natural history', of a morbid state in a multi-cellular organism has its counterpart in disturbances of the existing order of a human civilized community, there must be certain universal features of the first that could be applied, and then shed light, upon the second. Let us take the case of a cancerous growth. This nosologic entity consist of a group of cells, from one of many possible tissues of the body, who escape control from the regulatory mechanisms which orchestrate all physiological systems and commence to grow and spread in a 'disorderly' fashion to distant sites, frequently resulting, because of the functional disruptions it causes, in the death of the metazoan. The 'malignant' cell's 'hubris' ultimately, then, can give away with life itself, and in the process bring about their own destruction. Death is the price for victory.

The neoplastic cells originate in one of many possible cell lines and, as we said before, one of their fundamental characteristics is their lack of response to the restrictions and limitations that communal life imposes: a freedom, precisely, from those regulatory mechanisms which are essential to the survival of the afflicted animal or plant. The eradication of the malignant process requires a surgical resection, chemotherapy or radiotherapy, depending on technical factors irrelevant to our discussion. It is worth noting, however, that with the present therapeutic resources, IN NO WAY THE CURE OF THE CANCER, AT LEAST AT PRESENT TIME, IS EFFECTED BY THE RETURN OF THE GROUP OF CANCEROUS CELLS TO THEIR PREVIOUS STATE OF OBIDIENCE AND HARMONY WITH THE WHOLE. ONCE THE CELLS DEREPRESS THEY WILL REMAIN IN THIS CONDITON IN THE VAST MAJORITY OF THE CASES, insensitive to regulatory influences, oblivious to the interests and demands of the organism to which they belong, egotistically trying to advance their individual urges. A cancerous cell LACKS ALTRUISM; that capacity to cooperate with others for the common good, the sacrificial spirit and willingness to surrender individual urges critical for survival of the metazoan.

Likewise, in a human society, occasionally a number of their integrating members develop attitudes and behaviors opposite to the best interests of the community to which they belonged; what we can call brigands or antisocial elements. THE EQUIVALENT TO CANCER CELLS IN A HUMAN COMMUNITY ARE THOSE ELEMENTS OF THE SOCIETY WHO, BY THEIR ACTIONS, TRY TO DESTROY ITS FABRIC FROM WITHIN. This upheaval in a social fabric corresponds, in every respect, to a DEPRIVATION OF HEALTH in the biological domain, a disruption of a healthy state in a living organism.

The parallel between cultural and biological organisms is even more enriching. A 'war', that is, an armed struggle of a nation or civilization against another, or even the quiet and often slow invasion of a civilized society by members of a different human group which at first surreptitiously, and later more openly, disrupt the social balance, sapping its 'energy' and ultimately even provoking a collapse and dissolution of the 'body social' of the cultural supra-organism, could be compared to the ravages of an infectious disease. For instance, a disease like lethal pneumonia could in the socio-communal case be compare to the sudden destruction by foreign invaders of a nation or civilization; like, for example, the downfall of the Aztec Empire by the Spaniards. In other cases the process is more akin to a chronic fatal infection, like tuberculosis, as was the case with the progressive infiltration of the Western Roman Empire by the barbarians, a process which eventually led to its downfall.

However, as with an infection in the biological realm, the infiltration by invaders of a human community do not necessarily has to result in a national collapse; sometimes the invaders are repulsed, a 'cure' of the social 'ills' is effected and the socio-cultural supra-organism survives. Typical cases are the slow penetration by nomadic invaders of bronze-age civilizations, which conquered them only to be ultimately overthrown and repulsed: Like the case of Hyskos in Egypt, Mongols in China and Elamites in the Sumerian cities. These are clear examples of restitution of communal 'health' after such invasions (although in Mesopotamia, after a protracted struggle lasting several centuries, the Sumerians ultimately succumbed to the invaders following the fall of Ur). Another case in point was the "revival" of the Roman Empire after the crisis of the III Century by the concerted efforts of the Illyrian Emperors and later on by Diocletian and Constantine, who strapped the Empire in the straight jacked of a caste system. These comparisons, of course, could only be approximations. The civilizational hierarchical level only keeps a rough similarity to the biological counterpart. Biological cellular behavior lacks the 'deliberate intention' or 'premeditation' of human acts, or so we think, but in general the correspondence is valid.

We have been commenting, up to here, about the similarities between biological and cultural organisms, but there are also some very significant apparent differences. As we have pointed out before, the 'fate' of a cell in a multi-cellular organism is ingrained in its morphology. They, invariably, have a specific structural make up and function according to their assigned roles in the metazoan animal or plant. This role cannot be transformed or changed into another, IT IS FIXED for the life of the cell inasmuch as it is part of the phenotypic expression and, as such, PREDETERMINED. (This situation is currently changing with the successful transformation in the laboratory of human stem cells into specific tissues). This, of course, does not appear to be the case with the integrating elements of the human cultural supra-organism: Man. Man's plasticity, we have already said, indicates that ultimate 'fate' cannot be predicted from 'look' or dress, that in fact his role in the human community could be changed if He so 'desire' and environmental circumstances allows it to happen. (Paradoxically, although man, the individual, appears to be able to change his role in the human community, social classes do not.)

THE RULING CIRCLES OF A SOCIO-CULTURAL SUPRA-ORGANISM (THE POLITICAL PARTIES IN A DEMOCRACY) ENDORSE A RATHER PERMANENT SET OF VALUES THAT DETERMINE THEIR VIEWS IN SOCIO-POLITICAL AND ECONOMIC MATTERS AND DEFINES ITS POLITICAL GOALS AND ACTIONS IN GOVERNMENT, WHILE THE INDIVIDUAL, ON THE OTHER HAND, IS ABLE, IF HE SO DESIRE, TO CHANGE HIS OR HER POINT OF VIEW AND POLITICAL AFFILIATION. This last situation is equivalent to a cell being capable to decide to which organic tissue she will belong.

It is, precisely, this property what has permitted the enormous success of Man by allowing his rapid adaptability to environmental challenges of every sort AS A MEMBER OF THE HUMAN GROUP after escaping with his culture THE TYRANNY OF THE GENES. In fact, a human is perfectly capable, and often does serve, several roles or 'duties' for the community. He or she can, for instance, be a hair-dresser during the day, play a musical instrument for an orchestra at night and, perhaps, even function as a leader in various capacities for the group. It is also possible that a person takes different roles at different times or periods of his or her life. This versatility is unheard of in their biological equivalent: the cells. Even those capable of multiple activities within the frame of an organ (like the liver cells which does synthesize glycogen and excrete bile pigments among other functions) do so by genetic commands, always within restricted set of options, and could never be 'promoted' to a governing or ruling position like Man does in a modern society. There is not such a thing as tissue 'communalism'.

However, it has to be clarified that not even in the unlikely event that a person would be able to change his profession and even his perceived role in society it means that he is free. THIS ILLUSION RESULTS FROM

OUR INCAPACITY TO PREDICT INDIVIDUAL BEHAVIOR. Individual human freedom, it has been said before, is an illusion. I contend that if the totality of neurological stimuli determining behavior at a given instant are known, behavior would be ABSOLUTELY predictable. That is, if the sum total of all the sensory impulses (including those from the higher association centers) impinging, at any given time, upon the efferent neuronal apparatus were COMPLETELY KNOWN, the response of the individual would be anticipated with the same accuracy we can display in predicting the response to the most simple reflexes, like the knee jerk reflex. This, of course, does not mean that another human given the same set of stimuli upon his efferent neuronal pathway will act in like manner. In each case behavior is the consequence of individual neuro-physiologic characteristics of the nervous system which determine the final response. Human actions are unpredictable (here the notion of freedom) BECAUSE WE IGNORE THE EXACT COMPOSITION OF ALL NEURONAL STIMULI CONVERGING UPON THE 'VOLITIVE' EFFECTOR CENTER AT ANY GIVEN TIME, AS WELL AS THE DIFFERENT NEUROANATOMICAL AND NEUROPHYSIOLOGICAL CHARACTERISTICS OF EACH INDIVIDUAL BRAIN, THAT IS, THE INNER WORKINGS OF THE INDIVIDUAL RELATIONAL APPARATUS. Collective responses of human groups or social classes, on the other hand, are frequently accessible to predictions in view of the fact that they are historically and culturally conditioned and sufficient number of individuals will react in a similar manner to socio-political events; the factors at work are known and outliers do not have enough power to alter the behavior of the group.

Another very significant difference between biological and cultural organisms is in what refers to the 'retribution' received by the individual constitutive elements (cells or humans), for the rendered services in behalf of the group. In the former case the cells of the various tissues are only expected to be provided with their 'nourishment', in other words, with the necessary means to proceed with their 'work'. This nourishment is conveyed by way of a system of channels (the blood vessels) carrying the necessary substances (nutrients and oxygen) to sustain their lives and also serve as a means for the disposal of toxic metabolic wastes (another survival necessity).

This situation is quite similar to that of AN SLAVE in a human society, the condition when a person was only expected to received, in exchange for his or her labors, the daily minimal sustenance capable of allowing for life and reproduction to proceed and more work to be done. But in a human community the process of retribution is much more complex than this. Man has created the notion of VALUE and a way of assessing and comparing worth of services rendered by referring to a common denominator fulfilling the purpose, not only of VALUE SCALE, but also as a transaction vehicle or 'facilitator' of exchange of goods and services among members of the society: MONEY.

A first temptation is to compare 'money', in the communal realm, to 'energy' or calories, in the biological one. The distribution of the latter is made in an equitable manner according to needs and, if a 'surplus' take place, it is 'stored' in special units, the fat cells, for subsequent utilization as need arises. Not so with money in human transactions. Although it also gets stored in specific places (banking institutions), still belongs to the 'depositors'. This sense of 'property' is alien to the biological field.

Money serves not only as a common denominator to the worth of human skills and products but, in its turn, confers POWER to the possessor, precisely by this quality of been accepted in ex-change for any existing and imaginable material object, comfort or necessity. This is the reason why money not only satisfy the basic human urge to possess, but also conveys to their possessor a measure of control upon his environment and life. If to that is added the inherent unequal distribution of this precious commodity (because of differences in skills, training, industriousness, ambition, education, access to markets or even luck) we will be able to appreciate the lack of parallel between societal and biological 'economy', where, as it was said before, a sort of ingrained 'egalitarianism' and unselfish dedication in the carrying out of the cellular metabolic 'duties' prevails.

Ambition is one of the roots of human motivation and money enhances these urges by bestowing gratification and satisfaction to those who have it. It is money then, indirectly, the article that, by propitiating the social stratification of a modern human community, strongly determines the makeup of the governments, whether they are a capitalistic or communist society (in the latter case the 'party', at least in theory, is the one holding the economic and political power). It is fair then to assume that A MODERN SOCIO-CULTURAL SUPRAORGANISM, AS TIME

ELAPSES, RESEMBLES PROGRESSIVELY LESS ITS BIOLOGICAL COUNTERPART. The modern open society is a radical departure from the times of the hereditary ruling circles, so prevalent until very recently, when servitude and/or slavery were prevalent. Again, this change in the basic mettle of the socio-cultural entities has revitalized and strengthens seemingly decadent communities. It is equivalent to an animal that grows a new brain!

Finally, a metazoan has a discrete existence as a living Being, an existence terminating, rather abruptly, in time with death. Fundamentally, when a metazoan dies its constituting cells will in their totality die also but at different rates. Some will do so in a few minutes (like the nerve cells), but others will take several hours and even days to die (In fact recently it has been discovered that some stem cell can survive for up to 17 days), depending on their respective requirements for nutrients and oxygen. On the other hand, the 'death' of a society (nation or civilization) does not necessarily imply the concomitant 'passing away' of its constitutive members, that is, of the members of the community. Many could survive and, if the cultural demise is not violent, they frequently would not notice an immediate difference. THE TRANSFORMATION WILL NOT NECESSARILY BE EQUATED WITH THE EXTINCTION OF ALL THE CONSTITUTIVE HUMAN ELEMENTS FORMING THE SUPRA-ORGANISM AT THAT TIME. As it was mentioned before, the Roman Empire, for instance, by every historical evidence was dead (in the west) by the V Century AD, but people who lived then within its confine endured the hardships of the times and continued to carry on with their normal daily activities unaware of the momentous importance of what had happened . Yet, the inhabitants had ceased to function as integral part of the deceased society, something they were ignorant at the time. IT IS THIS CEASING TO BE MEMBERS OF A COMMUNAL GROUP AND NOT NECESSARILY PHYSICAL DEATH WHAT IS COMMON TO ALL THE HIERARCHICAL LEVELS OF BIOLOGICAL EXISTENCE AND WHAT DISAPPEARED WHEN THE ORGANISM, WHETHER A MOLECULE, PROTOZOA, ANIMAL, PLANT OR HUMAN SOCIETY PERISHED.

Notwithstanding these differences among the biological and social orders, the view of a human community as a cultural supra-organism is valid and, as we will see in the next Chapter, it has the merit of permitting historical predictions hitherto impossible.

This need to define the boundaries of an object of higher dimensional order creates natural ambiguities, giving a character of arbitrariness to any attempt to map the tetra-dimensionality of a human community. The perplexity results because of the vagueness inherent and the need to clarify the meaning of terms frequently used by historians like, for example, civilization, culture, nation, country, etc. In order to proceed with our discussion we need, now, to explain the meaning of these terms as they are being applied in this work.

We have to attempt the identification of the irreducible societal unit that undergoes the above mention evolutionary changes of growth, maturity, decay and death. Although semantically the nouns CULTURE and CIVILIZATION are used many times interchangeably, we are going, for descriptive purposes, to give different connotations to each one. A CULTURE, AS USED HERE, WILL MEAN THE SUM TOTAL OF TECHNICAL, ARTISTIC, LITERARY, MUSICAL AND RELIGIOUS EXPRESSIONS OF PEOPLE INHABITING A GEOGRAPHIC LOCUS OR EVEN SCATTERED TERRITORIES DURING A GIVEN TIME FRAME. CIVILIZATION, ON THE OTHER HAND, WILL REFER TO A SPECIFIC HUMAN GROUP BOUND OR NOT TOGETHER BY SOCIO-POLITICAL TIES AND WHO SHARE, OR PARTAKE, IN A GIVEN CULTURAL TRADITION.

For example, in the region which historians call today Mesopotamia, the 'land between the rivers', a CULTURE arose 5000 years ago and 'lived' uninterruptedly for approximately 2500 years. It gave 'birth' to several distinct CIVILIZATIONS (Sumero-Akkadian, Old Babylonian, Assyrian, etc) with similar roots but differing somewhat in cultural specifications, that is, in the details of their 'expressivity' (whether in art, religion, literature etc.). CULTURES, THEN, COULD BE CONCEIVED AS HISTORICAL SPECIES OF WHICH THE CIVILIZATIONS ARE THE INDIVIDUAL SPECIMES. There are occasions, however, when the geographic locus of the culture is EXHAUSTED by one single civilization; like in the case of the Egyptian, whose sway was practically identical with the physical location and territorial expanse of its culture. In such cases is when we will use interchangeably both terms. In reference to the nouns NATION or COUNTRY they will be here utilized in their traditional sense, to represent defined regional areas with political frontiers and unified governments. These political 'units', in some cases, could be equated and in fact overlap the geographic locus of a civilization and even a culture, like in the case of China (although their physical boundaries had fluctuated over the years), but in other cases several of them are included in the geographic and cultural confines of a civilization, like is the case with the Western European nations today. On the other hand, the term Western Christian Civilization, includes not only the European nations but also encompass countries descending from the European cultural stock, which includes today not only all the American continent but also Australia.

The modern 'country' or 'nation' shares, with their sisters, in the cultural heritage common to a given region and, singly or as a group, undergo the historico-biological evolutionary cycles we have already mention in all 'living' entities. England, Italy, Spain, Portugal, France, etc., had already experienced at different times their periods of growth, apogee and decline. Because they are relatively 'young' none has yet 'died' or disappeared from the historic scene and, although every one of them had left behind their periods of maximal power and splendor in world affairs, they are still very much 'alive' and the possibility of a future 'revival' certainly could not be ruled out. On the other hand, it is entirely possible that none of them would truly 'die' until the passing away of the civilization to which they belong. This is a case of social interdependence and mutual help to delay the ultimate unavoidable fate. Typical examples are the already alluded European nations, so much at each other throat for centuries, and now clinging together for mutual survival, something unheard of in the past, probably having to do with the development of modern weapons of mass destruction.

That civilizations, and countries, before their historical demise, can endure periods of decadence alternating with others of grandeur is an established fact. The classical case of such happening is the ancient Egyptian civilization, which suffered two epochs of frank cultural decline (one between the Old and Middle Kingdoms and the other between the Middle and the New Kingdom or Empire) before falling into the prolonged agony of creativity preceding its ultimate disappearance from the historical scene as a viable socio-political entity. Besides the periods of major decline there were numerous lesser episodes of relative decadence during the rule of uninspired monarchs.

Something similar happened to other major civilizations, like the Indian which, as will be seen below in more detail, after a major efflorescence in the third millennia BC in the Indus Valley, went through a prolonged dark age only terminating in the V Century BC when works in Sanskrit appeared, followed by the mastery of carving in stone heralding a cultural renaissance. Another case in point is China which, as also will be analyzed later on, endured during its long history several protracted episodes of decline and resurgence. (For reasons to be analyzed later on the Medieval Epoch is NOT considered here a temporary downturn of an existing civilization, but rather a period of gestation of a new one: Western Christian Civilization, an offspring of the Greco-Roman world).

It is an interesting historical fact that no human group smaller than a modern 'country' presently undergoes the cyclical evolutionary changes alluded to before. This is in contraposition to earlier periods when, often, the 'cities', at least during part of their history, used to be the geographic locus which underwent the cycles, inasmuch as a country frequently WAS a city (and even occasionally defined a civilization), with the immediately surrounding countryside functioning as an integral socio-political unit. Summer, Babylon, Athens, and even Rome at the beginning, are but few examples attesting to this geo-political fact.

As important as the geographic locus of a nation or civilization is, the notion of its temporal boundaries also is of paramount importance, but something frequently difficult to establish or apprehend concretely. Let us take for the sake of clarification the previous example of the Egyptian Civilization. When we refer to it we have in mind an ancient human group technologically advanced for its time which developed distinctive artistic, literary and architectonic achievements. It grew in the Valley of the Nile approximately 5000 years ago, historically surviving as a cohesive cultural group for a period of about 3000 years. But when we refer to Egypt the 'nation' today, the meaning changes completely to represent a distinctive geographic place with defined political frontiers, where a community lives under a unified government with codified laws and a set of social institutions. Although the geographic locus of the ancient 'civilization' approximately overlap that of the 'nation' today they are different 'things', because now the population is predominantly Arabic and the culture Islamic. There might still be some cultural and racial traits of the original inhabitants, those who found the previous 'civilization', but so diluted them must be as to become practically unrecognizable. After the 'hellenization' and 'islamization' of the land few identifiable remnants are left of the original people and culture.

The problem arises when we try to establish the concrete temporal boundaries of this ancient civilization. When the 'demise' of the Egyptian Civilization did occur? Was it at the end of the reign of Ramses XI when the Empire was dissolved, or rather with the Saites and Greek dynasties much later? Can we pinpoint an exact DATE for its historic demise?

The same situation is faced when we seek to define the temporal boundaries of Classical Greece. When it was that this civilization disappeared? We know that the land of Pericles, Solon and Socrates was different to the abode of the Byzantine Emperors, but when are we to declare it defunct: with the invasion of Alexander, the rise to power of the Antigonian, Ptolemaic and Seleucid dynasties, or rather with the conquest by the Romans? Could the Hellenistic World still be considered part of the same civilization as Classical Greece and, if not, when it transmuted into it? All that we can concretely say is that the latter dissipated slowly into history as part of a continuous transformation, the consequence of complex geopolitical and social changes that took place in the Mediterranean basin, and not before cross-fertilizing its cousin the Roman Empire, forming what historians call Greco-Roman civilization. The fact of the matter is that, in many cases, it is impossible to clearly ascertain when the 'character' of the human group changes, the historical 'moment' of its transmutation into something else.

Yet in some cases, however, this is entirely feasible. Carthage, the nation, ceased to exist when Scipious Africanus laid waste to the city in 146 B.C. and their inhabitants were slaughtered or sold into slavery. The site of the city was reoccupied later on during the Roman triumvirate

Miguel Ochoa

by Lepidus, becoming under Julius Cesar a colony of landless Roman citizens and later on under Augustus transforming into a prosperous center for the administration of the North African territories; but its population and culture were totally different and therefore not a part of the original socio-cultural supra-organism. It could be cogently argued that Carthage was the last VITAL offspring of the Phoenician culture, which besides the invention of alphabetic writing is credited with the development of the technique of glass-blowing, granulation in gold work and, as behooves masters seafaring people, the design of a prototype of ships rowed by tiers of oarsmen which, even, allowed them to sail into the Atlantic Ocean and probably to circumnavigate Africa. Likewise, the end of the Byzantine Empire can be concretely dated to 1453 AD with the fall of Constantinople to Sultan Memmet, and the conversion of the city to the Istanbul of the Ottoman Empire.

The spatio-temporal confines of socio-cultural supra-organisms could, then, be either sharply defined or fuzzy depending on whether they have political frontiers (like modern nations do) or not (ancient civilizations) and on whether their temporal boundaries are or not demarcated by specific historic events, like conquests, revolutions or wars. These are the reasons why the occasional perplexity as to whether human groups belong or not to a given socio-cultural denomination, that is, whether they are located 'inside' or 'outside' of them.

The problem, as was said before, is one of hierarchical perspective. It would be as difficult for an small cell to precise THE EXACT MOMENT when the metazoan to which she belongs dies, as for a human being frequently to know whether or not the supra-organism to which she or he belongs is still a viable entity, or has already become a cultural corpse. We can 'see' a tree, a fly, or another man and detect when a change in their condition takes place. We can tell when a tree 'dries' or a man 'dies', but if we were microscopic cells within these multi-cellular organisms, although what it is 'happening' to them would be very important to us, we will not be immediately aware of their 'passing away', inasmuch as we will be INCLUDED within this biological entity. Our enclosed condition will impede us to 'capture' all the events forming the totality in proper order and to perceive the meaning of what is occurring at a higher hierarchical level of existence. Only from a DISTANCE could we

46

achieve the necessary information unencumbered by our dimensional constrains.

Perhaps another example from the physical world might help to further clarify the matter. Let us assume that we are passengers in a spaceship leaving the Milky-Way galaxy. At what point can we, conclusively, be certain of having 'emerged' from it, in other words, when could we be unambiguously sure of being 'out' of IT? Not before we can identify it's 'contours', the disc shape with the central bulge and extended arms of the galaxy. (To be 'out', for our purposes, does not necessarily imply freedom from gravitational effects and other confounding factors; it only refers to visual clues). What this means is that we cannot appreciate the 'concreteness' of a conglomeration of stars until the proper perspective allows us to do so. It would be completely impossible for the hypothetical sidereal traveler to clearly ascertain the EXACT POSITION of the galactic rim and, therefore, the precise moment when the spaceship trespasses this cosmic frontier. There could be occasions, however, when there would not be any uncertainty; for instance if the spaceship 'falls' into a rocky planet. In this case the putative traveler, if she or he survives, would have no doubts as to where they are. The clear visualization of the rocky planetary surface will preclude any perplexity about it.

It is, therefore, THE CONCRETENESS OF THE HISTORIC EVENTS what allows the inhabitants of a socio-cultural supra-organism to determine their place in reference to It. The citizens of Tenochtitlan knew that the Aztec Empire was dead when after a prolonged siege the Spaniards overran and destroyed the capital. But as we said before, in the case of the Western Roman Empire it would be impossible to determine the precise instant of its historic demise. The Empire is a distinct historical corpse, a veritable object in the socio-cultural domain, but like the case of the galaxy in the physical ambit, the boundaries are imprecise BECAUSE OF THE LACK OF A CONCRETE EXISTENTIAL EVENT TO RENDER IT SO. Any attempt to draw a line of demarcation around the temporal component of the socio-cultural 'body' of the Roman supra-organism will be tainted with an element of arbitrariness.

Many authorities viewing history with the perspective of an outsider place Rome concluding days with the climbing to power of Odoacer (476 AD), who quietly "displaced" the last legitimate ruler. No great commotion marks this day, no political upheaval, conquest or act of violence of any kind took place which would allow the inhabitants of The Empire to suspect that their Nation had 'passed away'. After all, by then for over 70 years barbarian leaders in the West had been the de facto rulers under the services of weak emperors. Only with the perspective of our temporal vantage point can we resolutely establish the disappearance, at ABOUT this time, of the Empire as a viable historical entity. No clear cut boundary can be traced by us around its temporal dimension for the same reason that we cannot do likewise either with the spatial frontiers of a galaxy. But the fuzziness of a clearly detectable boundary does not mean lack of reality. (It has to be emphasized that 'distinctness', 'fuzziness', 'definite' and 'indefinite' are relative terms, and also depend on the hierarchical level and relative dimensions of the elements in the compared systems).

Again, the problem when referred to Man and its society is one of perspective. We, as tridimensional Beings, can adequately precise what the physical boundaries of a metazoan are, in other words, the spatial limits and a clearly perceived surface of such an organism. A very different task, however, is for us to determine the tetra-dimensional confine of a social group. We are hampered by our tri-dimensional spatial constrains and our necessity to view the fourth dimension AS TIME. It would be impossible for us to BEHOLD its totality; only a tetra-dimensional spatial Being would be able to do so.

Occasionally, also, spatio-temporal proximity can deceive us. Just as two separate but distant starts can appear as one by the fact of being superimposed in the line of sight of our telescopes, two different socio-cultural supra-organisms, because of geographic and temporal overlapping, might seem to us as constituting the same entity. In the case of the stars only careful observations requiring the use of special instrumentation, like the spectroscope among others, will permit the astronomer to discern the existence of two, rather than one, star. Likewise, only careful cultural and historical analysis could let us discover the presence of two different human groups when because of spatio-temporal confounding factors in a perfunctory investigation they would appear to be one.

The conception of cultures AS SPECIES OF HUMAN SOCIETIES OR COMMUNITIES establishes the possibility of a COMPARATIVE CULTUROLOGY entirely similar to the field of Comparative Anatomy, capable of establishing lines of descent which would permit, not only an analysis and evaluation of cultural traits, but also serve as basis for rational classificatory attempts between nations and decide whether or not given countries belong to the same socio-cultural supraorganism. This kind of 'cultural phylogeny' will also reveal such an abundance of extraordinary similarities among different cultural denominations, even among seemingly disparage and geographically distant groups, as to raise the notion of COMMON ANCESTERS (see below) among all living human communities. In the same way that chordates have a common amphioxus-like forebear, there appears to be a common proto-culture pervading every remote corner of our planet, at least since the Middle Pleistocene.

Now, it is common knowledge that there is nothing in the body plan of chordates INDISPENSABLE for survival on Earth. Other adaptive solutions could be found. We know this because we are aware of the existence of other types of metazoan (the invertebrates) who also live, frequently quite successfully, in numerous ecological environments. In the case of cultures, because of the absence of different cultural modalities or prototypes, it is impossible to imagine how these radically different cultural models would be like. A society without religion, music or art, would be very difficult, if not impossible, for us to conceive, in view of the fact that we have come to identify them with the human condition. Yet this do not make any of these categories indispensable to civilization, but for us a culture without those attributes will be very difficult to phantom, because we had never known of one without them. Likewise it is impossible for us to conceive the body plan of many strange creatures that had disappeared eons ago, and yet we know, by their fossilized remains, that they existed in our planet for millions of years and there are some that still live today. Hardly a year goes by without the discovery of new strange forms of life with no skeletons mostly from the depth of the oceans, but not limited to them.

Even at the molecular level there are questions of this kind. Is there a biological necessity of why the genetic code has to be the way it is? We have no prove that in Earth a different code never arose, and the possibility that it did and eventually disappeared could not be ruled out. In molecules, like with soft-body organisms, unfortunately, there are no fossils and therefore no possibility to search for traces of a different genetic makeup.

It could very well be, then, that the universal similarities of cultural traits, the apparent evidence of a 'master plan' shared by all civilizations known from the historical and archeological record or existing at the present (in every respect comparable to the 'body plan' of biological creatures), indicates DESCENT FROM A COMMON PROTO-CULTURAL ANCESTER probably identifiable with the strivings of Homo Erectus, but that could even be more remote, after the extinctions of other human prototypes, thus explaining strange cultural similarities among widely separated human communities. This phenomenon is not surprising when considered on the light of biological evolution with its periodic massive extinctions followed by new radiations. Many similarities of the cultural product should not, then, be considered a fortuitous event or prompted by 'practical necessities', but rather could be the result of CULTURAL EVOLUTION which parallel biological evolution but at a higher hierarchical sphere.

CHAPTER IV

What have we learned with this comparative analysis of the organic and cultural fields? What important 'lessons' can we derive from the first into the second? If no significant revelations could be extrapolated from one into the other we would be engaging solely in useless and wasteful speculations. Our hypothesis, however, carries TESTABLE PREDICTIONS which are based in the underlining 'fabric' and 'texture' of human society.

For instance, according to this thesis, the Latin American countries will never effect the necessary economic development under a laissez faire 'free enterprise' politico-economic system. The reason for this assertion is the fact that the 'middle classes' in these countries, the generative force for economic growth in a capitalist society, cannot be equated with the European bourgeoisie which is reputed with triggering the Industrial Revolution. This is because these 'middle classes' are the heirs of the Spanish and Portuguese equivalents, which are known historically to have lost their zest shortly after the conquest of America, when their outlook of life and mores were co-opted by the aristocratic classes of these countries, which then still possessed a medieval ethos. (Many historians attribute this socio-political phenomenon to the persecution and eviction of Jews and Moslems from the Iberic peninsula in the XVI and XVII centuries. Others attribute the Spanish downfall to the negative impact in their exports by the inflation resulting from the large inflows of precious metals from America.)

Although, as it was said before, individuals can change their role in society the 'character' of a social class and therefore the agenda of their political representatives is immutable. Human society and their integrating parts are 'organically' associated and, therefore, suffer structural constrains which render modification of its basic mettle outright impossible (as much as it would be for one kind of body tissue to transform into another). SOCIAL CLASSES SERVE PERMANENT FUNCTIONS IN THE INTEGRATED FABRIC OF THE SOCIO-CULTURAL SUPRA-ORGANISM. WHEN THEIR ROLES DECLINE IN SURVIVAL IMPORTANCE THEY WILL INVOLUTE AND

BECOME VESTIGIAL OR MUTATE INTO SOMETHING DIFFERENT TO ACQUIRE NEW RELEVANCE IN SOCIETAL DYNAMICS.

Unquestionably, the European bourgeoisie was largely instrumental in the spectacular economic growth of Western Europe during the XVIII and XIX centuries (some authorities see an earlier version of this class in the merchants and bankers of the Italian city states during the early Renaissance) which many attribute to the laissez-faire capitalism expounded by Adam Smith and followers, the system credited with freeing society from the grip of the Old European Regime.

It will be erroneous, however, to equate economic growth in many modern developing societies with a similar dynamic. If we focus in those countries whose middle classes descended from the conquering Spanish and Portuguese colonizers, and who never underwent changes similar to those in Northern Europe, it emphatically can be stated that this 'middle income sector' could not be compared to the European bourgeoisie that set in motion the miracle of the Industrial Revolution. The economic growth of these nations is based mostly in selling raw materials and commodities, something, at the present, only benefiting a relatively small sector of the population.

This should not be surprising when we realize that this Latin American social class carries within itself the atavistic medieval stigmas brought to the 'New World' by their Spanish and Portuguese ancestors, for whom the only socially acceptable occupations were the Church and the Military. Landed property was the most logical and profitable investment on top of giving status to the owner. Commerce and industry remained looked upon with contempt.

This outlook of life, this ethos was inherited by them during the colonial time from their ancestors and although, at the present, the middle classes in those new countries do not look upon a career in the military or the church as necessary appealing, they in general are financially conservative, and still today avoid speculative investments and look at landed property and real estate as the more advantageous vehicle of capital formation. THE ELEMENT OF INVESTMENT RISK, OF SUCH PARAMOUNT IMPORTANCE IN THE RISE AND ULTERIOR DEVELOPMENT OF MODERN EUROPEAN NATIONS AND THEIR DESCENDENTS IN NORTH AMERICA WAS LARGELY ABSENT AND NEVER GREW IN THIS SOCIAL CLASS.

It has been long debated whether this zest of the original bourgeoisie resulted from the nascent protestant ethic (mainly Calvinism) forming in Northern Europe after The Reformation, or rather to advances in communication, banking and transportation; but this discussion is beyond the scope and purpose of this book. What has to be emphasized is, as is the case in biological organisms, the INHERITABLE NATURE OF ACQUIRED SOCIETAL TRAITS, TRAITS THAT EVEN MIGRATE WITH THEIR POSSESSORS FROM ONE GEOGRAPHIC LOCUS TO ANOTHER. This is an additional prove of the pervasive biologism permeating Culture.

But changes in the underlining set of values of a social group can take place and are akin to mutations in the biological field eventually giving birth to something different: A new social species. Is that happening today in Latin America? Modern technology and finance are changing the geopolitical equation and it is possible that a new social species eventually will rise, but still it is too early to tell and I can't see it happening in the foreseeable future. Certainly some Latin American countries are developing their economies, but largely with foreign capital and thanks to export of commodity goods whose prices fluctuate, sometimes considerably. Whether the outlook of life for these societies will ultimately evolve and embrace spontaneously a materialistic tone akin to that of advanced capitalist countries, or if in order to develop their economies a radical political restructuration, entailing the eviction from power precisely of this ineffectual 'middle class', will be required, is difficult to tell. Judging by the slow social evolution in these countries due primarily to entrenchment of the existing order, stagnation could be a more likely outcome, if no radical change takes place. It was futile to expect of the aristocratic classes in post- Renaissance Europe to SPONTANEOUSLY transform and erase the structural hindrances to the advent of the industrial age. As it was postulated above, for similar reasons it will prove equally impossible for the 'middle income sector' of modern societies to be the engine of economic growth of Latin America, unless it morph into a new social class with a different outlook and perspective . A spontaneous modification of a basic behavioral pattern in a social class, that is, without a triggering mechanism, like the radical religious and technological changes during and after the Renaissance, is not more possible than the transformation of one kind of organic tissue into another.

Yet, again, it should be emphasized that if a pacific transformation eventually supervenes it will be an indication that this 'middle class' had morphed into a different sociopolitical entity with a different outlook of life and societal dynamic, in other words, into a new social class within the fabric of the cultural supra-organism to which it belongs. There are, however, geopolitical and demographic indicators, like the increase in population couple with better education, giving rise to some degree of upper mobility not parallel by improvement in occupational opportunities, which are provoking considerable social unrest, particularly among the young members of this expanding 'middle class'. Whether this situation, in future, will generate a new mutation in the makeup of this social group is a moot question.

In this regard it should be remember that also by peaceful transformation was that the European bourgeoisie arose from the medieval tradesmen and shopkeepers in the Renaissance. It was a process of slow mutation taking advantage of the religious changes and technological advances which propitiated its growth, including transportation and the increasing use of money in commercial transactions. This new urban class revitalized the cities and gave rise to a prodigious political and economic transformation, first in Northern Italy and later in the Low Countries and England before spreading to the rest of Western Europe. But it has to be emphasized that this new dynamic class of entrepreneurs, merchants and professionals, those who created wealth by investing and risking their capital giving rise to modern 'Capitalism', represented a true social mutation in the body corpus of their societies, a new social class with an entire different view of their social and political roles and with a different set of values and outlook of life that their Middle Age forbearers.

An intriguing phenomena is what is happening in Modern China where IT IS THE GROWTH OF THE ECONOMY LARGELY RESULTING FROM GOVERNMENTAL GUIDANCE WHAT IS GIVING RISE TO A MIDDLE CLASS OF CONSUMERS. Here again a 'middle income sector of society', like what is happening also in other areas of the world including Latin America, is represented at the present time by educated workers, professionals and bureaucrats who cannot be equated with the dynamic enterprising bourgeoisie of Europe. The modern 'middle classes cannot be trusted to economically develop their societies. Their only role is to consume and in doing so unintentionally sustain but not create the economic growth.

In the case of a guided economy, like China, the economic development is effected by central planning. But in those countries where there is no such a thing, like in the case of Latin America, the passivity and lack of entrepreneurship of this middle class disqualify it as engine or promoter of economic growth, only serving to perpetuate stagnation and therefore giving rise to chronic poverty.

A novel social phenomenon afflicting this new 'middle class' in modern countries is the rise of a new breed of workers better known as 'white collar', representing the salaried employees proliferating in what is now called, perhaps presumptuously, the 'Post-Industrial State'; the one that ushered our present so-called 'Service Economy'. They constitute a disparage group of people lacking in general the 'class consciousness' and militancy of the workers industrialization gave rise to. Being better educated than their forebears they disavow the vociferous comradeship of their blue-collar ancestors and, instead, very often tend to repudiate unionization. This new social animal frequently embrace the standards and tastes of the affluent in society and refuse to create bonds among themselves, a lack of solidarity undermining with their divisionism the capacity to form a common front to defend their working rights and interests.

But there is a new geo-political factor to take into consideration and that might render irrelevant whether the middle income sectors of the underdeveloped world, including Latin America, will mutate or not into a new enterprising class. Up to the recent past those countries unable, whether for lack of capital, enterprising spirit or plain reluctance, to assimilate the needed expertise to industrialize eventually did become, willingly or not, the providers of raw materials as well as often the markets for the products that modern industry creates. Because of the relative cheapness of these materials in reference to the manufactured goods imported, the end result of the process had been the progressive impoverishment of a sizable portion of the population, which only made increasingly difficult for these nations, many constituting the vestiges of decadent cultures from the past, to overcome their prostrated condition and gain ascendancy.

A surprising new phenomenon made possible by modern technology and the globalization of financial markets, as well as the free flow of capital, has crystallized in recent times: namely the outsourcing by the rich industrialized countries of many manufactory and service activities to poorer and cheaper areas of the world, with consequent savings in the production process. This phenomenon had been possible because of new developments in societal dynamics propitiated by advances in communication, transportation and financial services. THE NOMADIC NATURE OF MODERN CAPITALISM OWES NO ALLIANCE TO ANY COUNTRY AND MORE THAN EVER IS MOVED SOLELY BY THE PROFIT MOTIVE. The old mercantilist colonial system, when corporations "belonged" to a country and their exports were sold to the "captured" economies of their colonies is by now a thing of the past. Could this new universality of corporate power be a prelude to a new kind of world order? Would this be in fact the agglutinating essence that by erasing political frontiers dominate and subjugate The Earth? Could this new phenomenon by "changing the equation" be beneficial to the underdeveloped world and finally permit their economic growth?

In some cases undoubtedly it has helped. We had already mentioned the "miracle" of modern China which has enormously benefited by allowing into the country Western corporations and industry. But this nation was quite advanced when it entered in decadence after the Manchu's invasions, and today technological and financial progress couple with a strong central government had permitted its spectacular economic growth by catering the tastes of the rich West. To a smaller degree something similar is happening to other mostly Asiatic economies, some of them miniscule splits from larger relatives; like Hong Kong from China and more recently Singapore from Malaysia. But could many other weak economies around the world be able to imitate the successful examples we had mentioned above and escape the tyranny of underdevelopment? Many human barriers will have to be overcome to make this possible.

Religious, cultural and racial hindrances will have to be erased. Yet, it need to be emphasized, the changes we are witnessing are the consequence of a westernization of the world cultures not a result of the revival of ancient models or the 'birth' of a new social class.

CHAPTER V

In order to undertake a 'cultural investigation' we need to analyze what are the factors involved, the different components of the 'cultures' in question, and determine which are those constitutive components that can be dispensed with and which are those fundamental to the identification of the cultural process, in other words, of what defines and differentiates one socio-cultural supra-organism from another.

Of all the elemental components of a cultural process language does not appear to be a sufficiently reliable characteristic to help us in our task, although occasionally a particular one becomes the medium of the literary corpus and legal cannons of a civilization or nation. Within them, sometimes, not one but several languages or dialects are spoken. It is hardly necessary to offer examples in this regard. Both in ancient China and India numerous dialects were spoken and, frequently, people from different geographic regions within the confines of the same nation were unable to understand each other. This fact, however, did not preclude the growth and evolution of their cultures, neither the development of a centralized government (which, in both cases, was often disrupted by protracted internecine warfare).Temporal evolution of a language is also consistent with the viability and continuity of a cultural tradition. In fact, there is hardly any modern or ancient language which has not undergone substantial transformation with time.

Race, also, does not seem to be a critical element in defining a culture. We know how in Mesopotamia, Semites, Indo-Europeans, and ancient Persian racial stocks partook of the same cultural heritage. Neither the Mongols in China, the Hyskos in Egypt, or the numerous ethnic groups forming constitutive part of the Roman Empire, disrupted the civilizations of these lands, although, certainly, they were, at one time or another, instrumental in modifications to their basic frame of traditions or to the evolution taken by their subsequent histories. In fact, sometimes even a term used to describe a race can suffer considerable semantic modification, like the term 'Jew' sufficiently documents. Originally signifying a specific ethnic stock, today it has lost its racial connotation and, instead, defines a human group sharing the same body of religious beliefs and a sense of belonging to a common historical tradition; a drama highlighted by persecution and a search for identity.

This brings us, then, to a third constitutive element of a human community: religion. Does the body of religious beliefs specify a Culture? In fact, some well known cultures are named after the religion they profess (notorious examples being Western Christian Culture and Islam). Greek and its descendant Roman Culture had their pantheon of gods which 'died' with their civilizations, and the same thing can be said of the indigenous American cultures and of the Egyptians. (Christianity, although heirs of Greco-Roman culture, presided upon the collapse of the ancient world and the rise of a new one.)

The case of Hindu culture is more complex and diverse. Although early equated with the Vedantic pantheon, splitting sects developed as early as the VII BC (mainly Buddhism and Jainism) mostly, it is assumed, as the result of the rigidity and ritual formalism of the Brahamanic priesthood. Ultimately modern Hindu Religion slowly evolved and eventually overcame the splinter sects, although Buddhism and Jainism still have followers in the land. It should be noticed, however, that these Indian religions were variations of one single 'theme', in a way similar to the sects proliferating in early Christianity and tagged as 'heretics'. However, an entirely different situation was the introduction of the Islamic Faith in the country (XII Century AD). This religion was forcefully imposed by foreign invaders and made many converts. Still today there are more than one hundred million Muslims in India not counting the millions in Bangladesh and Pakistan, all of which were part of 'India' and otherwise shared with the Indus the same cultural legacy. This religious split ultimately gave rise to social unrest and disastrous persecutions, finally provoking the present partition of the land; yet, despite of this division all the inhabitants of the Indian subcontinent partake of the same cultural background. Something similar happens in the Western lands where besides the Christian denominations an increasing array of smaller religious cults are been practiced today without altering fundamentally the basic cultural underpinning of the lands.

On the other hand a religious belief can be shared by several different ethnical and cultural groups, like the case of Islam which is practiced not only in the original Arabic lands but also in numerous communities which do not belong to the same racial and cultural background, like is the case of Indonesia, a populous Asiatic nation. Likewise Christianity is practiced in non-western cultural countries such as Philippines and Southern India, the Coptics in Egypt and, Maronites in Syria and Lebanon.

Another case in point is China, which also is peculiar and difficult to understand by western standards. Its beliefs are an amalgam of Confucian, Taoist and Buddhist principles intertwined with ancestor worship, an old practice in this land. It is common for the people to hold, simultaneously, views from all these religious-philosophical schools on account of the fact that they are not mutually exclusive; actually representing bodies of ethical precepts around abstract conceptions of a 'Supreme Being'. The lack of concreteness of form might have resulted from the ephemeral nature of mythological lore in China, which the experts ascribe to the policy of the Chou Emperors (XII Century BC), who very early, proscribed worship by the commoners of the principal deities; a prerogative they reserved only for themselves. From this situation apparently arose the ancestor religion tradition. Of the other three denominations we had mentioned, Taoism and Confucianism were native 'concoctions' which, although in many points of principle held opposite opinions, nevertheless became quite compatible to the Chinese, who found common ground of understanding between these two great ethical autochthonous systems.

On the other hand Buddhism was a foreign influence. It penetrated the country during the period of the Northern Wei Dynasty at a time of governmental weakness following the downfall of the long and stable rule of the Han emperors in 220 BC., and became very popular around the Third Century AD. Unlike what happened to Europe in the Dark Ages the years of schism and turmoil that followed, with the so-called 'Six Dynasties', were not of obscurantism but rather of brilliant accomplishments in fields such as medicine, mathematics and astronomy, among others. By the IX Century AD, when the persecutions against this cult began, it was already the most powerful religious movement in the land. Perhaps the endurance of the native culture eventually catalyzed the revitalization of previous cults, like Confucianism, propitiating the reversal of religious values that took place later on in the century and finally provoked a rejection of Buddhism. It is claimed that during this period of persecutions more than 26000 monks were rounded up, jailed or exiled and about 4000 temples plundered and destroyed. Identical fate, at the time, befell several other foreign beliefs (among them relatively small sects of Manicheans and Christians, which were equally attacked while the patriotic fervor of the late Tang emperors lasted).

Buddhism in China, therefore, although it took many years to be accepted it grew slowly, taking force after the collapse of the Han dynasty, reaching its major efflorescence under the Tang emperors before the persecutions, and after a period of revival during the Mongol domination (some of their emperors became Buddhist) this faith was finally reduced to a secondary religion denomination except for the land of Tibet which although part of modern China many authorities do not consider It to be properly Chinese. Buddhism, therefore, has never been totally eradicated from China, although its power and popularity never again rouse to the previous ascendancy. Today it is estimated that less than 17% of the population practice this cult, or at least was doing so before the communist takeover.

Chinese civilization, therefore, in what refers to religion, displays an amalgam of beliefs, some autochthonous and other received from neighboring lands. In this case, therefore, also religion could not define cultural denomination. Although foreign sects today only account for relatively small portion of the population, their diversity precludes any attempt to identify culture with any specific religious practice.

Interesting cases are those of countries in the periphery of major civilizations but differing from them mainly in religion and some other minor aspects of their culture. One typical example is the already alluded case of modern Pakistan, a country splitting geographically from India after the Second World War precisely as a result of religious differences. Pakistan at one time part of India, shares the same cultural-historic and ethnic roots with its larger neighbor, but endorses the Islamic faith which we have considered foreign to Indian original tradition. Similarly, Japan, an island country culturally an offshoot of the great mainland cultural center, historically has been a stronghold of Buddhism after this cult penetrated the country in the VI Century AD.

What all this boils down to is that religion, although in general a constitutive part of a culture (a product of a given human group), is not specific for any civilizational denomination and, therefore, could not be used as a 'gold standard' to identify and separate them, in other words, that it is not a DEFINITIONAL TRAIT despite of the fact that, as we had seen before, in some cases a civilization is named after the religion it engendered and practice.

What are, then, these traits? Where can we find them? The clue, perhaps, is in the cultural profile of a nation. Nobody today will have any difficulty in ascertaining the cultural underpinnings of either Pakistan or Japan, because what counts are the VISIBLE MANIFESTATIONS OF A CULTURE, what the country or civilization DOES OR PRODUCE; in other words, not only the body of beliefs and language but also the sum total of the literary, artistic, technological and intellectual achievements of a human community. It is what is EXPRESSED and, consequently, manifested what specifies and define a culture. The STYLE of a culture is also of paramount importance. Quite often a piece of pottery, a brocade, a paint, an sculpture, or even a fragment of carved stone, is sufficient for an expert to assign cultural origin and, even occasionally, discover the author of a work, (which, of course requires a PRIOR KNOWLEDGE of the given culture). That is not to say that this identification is an easy task. Even to the expert eye, occasionally, the source of a cultural item (literary, artistic etc.) will be hard to ascertain. It should be emphasized, therefore, that an object in isolation WITHOUT REFERENCE TO A GIVEN KNOWN CULTURE is insufficient TO DEFINE a culture (A finger print by itself, with no way to relate to a given person, is useless as an identifying characteristic. It is impossible to 'reconstruct' a building from a window, a door or a piece of roof).

It is, in conclusion, THE SUM TOTAL of cultural expressivity what is frequently necessary to identify cultures and their denominations (civilizations and nations), that is to say, to recognize and separate socio-cultural supra-organisms. This fact should not surprise us when it is consider that a person is not, in most cases, separable from others solely on the basis of a single physical characteristic, whether it be the shape and size of the nose, color of the eyes, skin texture, etc. Only by the totality of his, or her, anatomical peculiarities can we be aware of who the person is and, therefore, to carry out successfully the act of identification. There are many people with brown eyes, long noses, big set of ears and so forth, but only by taking into consideration all the individual physiognomic characteristics is that we can discover who the person is. The same process of recognition pertains to cultural phenomena. It is the ENTIRE CULTURAL CORPUS what allows the identification. No single cultural specification or trait taken out of contest is sufficient. Only the integration of every bit of available cultural information will be successful in this regard.

We can speculate that, actually, it is cultural diversity what permits evolution to take its course by allowing the cultural 'traits' to compete in a social Darwinian way with each other to impose its kind and, consequently, to provide for the 'heredity' of mankind. It could be argued that different cultural characteristics compete with one another in the same way that individual metazoan do, resulting in the 'survival of the fittest'. The evolutionary 'stuff' of society is the cultural determinants playing the same role that genes play in biological evolution. Cultural traits, therefore, escape the biological constrains imposed to other living organisms by establishing for Man a new type of evolutionary base (culture) and a novel evolutionary unit (the human community rather than a particular individual).

The power of culture to define historically a human evolutionary group is well demonstrated by those instances when a conquering nation becomes ASSIMILATED to the vanquished people. The typical case of such happening is the integration of Mongol invaders (basically a nomadic barbarian stock) into the mainstream of Chinese civilization, to the point of giving rise to the 'Mongol dynasties'. This integration was a kind of 'domestication' of the cultural backward invaders by the highly refined natives. Historically the development and evolution of China, after the invasion, continued its unrelenting faithful course. Similar fate befell the Hyskos after conquering Egypt, and the barbarians who infiltrated the Roman Empire. The culturally inferior, even if superior in the battlefield, will eventually, if enough of the losers remain alive, be co-opted by their more refined 'victims'(another evidence, if more are needed, for the notion that racial considerations are of little importance when it comes to the identification of socio-cultural supra-organisms). This phenomenon, in a lesser scale, is equivalent to the victory of a weak, but cunning and smart person, over a physically superior but less intelligent adversary.

The struggle for survival among human communities can display a variety of patterns, from an outright war to economic-political competition and exploitation. Were not because of these peculiarities of the socio-cultural supra-organisms culture itself would have not evolved or 'radiate' in its multiple forms, but, if it existed at all, would have been a universal stereotypical varnish over human societies giving rise to something similar to the beehives and anthills, that is, evolutionary 'blind alleys' without diversity of collective expression, still subjected individually to genetic selectivity, but sorely lacking the cultural underpinnings which allows selection and evolution of another and higher order. That is why, as it was said before, Man is the only species emancipated from the tyranny of genes and capable of a radically novel type of evolution afforded by cultural characteristics.

Diversity of the cultural trait 'pool' had served Man well. In the Fertile Crescent approximately 2500 years elapsed from the flowering of the first Sumerian cities to the conquests by Alexander. As we have seen, despite assaults by numerous different migratory waves of less civilized people the same cultural corpus persisted for all this time and radiated with minor modifications into Assyrian and Babylonian branches, and not disappearing before inseminating the Achaemenian Persians and subsequently Islam.

Similar thing had occurred to other great cultures of the past. Greek culture, by way of the Romans, influenced what we call today 'Western Christian Civilization' as well as Byzantium (which was also directly influenced by its predecessor in the Greek mainland) and in the process gave rise to a prolific radiation of artistic and architectural forms (As we will see, the original Greco-Roman temple, for instance, evolved in the West into the Romanesque and Gothic and, in the east, into the Byzantine styles). Cultures, like their counterparts the animal species, do not last forever, but cultural trait pools allow some of their salient features to persist and evolve into new forms selected for perpetuation.

But 'mutational paralysis' and failure of cultural evolution are not necessarily incompatible with prolonged historical survival. Phenotypic 'petrification', as we have seen, is not invariably equated with a short geological existence either. Many bacteria (anaerobes), fishes (sharks), reptiles (lizards and crocodiles), insects (scorpions and dragon flies) and plants (ferns) are today not much changed from the original stocks of the species. Trilobites, who first appeared in the Cambrian seas, survived for over 400 million years only to vanish mysteriously at the end of the Cretaceous. Likewise, some cultures do become evolutionary blind alleys known to have subsisted for amazingly long periods of historical time.

A typical example of this dictum is the already mentioned 'Egyptian Civilization'. This nation developed a remarkable durable autochthonous culture subsisting roughly for three thousand years. Yet, the Egyptians, as far as can be ascertain, were unable to exert lasting cultural influences in any other human community, that is to say, none of their 'cultural traits' seem to have survived in a recognizable form in any other contemporary or ulterior human group. Nevertheless, this civilization was very homogeneous, with a strong personality distinguished, above all, by its mastery of stone carving, its taste for the colossal and its preoccupation with the after-life. Perhaps the reason for its durability was the early political unification of the land, which allowed them to withstand repeated onslaughts by foreign invaders without suffering the lost of their cultural identity. Be as it may, the essential continuity of this resilient culture was maintained until the very end. No one of their major cultural accomplishments became perpetuated in other human groups, no other civilization became its 'heir apparent', as was the case of Rome to Classic Greece, Khmer to Hindu, Incaic to the Mochica and Chimu or Islam to the Persian civilization. It is true that some of their contemporary near eastern centers drew from the considerable expertise of Egyptian artisans (like can be noticed in Phoenician and Assyrian ivory carvings), but their styles were basically different. The Egyptians, we might say, did not leave any recognizable 'descendants' for posterity. In history we can confidently state that their culture is a 'closed chapter'.

The fate of the ancient Egyptians is very revealing in establishing the amazing parallel between cultural and biological evolution. Living forms, it is well known, undergo from time to time spurts of what has come to be named 'adaptive radiation', which is nothing but diversification of forms to fit different ecological 'niches'. (In this regard, for example, the mammals are known to have radiated exuberantly early in the Cenozoic Era, and in a relatively short geological span occupied the 'niches' left vacant by the vanishing dinosaurs). Then, for different periods of time, the 'branches' into which the original stock had subdivided survived, many to finally die-out without a trace while few split to different evolutionary destinations.

Ethnological and archeological studies show that modern Man began to radiate culturally in the Neolithic Period, this radiation becoming firstly manifested in the so-called 'minor arts', like pottery, waiving and pictorial representations, but soon spreading to other cultural manifestations. Language, religion, music and writing, of course, also were early targets of this radiation which turned progressively more elaborated, to become solid bulwarks of cultural idiosyncrasies. This evolution in geological terms also did not take too long. By the Third Millennia BC the process of cultural differentiation was well underway. In the following centuries human centers became well defined and even some secondary branching took place (as we had already seen in the case of Mesopotamia). Ultimately some of the cultures languished and historically perished, like the Egyptian did, while a few remained to become the ancestors of the modern world. This process of radiation was certainly helped by the socio-political fragmentation of the cultural universe. The 'city-state' was then the civilizational evolutionary locus both in the Aegean and later the Middle East. (Civilizational centers in the Indus Valley and China as well as in the New World appeared to be independent developments, but also followed the same general evolutionary blue-print)

CHAPTER VI

In order to understand the way that cultural evolution works and radiates some historic examples are necessary. (For the historic evolution of some cultural traits see Appendix I). For instance, the already mentioned original Akkadio-Sumerian cultural tradition evolved somewhat differently in Assyria, where the continuous bas-reliefs depicting historic events developed probably under the influence of Hittite rock carvings, than in Babylon, where the extensive utilization and perfection of the technique of glazing bricks and tiles took place, to be subsequently incorporated into contemporary Persian Architecture; as could be appreciated in the magnificent remains of Achaemenian kings palaces and, much later on, in the exquisite Timurid and Safagavid royal and ceremonial buildings. The arts of weaving and jewel making seem also to have been more fully elaborated in Babylon than in Assyria, whose art, on the other hand, excelled in palace fresco painting, carving stone and ivory.

It can be cogently argued that these subtle (and not so subtle) differences are comparable to the biological evolutionary changes which slowly transform the phenotypic expression of living creatures worldwide. Polymorphism in a genetic locus results from mutations giving rise to radiations of the common original form. Likewise, evolutionary changes in the basic patterns of cultural products (the 'traits' equivalents to a genetic locus of biological organisms), like style in ceramics, painting, textiles, metal works etc., could be considered the result of 'cultural mutations' which can transfer, and become further modified, from one human community to another. Although many of these 'traits' do not seem to afford evolutionary advantage neither do many biological markers.

It is this unrelenting transformation of cultural traits what explains societal evolution and the rise and fall of human communities. The rather rudimentary bas-reliefs of the Hittites became the magnificent renderings of the Assyrians and again their form reappeared, after many centuries, in the monumental rock carvings of the Sassanids. Like the genes, cultural traits occasionally remain dormant for long lapses just to reemerge again more or less suddenly in a new orgy of exuberant creativity. The traits, therefore, can subsist hidden from sight, like recessive genes do, perhaps buried in the collective unconscious of a human group, latent but alive, ready to jump again to the world historic stage at any moment.

The diversity of cultural manifestations, like the phenomena of genetic polymorphism, could be fundamental to the adaptability and survival of a culture by providing the means and necessary plasticity for adaptation to environmental changes otherwise insurmountable. Cultural, like biological 'vitality', depends on this 'flexibility' to adjust to new challenges, something made possible by the heterogeneity of the reserve 'pool', whether of genes or cultural traits.

Civilizations or nations, like biological organisms, could, when engaging in 'intercourse', blend their hereditary material to produce a new synthesis of forms and essentially becoming something 'different'. We only have to witness, for example, the fate of the Hellenistic Art when confronted with the orientalizing influence of the Near East. The highly personal, realistic and dynamic character of this art slowly transformed into the rigid, formalistic and stylized products of the Byzantines, strangely enough a Greek speaking civilization which viewed itself as 'heirs' in right of the venerable Roman Empire. (See also Chapter XIII)

The frescos and shimmering mosaics replaced sculptured forms as objects of worship, receding into insubstantial ethereal figures, which, with their frontal design, became not representations but actual 'extensions' of the latter. Also in architecture we can appreciate a difference between the Byzantines and their predecessors. A domed, central type of church with an interior feeling of 'falling heavens' eventually evolved in the East, ultimately differing notably from the cruciform basilicas with roofed arcades crystallizing in the West, which as we will see, after further elaboration eventuated in the soaring heights of the ribbed spiked vaults and removed monumentality of the Gothic style. (See also Chapter XII)

Armed with these concepts of what specifies a culture, let us resort to a cultural analysis as a way of investigating whether geographically related historic communities, like the 'Old' and 'New' Kingdoms of Babylon, belonged or not to the same socio-cultural supra-organism. (For another more complicated example see Appendix II). How are these temporally remote communities related? Is the land of Hammurabi different to the one of Nebuchadnezzar? Do they, like the distant stars, only appear as one because of their distance from us? The difficulty here is that all human groups inhabiting the Middle East before the III Century BC are strongly influence by the pervading cast of their prolific illustrious predecessors, the Sumerians, and in many respects their cultural manifestations could not be clearly separated from them.

The Old Kingdom, it is well known, was attacked and briefly invaded by the Hittite Empire and shortly thereafter overran, in the XVII Century BC by invaders, mainly Kassites from Central Asia. Although history tell us about the 'assimilation' of the new barbarians to Babylonian Civilization, these cultural interchanges are practically never a one side phenomenon and the influences are usually mutual. A 'Dark Age' of a sort then ensued, and there were no more cuneiform inscriptions until approximately 1450 BC. under the dynasty of a Kassite King. After the reinstallation of autochthonous powers a protracted internecine struggle between the rival neighbors of Babylon and Assyria took place, the latter becoming the prevailing nation, even at one time razing Babylon to the ground and flooding the city by diversion of the course of a nearby river under Sennacherib, only to be rebuild later on by his son Esarhaddon. Babylon, however, subsequently defeated the Assyrians and experienced a final efflorescence, lasting slightly more than a century, under the Chaldean Kings (the New Kingdom), before succumbing to Cyrus of Persia in 539 BC. Not that Babylon disappeared immediately, in fact under under the Achaemenian Kings it became quite prosperous, but after the Macedonians invasions it lost vigor and began to depopulate, ultimately to be abandoned completely. A pile of ruins, finally, replaced a city of more than 2000 years of continuous existence.

Did the inhabitants during this prolonged span of time belonged or not to the same socio-cultural entity? As we had seen, the original Semitic stock must have intermixed, after the first fall of Babylon, with different proportions of indo-European as well as probably Asiatic ethnic groups, and later on with others like the Elamites, of Persian origins, and the Chaldeans or Arameans, also of Semitic origin. The latter were the ones who after beating the Assyrians founded the New Kingdom, whose language, slowly, since the turn of the first millennia commenced to replace the old Babylonian tongue (of Akkadian roots), although it remained in 'official' usage for edicts and legal documents in general.

In religion the neo-Babylonians still worshiped Marduk and the other Mesopotamian divinities common to the Old Kingdom, this religious identity being through the ages one of the reasons for discord and frequent upraises against foreign rulers. Also in architecture and art there was an obvious revival during the latter period of the former grandeur, with the building of the great ziggurat as well as numerous palaces and temples (including the famous 'hanging gardens'), following in general the traditional style of earlier epochs.

Because of the numerous wars and invasions suffered by the city not many remnants of the original Babylonian art remain extant today. One precious example though, is the stele containing the code of Hammurabi. In the neighboring city of Mari, also under Babylonian control at the time, frescoes, sculptures and cylinder seals depicting people offering to the gods had been found. In general, however, their art is difficult to differentiate from other Mesopotamian contemporary settlers. Something very similar happens with the Neo-Babylonians whose art also was difficult to separate from the Assyrians except in their taste to decorate the inside and outside walls of their temples with glazed colored tiles (see also Appendix I) depicting flower arrangements, trees or real and imaginary animals forms: Like the one in the throne room of the palace of Nebuchadnezzar II, or the lion in the renown Ishtar gate. In glyptic art and sculpture there is a dearth of archeological findings in this period, but their ceramic objects were highly appreciated by their conquerors the Persians.

It is fair to conclude, therefore, that in cultural expression, except for the usage of glaze tiles, there appears to have been a continuity and clear relation of cultural forms between the Old and New Kingdoms, spanned by the Kassite dynasties and the protracted struggle with the Assyrians, with whom they culturally interrelate. These two nations borrowed deeply from the original Sumerians, whose pervading influence lingered in this region for more than 1500 years after its disappearance as a viable socio-cultural entity. Linguistically, there appears to be a progressively widening gap between the scribal classical tradition and the Aramaic speaking population, a fact blamed by many historians for the final obliteration of Mesopotamian Culture. Ethnically, as was already mentioned, during the two thousand years this civilization lasted there was profuse racial intermingling with other neighboring human communities.

Yet, as it was said before, these linguistic and racial differences do not ruled out cultural identity. According to the specifications mentioned above, therefore, the Old and New Kingdoms of Babylon belonged to the same socio-cultural phenomena, that is, form part of the same supra-organism inasmuch as they shared a common CULTURAL CORPUS. Architectonically, in religion and the minor arts there are sufficient similarities between the inhabitants of the old and new kingdoms to conclude that the two belonged to the same cultural entity or supra-organism, despite of the prolonged temporal interval eliciting between their periods of maximal efflorescence. Actually, it can be said with confidence that the 'soul' of this city was the same during this period of time. This opinion is reaffirmed by the numerous uprisings in Babylon, even after the fall of the New Kingdom, while the city was occupied by the Persians, who even in one occasion enticed Zoroastrian zealots to burn the famous ziggurat; something which gives an idea of the religious militancy of the worshipers of Marduk, still at that late time the tutelary deity of the city. (Something similar could be said of Chinese Culture which kept its cohesiveness through the ages despite the Mongolic and Manchu invasions notwithstanding the numerous dialects spoken in mainland China. This is also the case with our Western Civilization that has kept its unity despite of the numerous languages spoken in its constitutive nations)

The sum total of cultural specifications, to repeat again, is what provides for the identity and defines the spatio-temporal confines of nations and or civilizations, in the same manner that CELLULAR COHESIVENESS does for metazoan organisms. CULTURE, UNDERSTOOD AS THE CREATIVE EXPRESSION OF A HUMAN SOCIETY, BECOMES THE PROBE WHICH, BY BEING THE INSTRUMENT OF HISTORICAL ANALYSIS, ALLOW US TO DECIDE WHETHER CONTIGUOS OR OVERLAPPING TEMPORAL AND OR

Miguel Ochoa

GEOGRAPHIC COMMUNITIES BELONG OR NOT TO THE SAME SOCIETAL SUPRA-ORGANISMS. It is this manifestation of human activity, this rendering of something special and unique by men of a given cultural denomination, what makes them different from those of other societies, giving to the human community its specific character or 'personality'.

CHAPTER VII

Nowhere, perhaps, can the phenomenon of 'unspoiled' cultural radiation and its locus in politically disparate and independent communities be better studied and recognized that in the fertile soil of Meso-America. Authorities are in general agreement about the level of cultural sophistication of the human groups which began reaching the continent during the last glaciation: Lower Paleolithic. The general consensus of opinion is that ALL the advanced civilizations subsequently evolving in America (North and South) were indigenous, emerging from a Neolithic horizon supporting a progressive system of cultivation; including such common plants as corn, avocado, chili and squash, among others. Slowly, in the Pre-Classic epoch a quite distinct culture commenced to take shape. This proto-civilization was typified in general by things like the polishing of obsidian, rafts with gourds floats, the building of steep pyramids, use of rabbit fur for decorative purpose, two kinds of calendars and religious practices which included human sacrifices and ritual cannibalism.

In Meso-America is from this pre-Classic front that more than two thousand years ago the great cultural groups of this geographic region (entirely comparable in this regard to Mesopotamia before), like the Olmecs, Zapotecs and Mayas, among others, began to differentiate. Linguistically each of these cultural groups was also different, and three main families of languages (Zoque-Mayan, Macro-Otomaguean and Nahuatl) are identified, which further ramified into a diversity of dialects, some still even spoken today.

Like in Mesopotamia also these human communities underwent the typical historic process already alluded (growth, maturity and decadence) independently of each other and invariably related to the fate of the urban center serving as civilizational nucleus (La Venta for the Olmecs, Tenochtitlan for the Aztecs, Monte Alban for the Zapotecs etc.). Although at the time of the conquest of America most of these societies had past their zenith, quite a few were historically still 'alive' and the indian communities could be culturally identified. Be it as it may, for our purpose what is important is the evidence of considerable cultural radiation among the different branches arising from the already mentioned original Mesoamerican proto-culture.

The Olmecs, judged by many to be the 'mother culture' of Mesoamerica, were characterized by the solidity and massiveness of their art. They were supreme sculptors and carved mysterious colossal basalt heads with negroid features, and also stelae and statuettes in human and animal forms. It is in Olmec Art that the jaguar first appeared, to become a recurrent and frequent theme in all artistic renderings of this geographic region. Carved jade pieces, many representing cripples or aristocratic personages, were profusely produced and had been recovered at sites throughout Mexico and Centro-America, attesting to the wide influence of this earliest of classical Mesoamerican civilizations.

Teotihuacan was the largest urban center in pre-Columbian America. In its heydays in the pre-Classical Period its population was estimated to be around 150000 inhabitants, and included groups from many other districts of Mexico. Evidently its economic, military and cultural power was extensive and extended well beyond the Altiplano region of central Mexico. Intriguingly, nobody knows who the original inhabitants were. The Aztecs found the ruins when they reached Central Mexico many years after the site was abandoned.

The unearth buildings of the city consist of palaces, temples and probably administrative buildings. The houses were made of adobe bricks and volcanic stones lined by lime plaster, frequently displaying magnificent frescos with bright colors. The Teotihuacan people are credited with the development of the 'talud-tablero' type of construction (sloping and vertically projecting walls which they used in their great pyramids). A great engineering accomplishment was their drainage and water supply systems. The economy of the city was based in the obsidian extracted from local mines. With it they made spears, dart points and human figurines among others. They also sculpted stone masks made of basalt, jade and other materials with eyes inlaid in obsidian rock or sea shells. Their ceramic was in high demand and they produced a cylindrical pottery vase with slab-shape feet and objects of clay including vessels shaped like flowers. Other objects among their amazing manufactures included incense burners, mold-made figurines and clay pellets used for hunting.

The Zapotecs, who developed a glyptic writing, perhaps the first to do so in this area, erected very impressive ceremonial centers consisting of buildings with great central courts, tombs and burial urns in the shape of men and gods. They also constructed with volcanic stones pyramids similar to those of the contemporaneous people of Teotihuacan, utilizing the same principle of panel and slope which pervades the architectural style of this region. Pictorial representations with renditions of religious or mythical subjects, including priests, gods and, of course, jaguars were also typical of this nation. Their pottery was very original, of the flat-based tripod type with elaborate decorations in paint-cloisonné and stucco inlays.

A very personal form took the art of this period in the low lands of Vera Cruz. The lines became curved and sinuous rather than straight as in Monte Alban and Teotihuacan. Here, at El Tajin, clay figures had smiling faces instead of the almost somber depictions of the other sites. This gave to their cultural renderings a distinction and almost care-free elegance, also repeated in the original design of their pyramids (square structures decorated with panels incised with rows of 365 deep niches, one for every day of their solar year).

No Mesoamerican cultural denomination, however, achieved the scientific and artistic sophistication of the Maya people. They developed a complex scriptural system with 270 known characters, realized amazingly accurate astronomical observations supported only by the naked eye, and excelled in architecture as well as in mural painting. Their pyramids were steep and often surmounted by temples, terraces and palaces. Decorations and relief carvings were richly ornamental with no empty spaces, and stucco inlaid were also amply utilized. Mural painting was surprising by its expressive force based in flat colors, the human figure drawn with heads in profile and bodies turned sidewise, frequently with considerable dramatic results. The minor arts were also profusely represented. Pottery was supreme, often decorated with abstract designs of deities and ceremonial motifs. Gem carving attained also quite an advanced degree of perfection with their best works in jade.

Maya's classic culture had a strong distinctive character of poise, harmony and vigor, impossible to be fully explained with words. The decorative designs and steep pyramids have a vague resemblance to some of the Hindu and south East Asian sites. The Mayas shared with other Mesoamerican civilizations many common traits, but their masterpieces exhibit peculiar features, a personal accent very singular and vigorous. This human community was in frank decadence by the time the Spaniards colonized the New World and many ancient centers had been, by then, mysteriously deserted, leaving for posterity the legacy of a sumptuous art of great singularity.

In the cordillera in the Post-Classical period irrupted the Mixtecs, who were masters of decorative and pictorial techniques including gem carving, pottery, wood, bone modeling as well as mosaic decoration. Metal objects were also a predilection, which they finished with a very peculiar repose style. After overcoming the remnants of the Teotihuacan settlements they penetrated Oaxaca and overran Monte Alban coming, therefore, for a while in control of most of Central Mexico. Their art, again, was distinctive and influential, with predilection for the small crafts and painting rather than for monumental enterprises, indicating a strong radiation from common Mesoamerican custom.

The succeeding Aztecs, on the contrary, adored massive architecture and sculpture, which was vigorous but brutal, at times almost loathsome. Their naturalistic representations of rattle-snakes, otherwise a popular subject in Mesoamerica, were of remarkable quality. But this nation never reached the virtuosity of the Mixtecs in the small crafts; in fact, many of the objects worn and used by them were of such origin. A magnificent and tantalizing object of their make was the 'calendar stone' found in the temple site of Mexico City. The Aztecs also were not outstanding in painting, but in martial arts, however, they surpassed the standards of any other contemporary indian community. They ultimately conquered all central Mexico up to the frontier of what is today Guatemala and collected tribute from many neighboring indigenous groups.

There is a great controversy as to whether the human group called the Toltecs actually has historic validity. We learned from them by the myths of the Aztecs about the struggles of Quetzalcoatl and Tezcatlipoca. The truth is that, according to some experts, the Toltecs probably were one of several Nahuatl speaking city states. In fact there were several possible post-classic settlements by the name of Tula, its assumed capital. The one that is considered to be the most probably site is largely in ruins. Still extant at the site there is a large stepped pyramid built in five stages and displaying panels with friezes of the mythological plumed serpent, the indispensable jaguars and eagles eating human hearts. Behind the pyramid is the gruesome, so-called, 'serpent wall' with carvings of rattle-snakes also eating human remains.

The post-classical culture of the putative Toltecs shows signs of decadence in comparison to the classical renderings of Teotihuacan. Their pottery included human and animal forms, but it is reputed to be the only glazed pottery produced in Mesoamerica.

———

We can conclude, therefore, that in Mesoamerica, like in Mesopotamia before, the Bronze Age cultural complex which emerged from the Neolithic foundation radiated early, giving rise to several different but related groups, each accomplishing independently the historic evolutionary cycle we had learned to identify with a socio-cultural 'supra-organism'; in other words, the irreducible human communal nucleus which undergoes the already mentioned vicissitudes of a 'life cycle'. Each of the groups had its own 'personality' given by its cultural peculiarity, that is, by their idiosyncrasies in art and architecture. Furthermore, every one of them, after a period of maximal efflorescence, was then superseded by another group until the arrival of the Spaniards when the Aztec Empire was reigning supreme.

It is impossible, of course, to know whether these Aztecs would have accomplished a true political unification of Mesoamerica, but after three thousand years of cultural radiation it is doubtful this would have been feasible. In those regions where such unification had occurred, like Egypt and China, once the stage of Bronze Age Civilization had been reached, it was a matter of, at the most, few centuries before the consolidation of the union was attained. To be sure times of internal dissolution do alternate with others of political unity, but it seems that once the latter is secured a new 'conscience' takes shape that erases the differences and discourages, or impedes, significant divergence from the common mold. In Mesoamerica, as in Mesopotamia before, the warring proclivities of the inhabitants probably impeded the process of socio-political unification, but we will never know for sure, in view of the abrupt end to their cultural evolution brought about by the Spanish conquest.

It might be argued that Mesoamerica, at the historic stage when the Spaniards arrived, was evolutionarily roughly at the same cultural level than Mesopotamia in the VI Century BC when Ashurbanipal Empire controlled most of the Middle East. It is also perhaps a strange coincidence that both the Assyrians and the Aztecs were war-like and cruel to the extreme. (Some historians will argue that this apparent cruelty of the Assyrians was the result of their assiduous recording of deeds in stone for posterity). But the parallel does not end there. Their Culture, in one case as in the other, was finally obliterated by foreign invaders never to rise again. Their Bronze Age civilizations are 'dead' and their corpses engross the list of casualties in the roster of world human societies.

The evolutionary radiation of Mesoamerican cultures was spectacular, in a few centuries producing several centers with distinct cultural traits which, in general, kept their autonomy and traditions until they vanished, or until the rise to supremacy of the Aztecs shortly before the arrival of the Spaniards. (As it was said before Mayan Culture was also still 'alive' but decadent). Yet, despite the notable degree of progress and refinement reached by these people they were impeded to leave descendants, on account of their complete obliteration at the hands of the newcomers. (Here the situation was completely different to Mesopotamia where the invaders adopted many of the technical advances and styles of the defeated nations, because in Mesoamerica the Spaniards were technologically much more advanced than the natives.)

We can summarize, then, by stating that from the late Neolithic horizon arose in Mesoamerica a Bronze Age cultural complex from which radiated several socio-cultural groups, broadly classified in two geographic branches: one in the cordillera represented by the Zapotecs, Teotihuacans, Mixtecs and Aztecs; the other in the low lands of the gulf of Mexico, being constituted by the Mayas, Veracruzans and Olmecs; the latter being the first to differentiate from the underlining proto-cultural substratum and strongly influenced the others. Linguistically, as we had seen, there were three main groups, maybe indicating some degree of geographic convergence of the human communities which had differentiated earlier.

Besides their warring proclivities another reason for the failure of social amalgamation of these societies might have been this linguistic heterogeneity, which could have impeded the formation of a central government. Even within the confine of a group (the Mayas for example) different centers were politically autonomous to the point of evolving disparate architectural styles (Pete, Palenque, Rio Bec, Chenes etc.), perhaps an early sign of further cultural radiation. In this context it will be erroneous to confuse the Post-Classical Aztec Empire with a unified nation. There was not a 'united conscience'; the occupied territories were considered as conquests of 'foreign lands'.

The fragmented Mesoamerican universe represented a collection of socio-cultural supra-organisms belonging to the species 'Mesoamerican Civilization'. In this respect, as we had mentioned, it strongly resembled Mesopotamia or the conglomerate of nations proliferating in Europe after the downfall of the Roman Empire in the West. Many of these supra-organisms were gravely 'sick', or had already disappeared by the time the Spaniards arrived in the New World and precipitated their historic 'demise'.

The rise of autochthonous Bronze Age civilizations was not limited to Mesoamerica; it also occurred in the southern part of the continent. Cultural evolution there was very similar to their northern counterpart with one caveat: eventually a large empire coalesced in the cordillera shortly before the arrival of Europeans.

The linguistic roots here are as numerous as in the Northern Hemisphere. Qhechua, the language of the Incas, Guarani and Aymara in Paraguay and Bolivia and Mapudungun in Chile are still spoken by native communities. Among other family groups are: Tupi, Chibcha, Pano-Tacana, Arawak and Chon; to mention only few.

The early manifestation of this culture was in textiles. Without a loom they achieved complex abstract designs representing animals and also human figures. Some of these figures displayed feline features that vaguely resemble the pictographic designs of their Mesoamerican contemporaries; although the styles are different with more emphasis in abstract motifs. The original centers, dating from 900 B C are located in Chavin, Northern Peru. The art of these people lacked the monumentality achieved by other indian groups, but in general are more meticulous in their details, although there are exceptions mostly from the post-Classic Period. Another characteristic of this culture was its pottery. Their vessels with a flat base and stirrup spouts as well as others shaped as human faces, shells, demons etc. are painted with geometric designs which are quite typical of this human group.

Toward the southern coastal plains of what is today Peru the Paracas partook of the general dedication of the Chavin Culture to textiles. They were used in profusion in their burial grounds, which frequently used caves where cadavers were mummified, a frequent practice in Bronze-Age Civilizations. The Nazca Culture which seemed to be and extension and evolution from the Paracas excelled in pottery. Their double spouts vessels are a defining artistic expression of this human group and certainly an evolution from the previous long-neck spouts of their ancestors. After the decline of the Chavin people there was a temporary cultural hiatus partially filled by the Recuay who were distinguished by their pottery with "negative decorations" consisting of black designs over red and white.

Further evolution of the Chavin style took shape in the northern coastal area at Salinar. Here there was additional evolution in the shape of the stirrup in pottery jars, which they manufactured with a long and narrow vertical neck adorned with red and white decorations. One curious characteristic is that some of these containers were designed to whistle when liquid poured out.

It was with their descendants the Mochica that the Classic Period in the northern lands of Peru reached its zenith of perfection. The profusion of shapes in their pottery, mostly funerary, was phenomenal and often decorated with low relief paintings. An intriguing characteristic is that some of the vessels are modeled like human heads, with physiognomic features that seem to indicate true reproductions of individual persons. The range of subjects in these decorations is very extensive including people, plants, life scenes and even macabre depictions of persons without limbs, and even erotic renderings.

Contrary to their predecessors, this culture had a taste for monumentality. They built large pyramids made up of adobe bricks and it has been claimed that in one of them an estimated 130 million bricks were used. Some of their large sculptures still remain, but numerous small carved objects of very good artistic quality had been found mostly in graves, as was the case with their cultural ancestors. Like the Chavin the Mochica also worked with metal but very few objects had been preserved; their level of workmanship was high.

Farther south in the shores of Lake Titicaca arose in the pre-Classical period a new cultural off-shot of the Andean civilizational complex: Tiahuanaco. Their artistic objects displayed a formal and stiff style differing in taste significantly from their cousins to the North. But they excelled in masonry and stone carving particularly during the Classical Period. The massive "Gateway to the Sun" displays in frontal pose probably their creator God Viracocha with condor and feline heads. To his side there are figures possibly representing attendants shown in profile and in motion, apparently running toward him. There are also several massive statutes in relief carving exhibiting the same formalized stiffness.

Their pottery was of a basic design similar to their cultural ancestors, but introduced a form of their own with long-neck beaker-shaped containers decorated with abstract geometric motifs sometimes representing fantastic animals or, like with their predecessors, outlines of condors and feline creatures. The cultural influence of this people eventually extended, during the post-Classical period, throughout the Andean region, particularly in the splendor of their textiles wrought in bright colors with geometrical designs so much popular among other American native groups.

The Tiahuanaco Subculture eventually declined, creating an historic hiatus temporarily occupied by the Chimus who settled in the northern coastal planes around the XIII and XIV Centuries. The site of Chan-Chan consists of well planned building complexes frequently surrounded by brick walls. They were skillful workers in metals, improving in the excellence of the finished products the works of their cultural predecessor. An array of artifacts, like ceremonial knifes, numerous types of beakers in gold with repousse designs, silver, cooper and bronze had been recovered from the ruins of their ancient cities. They also were very proficient in textile products and colorful feather work.

Contemporary to the Chimus the Incas founded the largest world empire in the Americas extending from Southern Colombia to Chile. They excelled in architecture. Their edifications including fortresses, walls and temples, were built of bricks and large slabs of stone so well positioned that often, still today, it is impossible to slide a knife blade between the blocks. How were they able to transport such immense blocks of stone without the help of wheel vehicles, and then able to carve the individual pieces to fit each other so perfectly is still a mystery. Also in some of the buildings, like the temple of Viracocha in Cuzco, their capital, frequently the stones were plated with gold. Their pottery was not particularly outstanding and one of their characteristic types was a jar with a conical base and long neck similar to the Greek aryballos. But in metallurgy they produced a profuse array of artifacts in gold and silver in the shape of Andean animals, like alpacas, llamas and also human figures. Another aspect of their technology, also common in other primitive societies was trephining, whether for religious purpose or therapeutic reasons. Tantalizing sculptures displaying physical deformities and other medical conditions had also being discovered.

Above all the Incas were masters in administration ability which helped them to create a vast empire. Their excellent road system that included suspension bridges and storehouses for food and other supplies certainly help, as also did a type of government which is reputed to be one of the first welfare systems in the world. There was no scarcity of food, and land was apportioned by the rulers according to the need of their subjects. A well developed method of taxation, which in general was just and fair, to be distributed among the royal class and religious orders was in place. From where they got their notion of justice is unknown, but certainly it was instrumental in the stability and internal peace of the community. Not that there were no problems with their neighbors, and the struggles for control of the empire between Atahualpa and Huascar shortly before the arrival of the Spaniards in the XVI Century are well documented to need comments.

In between the major cultural centers of Meso-America and the Andean cordillera there was a motley array of civilized settlements in Centro America and Northern Colombia. This geographic area was especially prolific in gold work of excellent quality. The only place in this general zone where monumental sculpture had been found is in

San Agustin in Southern Colombia, where numerous large stone figures (some over 14 feet in height) shaped in animal and human forms had been found.

Although the styles in architecture and the arts are different in the North from the South regions of the American continent (Mesoamerican communities are more given to monumentality in architecture while the South Americans use more abstract designs in their renderings), there are many cultural themes that are similar, suggesting an underlining common ancestor. The building of pyramids, the jaguar figure displayed frequently in artistic motives and the cultivation of similar native plants, like maize (corn), is paramount throughout the continent. Other plants like cassava, chia, squash, cacao and above all potato, first cultivated in Peru, to mention only few, were also broadly consumed and in fact their introduction in Europe had considerable geopolitical and historical importance in the Old Continent.

In music Native Americas developed an amazing assortment of instruments for their monophonic and pentatonic rhythmus, including flutes, several kinds of percussion instruments and even string devices, like the apache fiddler. Still today In the Andean cordillera different types of flutes of indian origin, like the rondador and the antara are in active use.

Religious manifestations evolved according to their cultural level of sophistication from an animistic phase in the nomadic inhabitants of North America (like shamanism, totemism, the ghost dances, the Earth Lodge, Drum and Indian Shaker rituals) to more elaborated religious beliefs and practices farther south. Of the advanced Bronze Age societies of Meso-America the Mayas and Aztecs worshiped a pantheon of gods (for example the Mayan Itzamna the creator sky god, or Kukulcan the feather serpent who seemed to be subsequently adopted by the Toltecs and Aztecs as Quetzalcoalt), hold elaborated ceremonies at times including, not unlikely other bronze age civilizations, human sacrifices and had a priestly class to carry out the religious ceremonies.

In South America the advanced Indian Cultures practiced ancestor worship and resorted to mummification of their rulers, like in Egypt. Also occasionally they engaged in ritual sacrifices to assuage their gods. Their pantheon, like in Mesoamerica, consisted predominantly of Nature deities like Inti the sun god ancestor of the ruling dynasty, Viracocha the creator, or Illapa the thunder god.

In religion, therefore, like in other cultural manifestations, Native American unfolded independently a pattern of religious evolution similar to that of other civilized centers in the World following, so to speak, a common evolutionary blue print which seem to indicate a pervasive biologism permeating human societies. As we have seen, a phase of animistic believes necessarily precedes more advanced polytheistic and occasionally monotheistic beliefs regardless of the geographic locus where humans conduct their life. (However, as it was said before, the possibility that cultural evolutionary similarities to other civilizations result from a common, remote, perhaps proto-human ancestor, could not be ruled out)

Is there any evidence that cultural achievements in pre-Columbian America instead of being autochthonous had somehow being 'imported' from somewhere else in the World? As it was mentioned before, according to present theories the inhabitants of the 'New World' reached the American Continent during the last glaciations, crossing the Bering corridor at an assumed early Paleolithic stage of cultural development. It is claimed that genetic and blood group evidence seemed to indicate an East or Central Asian origin of the population.

Linguistic studies do not seem to clarify the issue. Literally thousands of native languages and dialects were spoken before the discovery of America, but no clear descent from any other human stock had been conclusively demonstrated. As we have seen, some of these languages like Mayan (which bears the distinction of possessing a well developed glyph type of scripture), Guarani, Quechua and Navajo, among others, are still spoken today by descendants of the natives, but many others both in North and South America have disappeared forever.

Despite of many studies there is no scientific evidence to suppose that Native Americans had in the pre-colonial period any kind of contact with any other Bronze Age civilization. Any similarity, like the construction of pyramids, has to be considered fortuitous or a case of evolutionary convergence. (In the case of the pyramids, for instance, the Egyptians were mortuary sites while their American counterparts served religious and sacrificial purposes). IT HAD TO BE CONCLUDED, THEREFORE, THAT THE AMERICAN NATIVE CIVILIZATIONS HAD AN AUTHOCTONOUS DEVELOPMENT FROM A COMMON PROTOCULTURE that radiated widely throughout the continent, INDEPENDENTLY developing and perfecting the essentials for the existence, growth and stability of a human group: like pottery, building materials, utensils for hunting, war-making, and finally non-existential pursues like music, art and religion, therefore following a cultural evolutionary pattern similar to other human communities anywhere else in the world.

CHAPTER VIII

There are four major cultural species inhabiting our planet today: Chinese, Indian, Islamic and Western Christian, each represented by one or several modern nations occupying the original geographic locus of their culture. In order to understand the historic fate of human societal evolution, and thus to attempt some predictions of future events, it is imperative for us to undertake a brief comparative analysis of these relevant communal denominations.

Let us take first the case of Islam, a 'living' cultural presence which can be traced originally to the co-opting, by Arabic desert nomadic invaders, of the cultural richness they found in their conquered lands (originally Persian and Mesopotamia). This civilization is fundamentally characterized by its religious fervor and, of all its traits, precisely is this religion what has given name to this human group. From the already mentioned existing cultural species Islam is also the only that underwent a paralleled development to the West. Both cultures profusely cross-inseminated but kept their artistic, literary and religious independence, accounting for their radically different world perspective and ultimate fate.

It was without question the religious zeal of this people what apparently imbued the conquering armies of Islam with the passion required for the rapid subjugation of the Middle East and North Africa, followed, shortly thereafter, by the submission of most of the Iberic peninsula. The efflorescence of Islam under the Omayyad's rulers already displayed the specifications, mainly in architecture, which were to typify this culture up to the present time. The mosques, madrasas, caravansaries, palaces and mausoleums exhibit strong distinctive shapes, adorned by a highly personal decorative style consisting of the prodigal utilization of stalactite moldings, ceramic tiles and peculiar geometrical designs (arabesques). The distinctive arched doorways, the minarets and luster tiles are found almost everywhere in the Muslim world.

Islamic Culture kept a considerable degree of uniformity throughout their lands. Its cohesiveness was perhaps much helped by the free intercommunication that existed, despite divisions that arose after the downfall of the Umayyad Dynasty, among the Arab territories; something that permitted artisans and other artists to travel extensively not only within but, when possible, outside the Muslim World. In other cultural endeavors Islam also achieved notable progress. Literature and music developed a highly singular and peculiar expressivity, although, in this regard, there was much more variation on account of the non-Arabic nature of many Eastern Islamic communities (see below). All in all, however, the Muslim World was remarkably homogeneous and the nations the culture gave birth to (Moorish Spain, Egypt, Persia, Mogul India, the Ottoman Empire etc.), despite racial and linguistic differences, kept a basic cultural pattern; in a sense something similar to what happens, at present, in the 'West' notwithstanding its feudalistic origin in the 'Dark Ages'.

Not that there was lack of stylistic distinctions between the different parts of their sprawling world, as attested by the different architectural designs in the Moorish lands, which represent variations of an original Umayyad style. Delicate renderings in stalactite moldings and stucco work, as seen in the architectural masterpieces of the Almohads in Spain (the Alhambra of Granada), were the culmination of this branch of Islamic cultural tradition. The mosque of Cordova built in stages between 786 and 987 by the Umayyad rulers chased out of Damascus by the Abbasids Caliphs, became a prototype of architectural design in North Africa and Spain. The sanctuary of the mosque has aisles running north-south separated by columns bridged by double-tiered stone arches. The five-sided mihrab is covered by a huge stalactite dome decorated in marble. The horse-shoe arches became distinctive of this radiation of the original Islamic mold. Another architectural characteristic of North Africa and Spain was the square minarets, like the one in the Kutubiya mosque in Marrakesh and its twin sister the great minaret of the Giralda of Seville. It is being said by the locals in Morocco that the Almohads did not permitted any mosque in their lands to surpass the height of the Giralda.

Islamic literary works consisted mostly of poetry, typified by a metric system based in short and long syllables with the verse divided into balanced halves and the same rhyme repeated at the end of every verse. The poetic form was either a short one, usually used to extol war deeds or deprecate an enemy, or long, made up of many lines (usually more than sixty) and frequently of panegyric content.

Because early Arabic Poetry was an oral tradition disseminated by professional reciters (the rawis), it is difficult to ascertain how much of the extant compilations are real or forgeries. The most famous of them is the Mu'allaqat, in which almost every type of Arabian Poetry from the early formative period is included. The long verse (qasidah) became the prevailing kind in the Umayyad period although a love lyric kind also evolved. It was during the Abbasid dynasties that poetry experienced an exuberant development, and authors experimented extensively with the methods to reach new depths of expression. Many continued a traditionalistic approach with some modifications; like the addition of rhetorical tropes in the introductions of the long poems. Profuse usage of metaphors became common and some performers began to resort to plain popular language to better touch their audiences. In Spain a departure from classic style took place in the XI Century mostly in the large cities and population centers, like Cordoba and Seville. A new variety of strophic verse evolved there that included a rhyming refrain at the end of each strophe, and became very popular in the zajal (colloquial Arabic).

Persian Literature was understandably influenced by Arabic Language after the conquests of the region in the VII Century and the latter became the vehicle per excellence in cultural matters until the IX Century AD, when the Persian tongue finally became sufficiently matured to emerge as the natural medium of literary expression. Under the Saffarids and Samanids (X Century) panegyric and elegiac poems using the qasidah Arabic style were written and another shorter lyric form, the ghazal, soon became popular. Persian Language, however, was evolving fast and soon the development of rhyming couplets gave rise to original independent type of verses, the ruba'i and mathnavi, which permitted a broader range of poetic compositions including epics extolling the exploits of historical heroes from the pre-Arabic Era. In this regard very famous was the Shah-nama, which became the national epic of Iran, written by Firdausi in the XI Century and also the Zafar-nama where the author, Hamd Allah Mustaufi, a historian, recounted the history of the land from the times of Mohammed to the year 1331. Mystical themes were also frequently represented in epic form and brought to masterly perfection in the Mathnawi ima'nawi finished in the XIII Century by Jalal-ud-din Rumi, considered one of the greatest mystical poets of all times.

In Anatolia literary tradition was strongly influenced by Persian and Arabic sources. Because of fundamental structural differences between their tongues and Turkish Language the attempt to conform metrical conceptions and practices from the formers to the latter was fraught with difficulties, and resulted in the importation into Turkish Language of many Arabic and Persian terms and constructions with a corresponding debasement of originality. Nevertheless after the XV Century some outstanding poets, like Ruhi of Bagdad, Fuzuli and Baki distinguished themselves.

As far as Arabic prose is concern, its most salient feature is the utilization of a novel original modality proper to this language: the saj' or rhymed prose, which resorted to succession of pairs of rhyming phrases loosely balanced and without being bound by the rules of poetry. This seems to have been a very old linguistic tradition to the point that even the Koran is partially written in this style. After the VIII Century prose reached its apogee and Arabic works exhibited an unsurpassed degree of poignancy. About this time also emerged an anecdotal kind of narrative of a light genre that became very popular in succeeding periods, leading to a new literary form: the maqamat, a collection of short stories and tales of strong picaresque flavor.

Persian prose was, not surprisingly, influenced by the saj', which was introduced in the country by Hamid al Din in 1156, who also wrote a Maqamat with as elaborated a style as that of the original Arabic one. However, another simpler and purer form was being utilized since the X Century when Mansur I commissioned his vizier Bal'ami to translate the annals of al-Tabari. Works in history, theology and geography were also numerous during this period and some reached the degree of world masterpieces; like the Tarikh i Jahan-gusha written by Ata- Malik Juvaini (completed in 1260), and the Jami al-tawarikh by Rashid al-Din Hamadani, a monumental historic work drawing from European, Chinese, and Islamic sources as well.

In prose Turkish authors were active in epic religious narratives and some excellent chronicles, like those of Ibn Kemal and Hoca Sadeddin were written in the XV and XVI centuries. Literary activity during the

Republican Period had accused a great revival. In poetry the genre had been enriched with the introduction of free verses and in prose there had been an outpour of novels and short stories.

Islamic Literature languished during the XVII and the XVIII centuries but experienced a sort of 'revival' in the XIX, triggered by the Western political and economic revolutionary ferment. Westernization was intense, many works of European authors were translated and things such as newspapers, as well as the theatre, became introduced into the Islamic world. Classic canons were still favored by some but several attempts to reconcile traditionalism and modernism ended in failure. In the XX Century both schools had plowed independent courses, greatly helped by the vehicles of communication and production being introduced into these nations.

It is still questionable whether a new genuinely Arabic, Turkish or Persian literary style will ever emerge from the present situation, or whether 'modernism' truly will come to represent, in the course of time, the final phase of their methodological and thematic originality, in other words, Western literature written in Islamic languages.

In music, like in other cultural activities, Islamic sources are multiple. As was the case with Western Culture, Islam superseded and integrated previous cultural traditions and, therefore, is not surprising that it was greatly influenced by them. Arabic Music, one of its main subdivisions, blended the folklore of the desert Bedouin, consisting mainly of songs of epical or panegyric content, with elaborated Persian and Byzantine elements after the nomads spilled over the contiguous civilized lands. By the VII Century a system of eight diatonic modes was already in use (resembling the European ecclesiastic compositions), which was later on modified to include a neutral (three quarter-tone interval) added to the pre-existing whole tone and semi-tone. This innovation permitted the introduction of numerous additional modes which, by the XIII century, were in total more than 30. The Arabic mode could not properly be compared to the Occidental octave, instead being composed of a limited number of smaller units and, consequently, could not be reduced to consecutive intervals. This concept of 'mode' (the Arabic maqam and the Indian raga) has no parallel in the West and it is difficult to grasp for the Western mind. The 'moods' are conveyed not only by melodic tones but also by specific spacing characteristics typical to each mode. Rhythm also has its modes and by the XVI Century there were more than 20.

Islamic Classic Music was fundamentally monophonic and no correspondence to a Western 'orchestra' is properly found. Nevertheless, a great variety of instruments are utilized in its execution. Among them are: fiddles (rabab, kamanja etc.), lutes (ud), flutes (nay), harps (jank), drums (tabbl, daff), psalteries (qanun) etc., which attest to the richness of instrumentality.

After a formative period of several centuries the musical traditions of the Middle East became fused (about the XVI Century) in a continuous more or less homogeneous toto, stretching from Palestine to Eastern Iran and probably to North Africa. Although small local differences are noticeable no radical departures from the general mold could be observed.

Like in other aspects of this culture, Islamic Music had been heavily influenced by the Western World after the downfall of the Ottoman Empire and, although folk music is unperturbed, no new styles had appeared and the classic denomination seemed to have ceased to flourish. Like with the other cultural modalities its ultimate fate is at the present very much in question.

As far as philosophy is concern, the main accomplishment of the Islamic Culture has been in the translation and interpretation of Greek masterpieces. In fact, one of the avenues in the rediscovery of Plato, Aristotle and many lesser known men was, curiously enough, the works of Avicenna and Averroes who basically expounded Aristotelian theories with a new Platonic flavor, mainly influenced by the works of Porphyry.

The attempt by Arabic Philosophy to provide relevant arguments for human existence and explain the Cosmo ultimately failed, smashed against the bulwarks of Islamic religious tradition and mystical thought. Whereas in the West, despite of religious persecutions, the conflict did not hampered philosophical and scientific development because tolerance eventually replaced repression (mainly in protestant countries after the Reformation), in the Islamic lands, after the confrontation of Al-Ghazzali (The Incoherence of the Philosophers) and Averroes (The Incoherence of the Incoherence), the subject slowly died down and lost relevance when the vision turned inward and the Koran was accepted as the only repository of ultimate truth. In the Moslem world an inquisition 'western style' was never necessary.

In the Health Sciences the Arabs and Persians were quite active. It is intriguing that the most famous Muslim Philosophers were also physicians, like Averroes, Avicenna, Razhes and the Jew Moses Maimonides (who traveled from Spain to the East and became the physician of Saladin, the man who stopped the tide of the Crusades). Medicine followed the speculative tendencies of the times and did not improve upon any contemporary methodology. However, theoretical knowledge in Medicine was, in the early days, as advanced as in any other culture, and Razhes published a comprehensive compilation of Greek, Indian and Mesopotamian Medicine in the X Century. Some shrewd observations were made by few astute workers, like the denial by Ibn al-Nafis of the existence of 'pores' in the heart septum and the postulation of the lesser circulation of blood, but his findings were not seized upon and the whole matter was quietly forgotten without further investigation. Nevertheless, the great Arab cities, Bagdad, Damascus, Cairo, and Cordoba in the West, were medical centers of great importance, with well furnished hospitals and numerous physicians, mostly the result of energetic sponsoring by the rulers. Yet, like in other cultural endeavors, Medicine ultimately became stagnant and finally incorporated the cannons of the West.

In science, as in philosophy, Islam in general was not too original. The works mostly consisted of elaborations of Greek theories, although it heavily borrowed from Indian mathematical knowledge and from Chinese technology (like printing, manufacture of paper and use of gun powder). Alchemy, like in other lands, was intimately associated with mysticism, and a sect of Sufis, the Brethrens of Purity, did most of the work in this discipline. Although in general their theories paralleled those of the Chinese and Alexandrian Greeks they, remarkably, used quantitative methods of measurements; but their work had a narrow scope and did not have a lasting influence. In astronomy, although their theoretical efforts were restricted to translations and interpretations of the Greek authors, in the practical side several notable observations and measurements were realized. For example, Al-Battani, from Bagdad, devised better recordings of the ecliptic and the precession of the equinoxes than those of Ptolemy, and in mathematics we owe to

Islam the introduction into our Western Culture of the Hindu-Arabic numerals popularized by Al-Khwarizmi in the IX Century AD, something that eventually permitted the freeing of that science from the shackles of Greek mathematics. Paradoxically, works in geometry providing more concise proves of problems worked out by old Greeks were also carried out during this fertile period of Arabic Civilization.

Islamic Culture and specially its branch the Arabic type served, more than anything else, the function of a repository and transmitter of the aggregated scientific and philosophical lore of the times by way of which, ironically enough, its 'sister', Western Culture, rediscovered its own half forgotten roots after emerging from the morass of the 'Dark Ages'.

Islam today is a spent force. It has lost vitality and originality artistically, literarily and architectonically. There is a dearth of quality and quantity, more noticeable after its acceptance of many of the norms and vogues of the 'West'. In the minor arts and crafts there is still some degree of productivity, but it is mostly imitative of the great masters of the past. Is this a temporary decline or the prolonged agony of a culture destined to disappear forever? This is impossible to tell, but the present fragmentation of the Muslim universe, as well as, the adoption of Western techniques and tastes does not augur well for this once prolific sector of humanity, the true catalyzer of our own great Western Christian Civilization. Yet, it is within Islamic societies where a semblance of resistance to the inroads of Western standards and mores, even to the point of violence, has been more noticeable in recent times, but its acceptance of Western technology, forms of government and in fact all other aspects of cultural expressivity is at present paramount.

CHAPTER IX

Another of the great cultures still 'surviving' today is the Indian, the one developing in the Asiatic subcontinent and achieving a considerable degree of sophistication as early as the XXV Century BC. Already, at that time, the geometrically laid out urban centers of the Indus Valley were flourishing and from their ruins had been unearthed beautifully carved limestone busts and intaglio steatite seals. The cities of the Indus Valley became mysteriously deserted shortly after the end of the Third Millennium BC. coinciding with the first waves of indo-European invaders, which was followed by a long historical and archeological hiatus.

We recover the lead of historic events in the V Century BC when a distinctive Indian Culture (also known as Hindu) had already taken shape and most of the country was unified under the Maurya emperors (332 BC). By then the great religious reformers, Mahavira and Prince Siddhartha (the founders of Jainism and Buddhism), had completed their works.

Indian culture, which had numerous fructiferous contacts with Hellenistic and Persian invaders (stone carvings, for example do not appear to precede the invasions of Alexander the Great), disclose in all its expressions an strong idiosyncratic flavor and original character, revealed in the rather numerous off-shoots of the main cultural traits wrought about religious motifs and inspirations, particularly, but not limited, to architecture and sculpture.

Nowhere is the expressive diversity of this culture better demonstrated that in the literary field with its linguistic heterogeneity. The early epics, like the Mahabharata, Ramayana, the Bhagavata-purana and the Puranic legends, were written in the Indo-European Sanskrit, a school of rhetoric that was also very influential in the later evolution of court poetry. Philosophical writings in this language became also very important in ulterior literary themes.

Southern India had an independent literary genesis, originally under the Tamil Language, first with short poems on kings as well as other secular subjects, and later on ethical matters (the Tirukkural).

The other languages of this region, Telugu, Ganarese and Malayalam also gave rise to important literary genres, mainly the latter, from which arose a peculiar style of macaronic verse: the Manipravala. After the VII Century AD, however, Sanskrit became a pervasive influence in the literature of these southern people, while in the North the different spoken languages, stemming from a common Prakit ancestor, also served as basis to an independent literary tradition.

In India, linguistic evolution is intimately related to the spread of religious ideas, indicating how profoundly these ideas influenced the life of the community. Pali, for example, was associated to Buddhism and Ardha-magadhi to Jainism. The literary genre also varied from region to region, with the song and the ballad prevailing in the North, while in the South the philosophic poem and the epic were mainly favored. After the Muslim invasions, and conversions, native literature declined temporarily while Persian became the prevalent language, thus determining ulterior literary direction. The ghazal, a short love lyric form, certainly was of Persian inspiration, influencing mainly Urdu authors. As so often happens during times of decline, poetry and long narrative poems revived again in the XIV Century AD, much of the early works consisting of translations of classic Sanskrit texts. In this period also crystallized several literary styles, like the heroic and romantic cycle in the North, such as the Marathi ballad and the Bara-Masa poems.

The XIX and XX centuries saw Indian Literature, like with other cultural denominations, fell under the spell of Western ideas. Prose turned into a powerful literary vehicle and novels became quite popular. Theater and cinematography grew into important expressive means. In general there had been an assimilation of Western ideas and techniques to all literary themes. In fact, what had been heralded as a 'literary revival' largely represents an adaptation of Western standards and methods for literary purpose; it is difficult to discover any spark of the original 'soul' in these renditions. Indian Literature seems to have lost its independence and originality and a future recovery of its lost vigor is very dubious indeed. The traditional genres of literary achievements, if not completely 'dead', have ceased to radiate or to render any fruitful descendants.

Indian musical lore is extremely ancient, actually rooted in the tribal lore of pre-Vedic tradition and the early importation of instruments like the harp, probably of Sumerian origin. With the Aryan invasions music became a religious vehicle as clearly demonstrated in the Vedas where the narrative takes place in chants and recitation. Slowly, with the merging of the Indo-European conceptions and the native Dravidian practices, what can be defined as true Indian Music took shape approximately 2000 years ago.

Their melody, like in the West, is based in an 'octave' of seven notes. This octave, however, is divided into 22 microtonal steps or srutis (in classical music there are also six and five notes forms).Two scales of seven notes are recognized: the sa and the ma, which are the basis for the melodic cells or jatis. In a system of progressive complexity the jatis, then, are the basis of harmonic structures called the ragas, which are the melodic basis of this music and number more than 130. The assumed moods imparted by them might even change with the time of day and night. As should be imagined the restrictions imposed by these theoretical conventions represent great challenges in the compositions.

Many radiations of the basic musical form had occurred throughout India, particularly between North and South, with the selection of ragas and the manner of performance differing substantially from one region to the other; the northern being strongly influenced by Hellenistic, Persian and Arabic notions and practices, while the southern remained less 'tainted' by foreign tendencies, more attached and loyal to its Dravidian and Aryan roots.

In execution Indian Music is also rich and boasts a profuse variety of instruments. Different kinds of stringed (sitar, sarod, fiddles, sarangi etc.), wind (cross and vertical flutes, shawms, reed pipe, shahnai, na-gasuaram, etc) and many types of percussion instruments are among the imposing musical armamentarium.

The music of this ancient and prolific civilization, like every other aspect of its culture, has been experiencing considerable change with the irruption of Western ideas. There has been a want of originality associated with infelicitous attempts to introduce Western harmonic notions into the fabric of this mature musical tradition. The fate of genuinely Indian Music is at the present in the balance, in peril of being submerged by the tide of Occidentalism.

Indian Medicine has a history as long as its culture. Its beginning is lost in the fog of time but it is well known that, originally, Vedic medicine consisted of magic formulas and incantations to exorcise demons, as mentioned in the Atharvaveda. According to the Susruta, an ancient text of basic Medical lore, emphasis was given very early to anatomical considerations, which oddly enough were associated with 'sacred' numbers. The body, according to this ancient text, was composed of 300 bones, 90 tendons, 210 joints, 500 muscles, 70 blood vessels, three humors and 9 sense organs. Diseases were the result of imbalances of the basic humors (spirit, bile and phlegm), and therapies consisted, not surprisingly, of emetics, purges, bloodletting, cupping an application of leaches. The Charaka, a compilation of herbal products from the II Century AD, was clearly highly speculative in its theorizing. One interesting and rather remarkable accomplishment, however, was the observation of the relation of mosquitoes to malaria, undoubtedly the first in its kind. Yet, the association was not acted upon and soon forgotten.

It was in the field of surgery that Indian Medicine excelled. There had been described 101 blunt and over twenty cutting instruments, including knives, razors, scissors, bistouries, needles etc. Among the amazing kind of operations they performed are included amputations, resection of tumors, repair of hernias, couching for cataracts, deliveries of abnormal fetal presentations and fixing of fractures, among others. An interesting procedure was rhinoplasty, a frequently resorted procedure in a country where amputation of the nose was a punishment for adultery. Blood vessels ligatures were done by three different kinds of needles with sutures made of hemp, flax, bark fiber and even hair. This array of surgical procedures is remarkable considering the lack of efficient antiseptic resources at their disposal and the primitive analgesia, which fundamentally consisted of different kinds of wine and the fumes of Indian hemp.

It has long been debated whether many of the medical procedures described in Indian texts preceded or not the contact of this ancient civilization with Greek culture after the invasions of Alexander. The absence in the Hippocratic writings of any mention of rhinoplastic procedures and methods for repairing anal fistulas, as described in ancient texts of Indian surgery, seem to indicate an independent development of this discipline. As in other aspects of its culture medicine in India, at present, has endorsed Western cannons and technology and its pharmacology is becoming vital in providing access to medications at 'reasonable prices' to their enormous population.

About the most original and profound roots of Indian culture are their religion and philosophy. Undoubtedly a strange, but autochthonous, creation of the Indian spirit this religion reaches heights of mysticism in many ways incomprehensible to the Western mind, particularly in its INTROVERSION and the preoccupation with the individual. From the early rich polytheism of the Indo-Aryan Vedic pantheon evolved the notion of an immanent ineffable God, quite distinct from contemporary Western conceptions of divinity. This stage was arrived at as early as the Upanishads, which ideas strongly influenced the later religious and philosophical development of Jainism and, of course, Buddhism. The image of the Indian 'ascet of the forest' reaching through meditation the complete release from the 'tyranny of the sensuous' (mosksha) to achieve total identification with the Supreme Being, had come to be equated with everything that is mysterious and 'irrational' in oriental beliefs. In reality, during the epic times, Indian philosophy had intriguing similarities with Greek thought, particularly with the Eleatics and Atomists. However, later Indian philosophical evolution remained at a highly speculative level and, unlike the West, never applied methodological rigor or use 'Reason' to reach its goal.

Indian epistemology, as exposed in the Nyaya (a late system which purports to be more critical and analytical than early religion-philosophies) has interesting points and indicates that, at least in the early phase of its development, the Indian mind, like the Greek, groped with the issue of what is knowledge and ways of gathering it. Sense perception, they believed, together with 'immediate apprehension' is an original source of 'knowledge', and a modified syllogistic method of reduction et absurdum was occasionally resorted to. But the Indian mind never came to grips with a rational outlook of the Cosmo and Indian philosophy became stagnant, eventually accompanying other cultural endeavors in the general present decline.

The science and technology of India showed considerable early originality. The early Indus Valley civilization already used a numerical decimal system and utilized a fast potter wheel similar in design to the Sumerian. Their approach to mathematics was algebraic, like the

Sumerians also and, therefore, different to the Greeks which was eminently geometrical. They attempted summations of arithmetic series for solution of quadratic and linear indeterminate equations, and used sines and angles to solve geometric problems instead of cords like the Greeks. The most important of these works were done by historic figures, like the Aryabathas brothers and Mahavira, who worked in arithmetical problems and was one of the first to use the zero (which according to some experts had its true origin in Greece).

Most of what is known about other branches of science in India seems to indicate a dearth of originality and considerable borrowing. They held a geocentric world view, with the Sun, Moon and planets moving in orbits energized by 'wind' around the Earth and more distantly the stars, whose periods of rotation, because of the constancy of their alleged speeds, was proportional to their distances. The use of epicycles to calculate the more complex planetary courses betrays the Greek influence, but in assessing the motions of the Moon they used methods akin to the Babylonians. A seemingly 'Western' methodological outlook is obvious in their alchemical principles of five fundamental elements (Earth, Water, Air, Fire and Ether), although its origins in the Vedas could be traced and was apparently associated with the resurgence of Brahmanism.

Truly Indian Science lasting contributions to posterity were, therefore, restricted to the field of mathematics, with the development of algebra and the legacy of a numerical system that by way of the Arabs, we still use today. The lack of methodological rigor and systematic reasoning, which also plagued other contemporary cultures, contributed to its progressive arrest and ultimate decline.

Nowhere, however, is more notorious this present decline of Indian culture than in the fields of art and architecture. In general, indigenous Indian Architecture is highly original, well known for the profuse utilization of stone as a construction vehicle as well as in decoration. In carving the style was very distinct: the human form voluptuous and sinuous with aversion of sharp edges, and the female figure sensually represented no doubt to symbolize fertility.

Buddhist India witnessed a great flowering of the arts. The stupa, originally a burial mound, was later on transformed into a reliquary of sacred objects. It was a dome shaped round structure made of stone, surrounded by a railing with gates facing the cardinal geographic points and crowned by a mast supporting an umbrella-like form. This basic design dating back to the times of the Emperor Ashoka could be appreciated in Bharhut and Sanchi (I Century BC- I Century AD), and was subsequently progressively modified by larger masts and an increase in umbrella-like elements. Even more characteristic of this culture was the building, during the Maurya Empire, of the cave-temples carved with great effort and workmanship in mountain sides. The complexes consisted of pillared halls and sanctuaries, lavishly decorated with wall paintings and sculptures depicting mythological scenes as well as animal life. Particularly important are the paintings at Ajanta, in Central India, where an evolution from traditional symbolic and detached Buddhist iconography has taken place. Humans and animals are represented in an amalgam of forms, a reassertion of Life as an expression of religious feelings, a discovery of the spiritual by way of the common place rendered in an exquisite blend of all living creatures.

The original representation of Buddha is assumed to be the Mathura version, which portrayed the saga as thick set, either standing and wearing monastic robes with the right shoulder bare, or seated in a yogi position with the hands in his lap. When Buddhism spread toward the northern reaches of the Indian subcontinent it was further influenced by Hellenistic standards, which ultimately resulted in the additional evolution and radiation of Buddhist Art with the foundation of a new school at Gandhara. The representations of the Buddha figure, in this region, were of apollonian inspiration, the saga being reproduced wearing long togas with elaborated folded draperies. Later on, however, the Gandhara and Mathura styles were reconciled and a new 'hybrid' type took place under the Gupta Dynasty. With the subsequent collapse and fragmentation of this empire Hinduism effected a revival, and Buddhism lost ground becoming relegated to a minor place in the Indian pantheon, but leaving an idiosyncratic legacy. Nevertheless this cult spread widely, taking force in contiguous human communities like China, Southeast Asia, Ceylon, and eventually Japan and Korea among others.

Stylistically Hindu Architecture taps the same underlining sources in the entire Indian peninsula despite thematic differences. Their temples display a similar general structural plan. The central shrine, the garbha griha, is surmounted by a large tower, the sikhara, and flanked by a hallway leading to a porch where musical and dancing festivals, in honor of the enshrined deity, take place. The temple is often surrounded by a courtyard filled with lesser shrines and even stupas, constituting conglomerates of very distinctive look (chaityas), which occasionally are also included in the rock carved temples.

Toward the close of the First Millennium AD Hindu architectural standards underwent a major evolutionary trifurcation. Undoubtedly there was considerable mingling of styles but the three main variations became clearly evident. The Indo-Arian sikhara was represented by conical convex spires, with the facades frequently segmented by horizontal lines of carvings, and vertically divided by masonry ribbings, giving the towers an appearance which had been compared to a beehive, which can be appreciated in the magnificent Lingaraja temple at Orissa in Northern India, a complex of buildings where the progressive development of this style is clearly demonstrated.

The Dravidian School grew in the southern part of the country and their sikharas climb in a series of stepped superimposed terraces (the bhumis). Typical examples are the Kailasanath temple in Kanchipuram and the rock-cut Dharmaraja complex near Madras, where each level of the ascending platforms includes dome-shaped structures. Finally, the Chalukyan style evidences both Dravidian and Indo-Arian influences, the structures being erected in profusely carved polygonal platforms with low pyramidal towers. Remarkable examples are the temples in what is today Mysore State, like those in Vijayanagar.

Rock-hewn temples continued to be built by the Hindus when Buddhism became decadent, with ever more elaborated sculptures of humans and beasts, as well as, abstract patterns enriching their walls. The custom culminated with the construction of the grandiose temple of Kailasa at Ellora, an architectural feat of major proportions, encompassing an area as large as the Parthenon but one-half times as high. It was conceived and executed as a monolith, with surrounding courtyards carved in the rock around a 25 feet high rock platform.

In the XI and XII centuries Afghan and Turkish Islamic invaders penetrated Northern India as far as Bengal, subduing the native population and systematically destroying their culture and razing to the ground the temples, for which the fierce iconoclasticism of Islam felt a strong repudiation. But the techniques of the vanquished survived and under Indian artisans stone was substituted for brick and marble inlaid, assiduously used in colored and glazed tiles. Stylistically the indigenous and foreign schools slowly blended with the emergence of a distinct Indo-Islamic Art, which had its culmination during the enlightened Mogul rulers with magnificent works in stone and marble: like the Red Fort of Delhi and the notorious Taj Mahal in Agra, where the extraordinary talent in blending cultural influences (Persian, Timurid and Indian) displayed by this inspired dynasty is well demonstrated.

After a pinnacle of splendor in the XVIII Century AD the Mogul Empire fragmented and ultimately disintegrated, heralding also a collapse in creativity from which indigenous architectural tradition had never recovered. In this case, like with other contemporary non-western cultures, the generative vigor had been sapped and replaced by Western notions and standards, without even a semblance of the 'blending of styles' that occur when vital and dynamic cultures make contact in space and time.

The story of other Indian art forms is very similar. We already mentioned the wonderful wall paintings in the caves of Ajanta from the Gupta period. This style lasted, and was invigorated by the Hindu revival, until it was eventually, like in the case of architecture, integrated into the Mogul School which also partook, not only in the vivacity of color of native Indian renderings, but in the attention to decorative linear detail of the Persians, and in some elements of western perspective brought to the awareness of the rulers by Europeans, mainly Portuguese traders. A final burst of creativity took place in the Kangra style, named after a Himalayan kingdom where the artists from Rajput fled during the fanatical persecutions of the Mogul ruler Aurangzeb. Here the rich colors, profile positioning of the subjects, minute decorative detail and sinuosity of lines preserved what was best in Indian pictorial tradition until the XIX Century, when an earthquake put an end to the efforts, only to be superseded by Western standards which constitute the main body of artistic influences in present day Indian works.

Indian bronze objects historically followed a pattern similar to the other artistic denominations. It prolifically radiated leading to great virtuosity of design with many intermediate 'hybrid' forms. In general, the representational standards already mentioned in sculpture and painting were also found in bronze. Three main ramifications or schools are usually described: the Northern, the Deccanese and the Southern. In the Northern the human body was slender and graceful, often covered by translucent garments. This tradition was developed and matured with the Gupta Emperors, radiating a freshness and energy of surprising vigor and naturalism which, in subsequent periods, was lost.

Deccanese creations resemble, and were inspired, in contemporaneous sculpture holding to more traditional Indian conventions, particularly in what refers to the Andhara and Chalukya modalities. Lastly, the Southern Dravidian School accomplished a great degree of expressivity and dynamic content with very faithful depiction of qualities such as tension, movement and even tranquility. With the advent of the Moslem dynasties bronze, like the other representational arts, went through periods of persecutions and essentially disappeared. It is ironic, and very revealing, that present day Indian bronze work not only is imitative of the ancient masterpieces, but in general of far inferior quality and design, an obvious sign of decadence.

There is little doubt, no matter how we look at it, that native Indian Culture, like we have seen in the case of Islam, is in frank decadence. Their modern cities are losing the 'flavor' and personality of previous epochs, and in general are acquiring a western 'varnish'. All their cultural radiations and sub-radiations appear today as evolutionary 'blind alleys' or 'dead ends'. To be sure, this culture is still 'alive', religiously and linguistically it is still 'operative', it has not yet 'succumb' to time as the Egyptian and Mesopotamian did, but its decline is evident. Although the possibility of a 'Renaissance' could not be absolutely ruled out it seems every day less likely in view of the lack of vigor, creativity and originality.

CHAPTER X

From the main cultures differentiating in the late Neolithic period only the Chinese today still keeps an uninterrupted history traceable back to more than 3500 years. (In the case of Indian Civilization there was a hiatus of more than 1500 years from the disappearance of the early settlements in the Indus valley to the evidence of renewed vitality about the VII Century BC). It is one of the most remarkable feats of this durable and prolific culture that despite invasions and wars its character persisted during the enormous lapse of time eliciting since its inception. It might be that the geographic isolation of this human community surrounded by culturally inferior people and nomads, as well as, the fact of being separated by way of the highest mountain ranges on Earth, and the immense steppes of Central Asia, from any other contemporary major civilization, has something to do with this surprising endurance; but still the mere fact of such a prodigious survival is an unprecedented phenomenon. Because of this isolation it is also very intriguing the apparent independent development of the techniques of bronze casting (of which there is ample archeological evidence not only in relation to its exquisite design but of its antiquity too), which was brought very early to a high degree of refinement among the inhabitants of this region. Their pottery, lacquer products and ivory carving also exhibited great technical skill, the clear manifestation of a very unique autochthonous and creative civilization almost from the beginning of the historical record.

For example, the manufacture of porcelain is a distinctive invention of these people, essentially an evolution from a white pottery which was been produced in China for, at least, four hundred years before it was perfected about the time of the Sung Emperors. Other kinds of stoneware were the well known celadon, which used a green glaze over a gray base, and the popular Tenmoku utilized by the Japanese in the tea ceremonies of Zen Buddhism. The proliferation of ceramic styles and meticulous attention to detail are in general quite outstanding and very revealing of the enduring and innovative capacity of this ancient society, whose superb workmanship was not surpassed at the time by any other cultural group on Earth. Like other artistic derivations Chinese ceramics has in recent times become commercialized, the present activity consisting only of pale reproductions of previous works. The decline is more noticeable because it has occurred when the international demand for the product had increased as a result of better communications and commercial facilities.

The major art forms also evolved a highly peculiar style, with painting and calligraphy becoming their prototypes. From the Han Dynasty, only tomb slabs painted with tempera remains today. Figures are drawn juxtaposed in a stylized landscape. But it was not until the latter part of this period that the typical impressionistic Chinese genre emerged, the human figure being rendered with the delicacy and reserved pose so notorious of this culture. Also stone carving first appeared about the same time and an early radiation between the styles of Shantung which emphasized profiles, and the soft molded brick carvings of Szechwan which attempted to portray space in a realistic manner, could be noticed.

In the following interlude of the Three Kingdoms and Six Dynasties it was that Buddhism's first impact on China was felt. Like in India before, cave temples were carved in cliffs and mountain sides, and in Northern Wei the redoubtable complex of the 'Cave of the Thousand Buddhas' was built at Tunhuang. The inspiration for these works was certainly of central Asian derivation and strongly influenced by the Indian 'chaitya' which mark can also be appreciated, whether in stone or wall painting, in the internal decorative motives of the caves. The compositions were still two-dimensional with the figures appearing divorced from their settings.

Contemporaneous with these developments was a taste for large and massive stone carving associated with the spread of Buddhism. Buddha figures ranging from the monumental (cut on rock faces) to small decorative objects inside the caves are still preserved, but it should be noted that the degree of voluptuousness reached by Indian masterpieces is conspicuously absent, the sinuosity of surfaces and sensuality being replaced by an air of restrain and composure. The human figure is never depicted naked. A sense of repose and peaceful balance had permeated the art of this great culture as far back as can be remembered.

While these occurrences were taking place in the North, in South China artistic growth was undergoing a quite independent thrust. During the Chin Dynasty portraiture reached a high degree of perfection. In 'The Admonitions of the Instructress of the Palace Ladies' (attributed to a copy from the IV Century BC court artist Ku K'ai-chih), a X Century AD hand scroll, the main features typifying the great works of later periods, like the delicacy of the lines, meticulousness about details, and the sense of compositional equilibrium, already can be appreciated.

During the Tang Dynasty China finally recovered from the disintegration of central authority suffered after the downfall of the Han Monarchs. It would be an error, however, to compare the times of the Three Kingdoms and Six Dynasties with the cultural hiatus overtaking the West in the Dark Ages. In fact, as we have seen, many artistic influences from Central Asia were then introduced and became perfected. Precisely BECAUSE of the collapse of central order considerable cultural radiation between South and North China took place. (Contrary to this Western Europe, after the downfall of the Roman Empire, never had the fruitful cross-insemination with another great contemporary culture that China, despite of the distance, was fortunate to have with India after the collapse of the Han's Empire).

The Tang Emperors continued to propitiate, by direct patronage, the arts. Buddhism still, at least at the beginning, did afford for the thematic inspiration and the degree of excellence reached could be appreciated in the exquisite sculptures in the cave temples at T'ien-lung and Lung-men, presently considered among the great artistic treasures of all time. Painting crystallized, along calligraphy, as the major artistic expression. In color, monumentality, vivacity and poise, the compositions achieved a degree of perfection characteristic of a mature stage. A true naturalistic or realistic 'flavor' became manifested and animal figures, as well as flower motifs, were significant elements in the pictorial renderings. The name of famous contemporary masters of the brush: like Han Kan, Yen Li-pen and Wu Tao-tzu, had been immortalized by history. A specifically Chinese way to represent space, the 'blue and green' style, was born during this period. It consisted in drawing the mountains as large rocks and the division of space was defined by the rise of eye level or by the usage of pictorial subterfuges, such as clouds, etc. The exuberant originality of this epoch was carried through the subsequent brief interlude of the Five Dynasties, when the technique of ink monochromes and a novel style consisting of large mountain landscapes with small human figures (which was to dominate Chinese painting for the following six centuries) evolved.

The next dynasty, the Sung, was a time of isolation and inward looking for China. The early emperors had a selective taste and were great patrons of the arts. This was the 'high tide' of painting and calligraphy, which were further perfected along the lines laid down by their predecessors. The Academy, an institution created by the scholarly class and whose roots dated back to the VI Century AD, provided for guidance and immensely influenced the growth and evolution of major art in the mainland, becoming very powerful under the auspice of enlighten rulers. In fact, some of the Northern Sung monarchs themselves became famous artists, like Hui Tsung who inaugurated a style of small format, flat perspective and harmonious blending of shape and lines. Of special interest is the creation, toward the end of this period, of the Hsia-Ma school, consisting of a clever manipulation of space, a way to unfold '10000 miles in a foot of paper or silk'. The effect was rendered with ink tones and deceptively simple techniques to capture mournful, forbidden landscapes that seem to climb into the horizon.

The ulterior course in the evolution of Chinese Painting is very complex. There was a proliferation of individual fashions beginning with the Yan Dynasty, after many great masters decided to boycott the courts of the Mongol rulers, although they continued even after the restitution of the native monarchies, their independent courses. Cross-insemination and eclectic forms were common but they endorsed the general standards and rules already laid down by their predecessors. Typical in this respect is the Wu School of XV Century AD, whose works reflect a blending of numerous pre-existing styles mostly from the Northern Sung and Yuan periods. With the coming of the Manchu Dynasty in the XVII Century and the attendant commercialization of the arts, Chinese paintings became largely imitative, losing originality and innovative vigor.

In architecture the Chinese also exhibited a highly individualistic and original design. Although the Great Wall is one of the greatest feats of engineering ever achieved by mankind its style is not peculiarly Chinese, in the sense that the typical structural features we have learned to identify with this great culture were, at this early time, only in gestation. Although no intact buildings had survived, judging by models in burial sites, it becomes apparent that traditional genuine Chinese Architecture became recognizable during the Han Dynasty, including the gabled roofs and the T-shaped beams; an innovation permitting variations in the slope of the roofs and the curvilinear profiles so distinctive of this great civilization.

With the introduction of Buddhism in China, the pagoda, an elaboration of the Indian stupa, first appeared. This evolutionary radiation from the original Indian design consisted essentially of a tower, first of wood and later on of stone and brick, usually three to seven stories tall. The original rounded and bulky body of these edifications underwent during the years of migration through Central Asia considerable structural modifications, morphing into a tiered structure with multiple eaves frequently of wood, and crowned by a rod-like metallic object referred to as 'demon arrester', obviously a further elaboration from the Indian masts of the stupas. It is interesting to mention that numerous variations of the original architectural design of the Indian prototype of this type of edification could be traced, following the progress through Central, North and South Asiatic routes taken by the Buddhist faith. Typical examples are the Ta-yen-t'a Pagoda in Shensi Province (T'ang Dynasty) and the Pai-ma-sseu Pagoda near Honan (Sung Dynasty), both imposing and elegant masonry structures that depart considerably from the original model. The pagodas frequently were included in the courtyards of larger temples and served the religious purpose of shrines. The taste of the Chinese for setting their palaces and courts as complexes of buildings in enchanting gardens originated about this time.

Chinese Architecture remained an eminently traditionalist endeavor and the further elaboration of its main themes enlisted the efforts of many generations. For example, the spectacular beauty of edifices erected by the Ming Emperors resulted mostly from colored effects. The pillars were painted bright red, brackets and beams rainbow tones, and the tiled roofs deep yellow. Decorations were also profuse giving to the works a general feeling of bright splendor, as could be appreciated in the compound of the 'Forbidden City' in Peking. After the conquest of the country by the Manchu's, architecture, like the arts, became decadent and sapped of creativity and originality, consisting solely of inferior imitations of the old treasures, pale reproductions of past artistic glories.

The fate of sculpture is even more intriguing than that of the other major artistic genres of China. It achieved very early a surprising degree of refinement, as attested by the life-size terracotta soldiers in the tombs of the Hans's Monarchs, and the already alluded renditions in stone during the apogee of Buddhist inspired art, but began to decline in the XIII Century AD after the Mongol invasions never to recover again the lost luster and masterly workmanship. The decline is already apparent in the colossal stone figures flanking the 'Ceremonial Way' leading to the burial grounds of the Ming Emperors. According to the experts, despite their monumentality, the figures facing each other at regular intervals, whether humans or animals, are static and lack the distinctive finishing touches that previous generations had imparted to their works.

About the time the Ch'ing Dynasty rose to power sculpture was in obvious decadence and largely ornamental. This might have been the consequence of the suspicious attitude of the Manchu invaders toward the scholarly class of China, but, intriguingly, the new aristocratic taste for the minor arts brought about an enormous appetite for carved objects in semi-precious stones, jade, and ivory. Yet in sculpture, like in the other major art forms and architecture, after the 'high tide' of the Sung Dynasty an slow decline became noticeable, at the beginning almost imperceptibly but gaining momentum with the Ming monarchs, when a 'vulgarization' of taste took place presaging the creativity vacuum of the Ch'ing period.

It was not only in the visual arts that the Chinese Culture demonstrated its original vitality. In literature also it displayed a long history of exuberant productivity which can be traced back to the last three centuries of the Chang Dynasty, as attested by inscriptions recorded in bone and tortoise shells. Even on that early date (the end of the second millennium BC), Chinese writing consisted of more than 3000 characters, the ancestor of modern Chinese scripture and evidently an autochthonous development.

The first great poetic compilation dates back to the V Century BC and includes about 300 songs (the Shih Ching) in a characteristic tetra-syllabic style. Another lyrical form arose almost simultaneously farther south (the Ch'u Tz'u), consisting of longer and irregular lines more adaptable to chanting than to music, as the former were. From these early beginnings the evolution of poetry in China unfolded such wealth in variations of lyrical expressivity as to rival any other extant culture. Poetry's golden age was during the Tang and Sung dynasties when a new kind of verse, the Tz'u, was introduced, reaching its apogee during the tenure of the latter emperors. Prose was also amply cultivated since the early Shu Ching documents and the writings of Lao-tzu, Confucius and Mencius, to include through the ages works in philosophy, critical assays, drama and historical themes.

After the fall of the Sung Monarch's Chinese Literature, in general, began to be afflicted with 'antiquarianism' and it has been in the vernacular that evolution is clearly discernible. Since the mid XIX Century, at least, both prose and poetry began to be influenced by Western standards and ideas, culminating with the so-called 'literary revolution' of the early part of the XX Century, which was sparked by the efforts of Hu Shih to 'write in the living language of the people'. It remains to be seen if Chinese literature will keep its independent evolution or, as other cultural categories of this most ancient of present day societies, will languish in the warm embrace of Western Civilization.

Chinese Music is highly original in melody and performance practices. Musical instruments, like lithophones, bronze bells and earthware flutes, had been excavated from sites of the Yin Dynasty (XV Century BC). Lutes of pear shape and circular designs with straight necks are known to have been used before the III Century AD, probably reaching the country from Central Asia. Zithers are the oldest string instrument of this civilization and known to be an ancient part of its musical lore, at least since the V Century BC. So characteristic is the repertory of compositions devised for it that it has been compared with painting and ceramics as prototypes of Chinese Culture.

Melodically this music is fundamentally of a five notes kind but with frequent intercalations of seven notes stretches. Its peculiar intonation, so strange to Western ears, stems, according to authorities in the field, from the use of non-tempered semitones and the technique of 'gracing' notes with microtonal on or off glides. When playing together as a band, flute, lute and fiddle, all act in unison, each in its peculiar way against a backdrop of percussion instruments. It has to be pointed out that despite basic similarities of musical instrumentation with the Middle East and India, the simpler rhythm, different timbre and typical five note melody places apart this music from the other Asiatic traditions. The use of a mouth organ, unknown anywhere else in the continent, was also widely employed to double the melody or to afford accompaniment; a custom which seem to be very old in the land and an independent musical development.

Taking into consideration all the available evidence it is clear that in instrumentation, performance, mechanics and melody, Chinese Music has been an innovative, rich, creative and independent tradition, one which did integrate early foreign conceptions into the mainstream of its cultural peculiarities. At the present, like in the case of literature, the music of these talented people has been strongly influenced by Western ideas and techniques, with the composition of 'cantatas' and operatic pieces played with native instruments. Whether this resilient culture would assimilate and integrate these modern pressures or, instead, be superseded by them as another manifestation of internal decay, only time will be able to tell.

Chinese Philosophy blends inextricably with their religious beliefs (like ancestors worship common also to many other Asiatic communities), and shares with its European counterpart the rare distinction of evolving into a deliberate organized body of thought to explain Man's nature and its place in society. The early beginnings of this discipline were as prolific as in the West and by the VI Century BC, it is claimed, that more than 1000 'schools' had flourished, of which the most popular were Confucianism, Taoism, Moism, Legalism, the Logicians and the Yin-Yang school which, as also will be seen, also heavily influenced medical lore. Confucianism, which expounded a humanistic theory about the supremacy of Man as an artificer of his own fate, as well as, the importance of the universal virtues of wisdom, courage and humility in modeling society and civilization, enlisted through the ages a large number of disciples. The early ones were the most influential, inasmuch as their efforts resulted in the ulterior derivation of two different branches: one social and political, the other psychological and religious (initiated by Tseng-Tzu and Tzu-Ssu respectively).

Taoism was a mystical body of thought deeply rooted in Bronze Age mentality about the subordination of Man to Nature, and became a profound undercurrent of Chinese thought up to the present times. It also was an important factor on the acceptance and elaboration of Buddhism after it penetrated the country. In fact Taoism subsequently 'degenerated' into a form of religion (the Yellow Emperor Lau Tzu cult), but remained a strong presence in Chinese thought, becoming one of the pillars of its cosmology. Its concept of non-being is strange to the Western mind and the idea of a 'one-ess' underlining diversity, as well as, the interpenetration of cosmic events, has points of similarity with the Eleatics and early Stoics.

The other lasting root of Chinese philosophy was the Yin-Yang school. These two basic 'principles' represented 'reality' and in fact were the generative sources of everything that existed. In the reconciliation of opposites, in the interplay of harmony and contradictions strangely reminiscent to modern Hegelian dialectic, the entire realm of this 'reality' was founded. Every other minor school (Moism, Logicians etc.), for all practical purposes, disappeared with the burning of the books about 213 BC.

The recent history of Chinese Philosophy represents little more than further elaborations and occasional attempts to integrate the seemingly disparate schools. The efforts to construct a solid epistemology has been marred by the burning of the books, but the fact is that its philosophical corpus remains to the present a body of ethical precepts for man in society and a voluminous inventory of metaphysical conceptions. The Chinese apparently never came to grips with 'Reason'.

Intimately intertwined with their philosophy were the medical disciplines. The clever Chinese physician is part of the lore of many Asiatic and Occidental nations. Among the most ancient of Chinese medical texts, and the source of much of what we known about their medicine, is the Nei Ching which is divided in two parts: the Su Wen (Plain Questions) and the Ling Shu (Mystical Gate). Originally representing, like in so many other cultures, practices intimately related to religious beliefs which consider diseases as calamities sent by the gods to punish mortals and the need to placate them, it was at a later period based in philosophical and cosmological considerations parallel to practical herbal medicine. According to Confucian cosmology Man is a microcosm composed of wood, fire, metal, earth and fire.

Another philosophical principle, and perhaps more important for medicine, was the Yin Yang School. These two components were conceived as 'fluids' and of their perfect 'flow' depended the state of health. Because the Yang (masculine principle) was the predominant one medications were prescribed to promote this component in an attempt to restitute their equilibrium.

The anatomy and physiology of the Chinese was largely based in beliefs and conceptions with little observational basis, except for a few mentions of dissections in criminals during the Sung Dynasty. Diagnosis consisted, intriguingly, in the determination of the 'pulse rate' of which two hundred were described. Treatment of diseases was mostly empirical and followed the cannons of the Yin Yang School. Yet, it is known that iron was used for anemia, arsenic for fevers and skin diseases, and mercury for syphilis. Interesting is the fact that some of the treatments that have been in use in the Western nations, like rhubarb for purgatives and opium as a narcotic, among others, were also used in China. As far as surgical procedures is concern ancient texts described a number of operations including harelip, castrations etc., although for obscure reasons surgery became stagnant at the time of the Tang dynasty.

Like in other scientific endeavors and contrary to the West, original Chinese medicine was highly dogmatic, divorce from observation and experimentation, attached to traditional practices and refusing to accept any challenge to its ancient roots and beliefs. At present, however, and after prolong contact with Western nations and standards, the native ways have become superseded by the new methodology and principles.

Modern Chinese Medicine, like in other aspects of their culture, had embraced Western standards based in the usage of modern technology. Surely, traditional ways, like in other cultures, are still favor by many and not necessarily by the poor or destitute. Yet, contrary to the case of other civilizations, there is an ancient procedure long practiced in this country which, in recent decades, has gain favor in Western nations, and in fact all over the world: acupuncture. It has been widely used for the treatment of pain and even in some places for inducing anesthesia.

Despite of the fact that Western Man has been incapable of finding a convincing reason as to why it works, it does, and despite opposition in many quarters for the lack of an 'acceptable mechanism' of action, it has been reluctantly accepted.

Also in other fields the technology of this ancient civilization, being of a 'practical' nature, made some early and lasting positive contributions. As we have already seen, bronze was magnificently wrought by the XV Century BC and silk weaving, as well as, a numerical and ideographic system were by then perfected skills. In the VI Century BC iron came into use. Paper was, about that time, invented and the polarizing effect of the magnet discovered. A primitive way of casting iron came then into use, and some basic observations in optics and mechanics were recorded. Alchemy, not surprisingly, grew early from the speculative believe in Yin and Yang, but for the Chinese, apparently, the main concern was not the transmutation of metals but the search for the 'pill of immortality', which was avidly pursued by many emperors until relatively recent times.

Mathematics evolved, like in Egypt and Mesopotamia before, out of a practical necessity for surveying purposes, commercial and accounting reasons. Enough sophistication in the handling of numbers was attained to allow the solution of geometrical problems, such as areas of triangles, trapeziums and circles. Methods to find volumes based in sides and viseversa were invented. They had a value for 'r' of 10, and algebraic methods (equations) were used in many calculations which were enormously helped by the invention of the first 'number machine' similar to the Greek abacus. Astronomical observations are ancient in China and the position of stars, the Sun, Moon and comets, were carefully tabulated. Many celestial recordings during the Middle Ages, when practically none was been made in Europe, helped in the clarification of several obscured sidereal problems. For instance, it has been claimed that the birth of a 'new star' described by their astronomers around the year 1000 AD, corresponded to the supernova explosion that gave rise to the Crab Nebulae.

But the Chinese inventions with greatest impact in World history and technology were, undoubtedly, printing (first in block and later in movable type) and gun-powder, which they manufactured from sulfur and saltpeter. These discoveries enabled both the dissemination of culture and a more efficient way to conduct warfare. In a sense it is ironic that this most ancient of present day societies would have provided mankind with both, the means for mass communication and annihilation, but such has been its legacy.

Despite of their formidable past accomplishments Chinese Science and Technology, like all other manifestations of this culture, had long ago ceased to give signs of vitality and to produce indigenous original works. What we call in The West the 'scientific method', based in careful observation, induction and experimentation, never took hold of the Chinese mind, which repudiated any 'theorizing' as useless and investigative activity as denigrating to a cultivated person.

It can be stated with confidence, therefore, that this most enduring of living cultures is at the present time in frank decadence, its fruitful achievements a thing of the past. Small artistic radiations during the lapses of dissolution of central power (for example: The Northern and Southern schools of painting and poetry) were not permitted to destroy the cohesion of this civilization once dynastic tradition was restituted. Political unity thus help to preserve the integration or synthesis of even seemingly disparate tendencies, but frequently stultified any further evolution by casting in a rigid mold any original striving.

Yet, it has to be emphasized, this culture is not dead. There are indications to assume that it is still alive, but creativity has declined significantly in quantity and quality. To be sure Western ideas and techniques have disseminated rapidly in China, and the country presently is undergoing vast political, economic and social changes. There is no doubt that China economic growth in recent times is spectacular, and the country is projected to become the largest economy of the world at the latest by the middle of the XXI Century. The question is if what is emerging culturally from the recent maelstrom is still the same 'thing' or not. The 'face' of the Chinese cities is taking a distinctive Western look; the big towns are been clutter by enormous skyscrapers. It is still premature to foretell if native Chinese Culture will survive the present convulsive period, and, if it does, whether it will leave any descendants or rather will depart the world forum without heirs.

In reference to the Mongolic, Korean and other human groups who inhabit the periphery of the main cultural center, the situation is similar to that of the Nubians and Ethiopians in relation to ancient Egypt, in other words, there has been assimilation and some further elaboration of the received cultural heritage but, as happens with the main Chinese civilization itself, these countries are suffering the same fate of the parental tradition, that is, they are been progressively westernized, albeit at different rates of change . (The case of Japanese culture is special and will be analyzed in the next chapter).

The geographic locus of what is China, the nation today, witnessed the rise of a prolific culture which, like the Egyptian before, was able with perseverance to keep a unification, and therefore an homogeneity of cultural expression under a single 'nation', that has disallowed evolutionary diversifications or large departures from a pre-established mold. This is a different outcome of what happened in the 'fertile crescent', which fathered the Sumero-Akkadians and their successors, Assyrians, Babylonians and Persians, or to the collection of 'modern countries' which today define our Western Civilization.

———————————

CHAPTER XI

Japanese Civilization, the main variation from the original Chinese kind, is running a fate paralleled to its mainland ancestor. The miraculous economic and industrial growth of this country in modern times could not be credited to its traditional culture. To believe so will be to distort and misrepresent reality. Original Japanese Civilization was simple, functional and blended with the surrounding Nature. Cultivation and bronze-age technology were introduced in the land about the III Century BC by the ya-yoi people, who apparently were immigrants from Korea and China. Their houses already, for what is known of them, exhibited architectural details which, with time, became fairly typical of the islands. Their houses were built in roughly circular or oblong stilts, a design soon adopted in the Shinto shrines. They also incorporated high gables and thatched slanted roofs to the sides of central pillars, a fashion that still could be appreciated, despite numerous reconstructions, in the shrines of Sumo and Ise. Their bronze objects included swords, spearheads, mirrors and distinctly Japanese dotaku, which were embellished with bas-reliefs of mundane scenes.

In the VI Century AD, however, with the introduction of Buddhism in the land, Chinese culture began to exert a profound influence in Japanese Civilization. Buildings began to display the symmetrical layout of stone foundation, glazed tile roofs with curved eaves, and painted woodwork distinctive of contemporary mainland examples. The Buddhist temples (shinetoji) had definite Chinese ground plans and the frescos in their walls, as the statues in the interiors, bore the marks of this geographically contiguous civilization. So strongly imitative of the Chinese was the Japanese art of the times that in some cases, when no examples are preserved in the mainland, the Japanese objects are taken as representative prototypes of the given art form of the epoch. A case in point is the painting in the Tachibana Shrine at Nara of Kannon the Bodhisattva of Mercy, a work that has been taken to represent the style of the Chinese Tang Dynasty for which no original models remain.

The ulterior development of Japanese Art and Architecture, although heavily influenced by China, retook and further elaborated indigenous trends and origins. Scroll and folding screen paintings reveal an obvious mainland inspiration and evolved into powerful creations. Their use of color, bold lines, as well as the pose and balance even of large compositions, were native and independent features not inherited from the original and genuine Chinese sources. The temples, palaces and houses continued to display the typical Japanese traits in various degrees of integration. Artistic schools were not static but dynamic and vital.

This is clearly seen, for instance, in the pictorial arts. By the XI Century, Japanese Painting had absorbed the influences from the mainland and began to plow on its own direction. Already at that time the most eminent representatives of landscape masterpieces had perfected the techniques of Chinese masters and introduced modifications of their own: like the more defined and detailed reproductions of mountains and the use of ink and strong colorings. Japan by then had severed relations with the continent and Buddhist Art began to create an independent sensuous style lacking in Chinese compositions. (In this regard what happened is very similar to the separate evolutionary course frequently taken by animal and plant species when an original group splits and the descendants become mutually geographically isolated.)

Pictorial works such as 'Death of Sakyyamuni', on the Kongobuji Monastery, and 'Twelve Delvas', in the Kyoo-Gokokuji counterpart, are representatives of this nascent autochthonous school. The new fashion literally spilled over the secular field with the further elaboration of the Yamoto-e technique (bold use of lines or fine drawings and color to fulfill pictorial effects). Much dynamism and dramatic feeling was conveyed by this latter style under the Kamakura Monarchs, as could be admired in the scrolls of the Heiji Insurrection. Many scenes of everyday life were then, in agreement with the realistic ethos of the epoch, drawn utilizing these methods.

A new 'opening' of Japan, which occurred about this time, exposed the islanders to the art of the Sung Dynasty of China and to the influence of Zen Buddhism; an historic event of great future significance, one that opened the way to the refinement of a new fashion inspired in the introverted beliefs and rituals of their practitioners and preachers. During the so-called Heian period Japanese painting, again, became heavily influenced by the continental choices of highly symbolic and abstracted subjects. Also, like before, after an interlude of 'assimilation' the natives, once the techniques were mastered, plowed along their own tastes. A typical case was that of Sesshu, who, after traveling to the mainland, perfected their designs and created a highly idiosyncratic form. Another was Kano Masanobu, who originated a school of painting inspired, not only on the Sung and Ming Chinese masters, but also on the Yamato-e artificers. Other varieties of painting born in the XVIII Century, like the decorative Ukiyo-e and the Bunjinga or literary men of painting (a light brush technique), also drew from the continent during the Ming and Ching dynasties.

After the Meiji Restoration, as with the other historical cases we had analyzed, Japan incorporated Western methods and ideas to a considerable, even overwhelming, degree. Although indigenous genuine works are still produced, no novel or original kind, no new school had flourished in recent times. Western modern aesthetic principles had seduced the Japanese imagination.

In sculpture the Japanese also were originally heavily influence by the Chinese. The early examples found are grotesque clay statuettes probably used by the primitive inhabitants as fetishes or religious ceremonies of some sort. Not surprisingly, historically, the early examples of Japanese sculpture were introduced into the country with the Buddhist religion and by Chinese sculptures. The early examples in Nara did have an strong influence from Chinese North Wei style as could be ascertain in the Horyuji temple. The following Hakuho period is reputed to be strongly influenced by the style of the Tang Dynasty which appeared to be devoid of the removed monumentality of the previous period, depicting the saga with more human attributes even with sensuous smiling faces and a grace vaguely resembling Indian works.

In the capital of Nara japanese sculptures assimilated the Tang's Chinese style and created their own which was called 'Tenpyo Sculpture' with the human figure rendered more realistically, even with the faces expressing human sentiments. From this period dated a remarkable official factory that produced sculptures for the temples. Stone, terracotta, silver , lacquer and bronze were used for the works of art.

In the so-called Heian period in the VIII Century the capital of Japan was moved to Kyoto and the official factory closed. Esoteric

Buddhist rites flourished and a new style based in wood rendering the figure with massive imposing proportions and almost menacing faces became popular. Subsequently, toward the end of this period with the Amida worship the statues were rendered with more gentle and peaceful demeanor, the saga depicted in a seating position with folded legs apparently in meditation as could be appreciated in the Byodo-in in Uji by the master Jocho

During the following Kamakura Period there was the Kei school which claimed descend from Jocho and who with a new technique of 'woodblock construction' strived to render realism to their works to which end they studied early Nara Period masterpieces and also works from the Sung dynasty of China. Many were the masters of this new genre including among others the prolific Unkei who among his many works are the portraiture of Indian priests in Kofuku-ji.

The following Muromachi period was a time of decline in quality and quantity of Buddha sculpture which lacked the stimulus and financial support by rich people and government patronage of previous periods. The carving of masks for the No theatre became very popular

After the 'opening of Japan, like in other cultural disciplines there was an strong foreign influence in sculpture mostly from France with the so-called Paris School and after the Second World War avant-garde techniques and materials capture the imagination of Japanese sculptures. Presently sculpture, like other aspect of their culture, have avidly adopted international concepts and ideas but there had been recently a genuine drive to return to more traditional motives, a drive to blend objects to Nature led by the mono-ha school. Whether this new trend will crystallized in a synthesis, and therefore in some genuinely new genre, or if eventually the tide of 'Occidentalism' will, like with other manifestations of their culture, drag away in its unstoppable torrent this art form is still too premature to tell.

In the field of music the situation is quite similar to that of the other cultural denominations. Mainland influences from Korea and China were prominent and far reaching. Liturgical melodies and numerous continental instruments were introduced with Buddhist practices, and by the time of the Tang Emperors several distinctive musical genres had emerged, some courtly and others popular forms, which grew side by side with the religious type. Some of its roots could even be trace down to places like Burma and India.

The Heian Period saw several distinct musical styles crystallized. The To-gaku represented the music from China and Southern Asia. It was played with bamboo flutes, reeds contrivances, organs, percussion devises and two classes of stringed instruments. The koma-gaku was the music from Korea and Northeastern Asia, which was played with a low-pitched flute and a six-stringed zither. Under the Kamakura Emperors Buddhist Music was transformed by hymns added to the bombai chants. This was the time when the No theatre was created and incorporated rhymes from the Tang period: the popular Kure-gaku and To-sangaku. Groups of wandering monks playing bamboo lutes took to the road influenced by Zen Buddhism. Finally, under the Tokugawa monarchs Western customs and ideas pervading Japan also left their strong imprints in music. The Kabuki theatre took shape and a long three strings instrument, the samisen, was introduced from Okinawa, attesting to the vitality and originality still exhibited by the music of this country even that late. Three secular schools (Naga-uta, Tokiwazu and Kyomoto) also sprung at this time.

In modern times, like in all other cultural denominations, the introduction of Western methods and standards was surprisingly rapid. Theoretical education in music was neglected to be replaced by Western notation and harmony. After the Second World War there has been a serious attempt to preserve the old cultural values and, although, it has met with some success no new musical forms had emerged other than some integration of western models with native lore; an adoption that has had so far mixed results and whose consequences are still impossible to foresee.

Genuine Japanese Medicine is not very original although it is reputed to possess considerable anatomical knowledge. The early period of mysticism and superstition was changed in the IV Century AD with the teachings and practices of the Chinese, who seemed to have originally entered the country as court physicians and soon became the dominant influence in the country, which adopted and assimilated almost completely their diagnostic and therapeutic methods to Japanese Medicine. Even in the X Century, when Yasuyori Tamba wrote his I Shinho, it was still apparent the great influence that China exerted over its geographic neighbor, to the point of almost complete obliteration of autochthonous models.

This situation began to change in the XVI Century when there was an attempt by some native physicians (mainly Tokuhon Nagata) to retrieve medicine from the hold of the Chinese, coinciding with the arrival of the Portuguese who introduced into the country European methods, which slowly penetrated the country. In 1857 the Dutch inaugurated a European type of medical school at Yeddo and since then medical sciences and practices have become thoroughly westernized. Today Japanese Medicine is as advanced as in any other Western industrialized country, producing excellent research and outstanding delivery of healthcare, but again, in its corpus there is no identifiable vestige of the original practices.

It is in the field of literature that a semblance of retained vitality is still observed. As with every other cultural category the islanders were enormously influenced by the mainland. In fact, their scripture originally was based on Chinese characters, which were the only available means of written expression before a grammatical corpus could be incorporated into language. The literary flowering taking place after that could only be categorized as formidable and rivaled those of the Western nations. By the IX Century AD, with the invention of Kana phonetic syllabary, a golden age in literature was inaugurated. A long syllabic form (choka) and a short one (tanka) were introduced, permitting an exuberant poetic proliferation. Two main compilations were produced: The Kokinshu addressed themes in a light vein and rather superficially being mainly concerned with poetical beauty, while the Manyoshu was an emotional and profound genre. In prose also great masterpieces were written during the Heian Period, the most famous being the 'Genji monogatari', a mature, complex and imaginative tale which set standards for posterity and perhaps was the first great novel ever written.

Under the Kamakura and Ashitawa Emperors another poetic form, the Renga or 'link verse', was devised by joining alternate verses: one in three lines and the next in two, giving rise to long chains. It was then that the No drama took shape and became popular. They were tragic compositions expressing subtle emotions with highly elaborated renditions, an indication of the richness and technical complexities achieved by the Japanese language at the time. The Tokugawa period was also artistically and literarily very fructiferous, witnessing the emergence of the Haiku as a new type of poetry, as well as a further evolution of the theater into the Joruri and Kabuki varieties.

With the Meiji Restoration the 'opening of Japan' took place, provoking the profound cultural changes we had alluded to before. Literature was no exception and an outpour of Western style novels, poems and theatrical productions of a 'modern' kind occurred. Also, like with the arts and architecture, a number of die-hard traditionalists continued to struggle with the old methods and ways; some even attempting to express modern themes, as well as social, historical and political issues. Undoubtedly Japanese Literature is not 'dead'. Yet, no genuine modern school or novel genre had appeared recently.

Nowhere is the eclectic mind of this civilization better proved than in the realm of ideas, where the Japanese essentially incorporated and assimilated the teachings of the Chinese masters, somehow adapting them to their own needs and beliefs, which were integrated with the original cults of Shinto deities. Taoism, Buddhism in all its branches, Confucianism and even the Yin-Yang School became intermingled among themselves to an incredible degree, perhaps serving as a typical demonstration of the inherent Japanese talent for synthesis. In fact, the syncretic product became a vibrant representation of eastern philosophical principles and speculative concepts.

As we have already seen in the case of other cultural endeavors, at the time of the Meiji Restoration a great influx of Western philosophical ideas and concepts penetrated the country and exerted a massive influence in ulterior developments. The irruption included ideas and notions from Renaissance men, figures from the Enlightenment as well as French and German masters up to modern times. The fact that the Japanese were able to integrate in such a short span, to digest in a relatively minuscule lapse of time, the masterpieces of several centuries of occidental philosophical thought has to be a tribute to the perceptiveness and adaptability of their culture and spirit. Like was the case with China, occidental ideas were manipulated to serve local needs and ultimately became ingrained with native principles in a remarkable and complementary form, again proving the eclectic talents of these people.

Two modern figures in the XX Century stand tall in this field: Nishida

Kitaro and Tanabe Hajime. They wrought a system of deeply intertwined Western Idealism and Buddhist spirituality of surprising coherence. Central to their thought is the conception of Absolute Nothingness, a notion difficult to grasp by the occidental mind, an strange contrivance foreign to our understanding of the world order but prevalent in oriental philosophical systems for which it represents an existing entity, a presence as 'real' as matter, substance or any other category of 'Being' we are familiar with . Leibnitz monadology, Hegelian dialectics, St Augustine Christian speculations, even Gelstad psychology and Existentialism, became integrated in the works of these people. Occidental Man, in his turn, was also influenced by them, particularly the late promotions of existential writers like Heidegger and Sartre .

It can be fairly stated that Japanese Civilization, which was rooted in the Chinese Oriental Culture from which it began to branch-off in the II Century AD, is running the risk, since the Meiji Restoration, of being obliterated and superseded by its Western equivalent; a process that has been accelerated after the end of the Second World War and embraces every single aspect of this cultural tradition. It appears that only in the fields of literature and philosophy it still keeps some semblance of vitality, given by some degree of originality.

It can conclusively be stated that Japan today is a thoroughly westernized country. Granted that these people could, and frequently are, strongly nationalistic and loyal to their fatherland and beliefs, but even this does not indicate an endorsement of the standards of classic indigenous Japanese civilization. In fact the native 'way of living' or 'life style' of the country today is strongly molded by occidental mores and customs. Many will argue that the fanatical zeal, loyalty and determination, demonstrated by this country in its modernizing success are native singular cultural characteristics, but I believe this is a fallacious conclusion. What they are is general qualities of the human community liable to change with time and not restricted to a specific society, therefore not exclusive patrimony of any culture.

This is not to say that the ancient ways have ceased to exist. Western table manners, utensils and house furniture, for example, have had a slow acceptance, but anybody visiting an urban center anywhere in the country today, would have a hard time in finding substantial physical differences to those of any Western nation. I believe that much has been made about the 'blending of styles' in architecture (Japanese tradition in their modern buildings had been largely limited to a token tribute in roof design) and the revival of the art of prints.

Whether traditional Japanese civilization could have, or not, the resilience and staying power to resist the onslaught of occidental ideas, survive and recover its vitality is, of course, a moot question in view of the fact that, at the present time, it is impossible to accurately assess all factors involved. Nevertheless, without question, this off-shot of Chinese culture is, like many other contemporary societies, in mortal danger of being completely co-opted by Western Culture, the one which should be credited for the miracle of modern Japan.

CHAPTER XII

When it comes to our 'Western Civilization' the proliferation of cultural forms is so staggering as to overwhelm the imagination. It constitute a heavily 'radiated' group of human communities, politically subdivided in 'nations' resulting from the inter-marriage of the Greco-Roman World with the barbaric societies co-habitating what is today Europe. Their ultimate cultural roots are to be found in the Achaeans and their Ionian descendents(and also probably Minoan migrants) who took refuge in Asia Minor after being displaced by the Dorian invaders and who, quite likely, were part of that drifting mass of humanity called by the Egyptians 'the sea people': A restless inhomogeneous lot credited by some historians, among other deeds, with the no insignificant one of delivering the final blow to the Hittite Empire.

There is something familiar about Western Man in the joyful 'bull acrobatics' reproduced so vividly in the magnificent frescos of the Minoan palaces, or in the grim determination of Mycenaean gold masks. The Achaeans seem to have been the first identifiable Greek speaking people, and their origins are obscure. Some of their metal works and architecture resemble vaguely those of contemporary populations in Anatolia and, therefore, their ancestors might have come from Central Asia, although other scholars consider them of European extraction. Their origin is therefore in question and ethnological studies have a long way to go. Be it as it may, Western Man descent cannot be traced, at the present, farther back than this before losing its identity in the Neolithic horizon.

There was nothing original in the cultural endeavors of the people populating the Greek Mainland and Western Mediterranean area in the Second Millennia BC., nothing that could foretell the momentous changes in the mettle of their collective spirit. Their communities consisted of small towns and surrounding tracks of land dedicated to cultivation, which were not different to contemporary similar centers in the Levant. During the so-called 'Dark Age' of Greek Civilization, however, many of these communities began to coalesce and a new conception of social life began to form. No longer was the king a divine figure to be obeyed and venerated, but his authority was superseded by the clans of the merging communities. Slowly the concept crystallized that the cities and surrounding lands were THE COMMON POSSESSION of all members of the community, and as such that everybody had to abide to a set of laws and to contribute to the common good. This was a new radical idea that became a foundation of Western civilized life, a true "mutation" of the human supra-cultural genome, a change in character that has survived despite innumerable attempts to vanish and eradicate it from the fabric of the Western soul.

The growth of the Polis and its social transformation, in part resulting from the demographic changes taking place with the displacement of many poor peasants from the countryside when the new cultivations of olive oil and wine by rich landowners began to take place, prompted the need to codify the "customs" and social rules hitherto hold by oral tradition in those communities, which slowly took the character of independent republics subject to the Will of their citizens. The law givers where not anymore demigods bestowing upon society the distillations of a Supreme Being, like in other contemporaries communities, but secular figures like Solon and Lycurgus. Democracy, therefore, born in the new social milieu of some of these civilized settlements, was a true emancipator from the priestly control, a manifestation of the new ethos fermenting in the human spirit.

The Greeks are also credited with the discovery of REASON, the conception that Man could search into Nature with his intellect and "understand" better his surrounding by using the mind capacity to recover the hidden truth. An early stirring of this faithful conviction could be already detected in the pre-Socratics, particularly the Pythagoreans, who dressed their discoveries in mathematics with the mantra of a secret cult, and believed that numbers had a physical reality. This conviction also ran deeply in the Greek veins of the Golden Age with the Platonic claim that knowledge could be obtain by searching into the mind. This strong belief, this reliance in the power of the 'intellect', never relented in the ulterior history of Western Man, and survived in a latent state religious persecutions and social upheavals of all kinds to become the foundation of the scientific and technological explosion characteristic of the present age.

One of the typical qualities of the socio-political units (countries) who share or are integral parts of Western cultural traditions is that they are the creators of 'modernism', in other words, the effectors of the modern world. We can hardly conceive any human activity or 'walk of life' which had remained unaffected by it. Western Man had been so successful that he is imposing his standards in everybody else, its influence hardly escaping any corner of our planet.

It has not been always that way. Our culture had an obscured and hesitant beginning in the 'Dark Ages' during the period of unremitting horrors following the disintegration of its predecessor the Western Roman Empire. Its birth was marred by the internecine feudal warfare, poor communications, lawlessness and occasional devastating epidemics, which decimated the population of Europe. This beginning, unquestionably, was inauspicious from every stand point, particularly when compared to the splendor achieved in a relative short time by its 'sister culture', Islam , as well as the grandeur and wealth of its other great contemporaries: India and China.

The struggle of Western Christian Culture with neighbors and barbarian invaders fills innumerable pages of world history, and religious persecutions at times reached a degree of paranoia and sadism difficult to reconcile with its moral accent. It is hardly believable that in such a convergence of apparently extraordinarily adverse circumstances arose one of the most vital and fecund cultures ever to set foot in our planet. Surrounded by enemies, in constant fear, harassed and decimated by wars and 'pestilences', it is hard to understand how Western Man was able to survive, let alone accomplish so much and against such insurmountable odds. But He did it out of determination and sheer courage, helped as it was said above, by the systematic utilization of the resource inherited from his Greek forebears: Reason.

The 'gestational' period of Western Christian Civilization, we know, took place in the historical vacuum left by the collapse of the Roman Empire, heralded by the progressive christianization of the barbarians who, for so long, confronted and fought the Empire without ever been completely integrated into its fabric. Religion finally succeeded in what centuries of wars and forceful attempts never did. It took the crumbling parts of Roman Civilization and institutions to create the sap that nourished the tender embryo of this new culture.

The early objects of art outside Italy in the Dark Ages were the Merovingian jewels and illuminated manuscripts with their decorations of plants, animals and interlacing lines, a pattern perpetuated later on and extended to other art forms; namely sculpture and architecture. During this time, because of the simple habits of the Frankish settlers, sculpture was only restricted to bas-reliefs and exhibited a rather poor workmanship. All in all this was an early formative age with the population still manifesting very little originality, while applying their efforts to learn and master the complex techniques necessary to attain a higher degree of refinement. Buildings, not too surprisingly for such nomadic societies, were of poor quality and the churches of renovated late Roman design.

With the ascension to power of Charlemagne Western Europe found itself again reunified, which brought a measure of stability and peace to a land ravished by internecine warfare, incertitude, and fear. There was an urge to revive the Roman Empire. The monasteries and churches were the centers of administrative and cultural activities, searching for the lost past and in the process becoming repositories for most of the artistic works of the age.

The basic church design was borrowed from the Romans: the basilica (copied from the roman 'Hall of Justice') built with a central nave flanked by two aisles separated from it by paralleled arcades and with an apse in one end. But the new cultural soul gestating in these lands was, at first, betrayed by small hints of what was to finally evolve in the marvels of the high Middle Ages. Charlemagne palace at Aachen, for instance, although an attempt to imitate the church of San Vitale in Ravenna, included small plain arches rather than arcade niches facing the central octagonal space, thus anticipating the Romanesque style.

Another example is the gatehouse of the Abbey of Lurch where the lower floor includes a series of arches and columns in the Roman taste, but the edification is surmounted by a second floor with narrow windows and external geometric patterns of decoration entirely alien to the Roman 'spirit'. Furthermore, there was in this period much experimenting with and modifications to the basic basilica design, as attested by the massive tower erected in the west side of the Abbey, an idea often repeated later on in the gothic churches. In Southern France, on the other hand, there was some mozarabic influence indicated by the horseshoe arches and square-ended sanctuaries, perhaps anticipating the Mudejar art of Spain.

Little remains from the Carolingian fresco paintings and monumental sculptures, but a profusion of ivory carved objects and illuminated manuscripts had survived to the present and, as in architecture, a number of cultural influences could be recognized in these works. In carving, for example, different decorative traditions could be identified. In the ivory covers of the Lorsch Gospels Late Classical and Early Christian derivations are represented side by side. In other cases naturalistic forms were produced and toward the end of this epoch elaborate decorations dominated the artistic fashion. Manuscript illuminations also varied considerably from a linear design to a more intense and dynamic type.

The jewelry and metal works leaned also toward elaborated workmanship, although this tendency frequently was veiled by a deceptive simplicity and austerity. The feeling was one of massive splendor in spite of delicate workmanship. Occasionally, however, the objects were showy and spectacular in a byzantine manner, nowhere better represented that in the crown of the man for whom the entire historic age was name: Charlemagne. Heavily inlaid with precious stones and decorated with gold filigree and enamel its opulence hardly keeps tone with the 'character' of the times.

The Carolingian Empire culturally was a period of gestation when multifarious elements, from late antiquity, Arabic and barbarian sources, met to shape the dimensions of a new and still distant era, and when the early stirrings of the Western Soul crystallized. We saw it in architecture with the synthesis of the old schools producing something new, and again in miniature painting where the static, frontal, human figure appears in a perspective-less background seemingly anticipating the Middle Ages.

The following Ottonian interlude saw Europe reeling back under the attacks of Viking raiders, Muslim, and Magyar invaders. But in the Germanic lands a time of stability allowed the perpetuation of an artistic tradition akin to the Carolingian, with some added Celtic and Byzantine overtones. If anything their paintings became more stylized, even motionless, but with a strong expressive force highlighted by the slender faces and large eyes which gave the compositions an aura of solemn spirituality.

After the chaos of the barbarians invasions subsided a new climate of peace fostered trade and travel. The cities as a whole grew in importance and pilgrimage to holy places became common in the new found safety. Not unexpectedly the church orders, which had become remarkably richer and more powerful by providing heavens from the insecurities of life during the preceding years of turmoil, embarked now in a fever of construction and expansion. The throngs crowding their naves grew and the size of the existing facilities was not sufficient to accommodate the new surge of shifting humanity.

Out of this situation the Romanesque Style was born. Again, the inspiration of the times was the architectural models and techniques of the vanished Romans. The barrel or tunnel and groin vaults replaced the wooden roofs of the Carolingians, permitting for more spacious interiors. But the walls to support the new heavy stonework required increasing massiveness and buttressing, something which enhanced the feeling of monumentality.

Another characteristic of the churches was the generous use of decorations, not only in the inside walls, but also in the porticos and façades. In fact sculpture, whether statuary or in relief, largely replaced wall frescos imparting a sensation of solidity and agelessness to the works. Like with the buildings, sculpture could not be described in other terms but monumental and the shapes retained the stylized and formalized form in the pictorial compositions of the preceding periods. Some of the representations were narrative, depicting scenes of the Bible or of the life of Christ and apostles. Romanesque sub-styles throughout Europe were numerous and important variations developed (Cluniac and Cistercian in France, Rhine in Germany etc.), this exuberant ramification serving as mute indication to the fecundity of this school.

It can therefore be affirm that the Romanesque Style, which had humble beginnings in the XI Century in Lombardy with churches such as San Vincenzo del Prato, reached its apogee in Burgundy thanks to the ambitious construction program of the monastic orders of France, and by the end of the XII Century it had spread throughout Western Europe, radiating explosively in the regional sub-styles already mentioned. But as so often is the case also in the evolutionary history of biological beings, only one single branch of all born at this time was destined to begot a worthy descendant, one which represented a "mutation" from the original cultural 'clone' and in its turn grew unremittingly to the point of replacing, or rather obliterating completely, the old models as the favorite type.

It was in Normandy during the XI Century where the early stirrings of still another new architectural conception were felt. The trait 'mutation' took place first at the town of Caen which was erecting two churches (La Trinite and Saint Etienne) utilizing a novel design of support that was denominated, for lack of a better term, 'rib vaulting'. It was only a matter of relatively short time before the revolutionary idea turned into full bloom. Every other variation of the Romanesque proved to be an evolutionary 'blind alley' and, like its biological counterparts, this style was destined to exhaust its creative vigor before being overrun by the new Gothic type.

From Normandy the novel cultural 'mutant' rapidly spread to neighboring England where the pointed vaulting was employed to procure greater heights, like in the Norman Durham Cathedral. It didn't take too long before the true purely Gothic shape came into its own with the Church of Saint Denis, also in Normandy. The vertical shafts and piers were supported by external flying buttresses that rendered unnecessary the massive walls and ponderous arches of Romanesque constructions, allowing the final culmination of Gothic Art, that which permitted a flood of natural sunlight to drench the naves of cathedrals and churches: the stained glass windows.

During the remaining of the XII and the following XIII centuries Gothic experienced a very rapid growth throughout Western Europe and underwent a remarkable evolutionary radiation, with many stylistic branches emerging and smiting every other existing art form including the Romanesque. The sheer size of the churches became colossal. The north tower of the Strasbourg cathedral was 466 feet high, that of Ulm 525 and Chartres attained 375 feet.

In England this architectural model was less conspicuous and devoid of the continental taste for spectacular heights. Although decorative concepts as well as the use of stain-glass windows were soon assimilated, it was not until the XIII Century with the erection of the Westminster Abbey that the tracery windows became finally accepted. As it is so often the case Gothic Style then became further elaborated, ultimately evolving into the curvilinear patterns of York Minster and the Carlisle Cathedral.

In Germany, on the other hand, Gothic was introduced slowly. Here the 'collision of styles' was more acute, with Romanesque refusing to give way. When it finally did the basic design had undergone idiosyncratic changes of its own represented in the 'hall church', a type of edification where nave and aisles had the same height. The Germans also simplified the general plan by abolishing the capitals of the piers, the moldings passing directly into the arches of the vault. But Germany, like France, was caught in the urge for monumentality as dramatically exemplified in the Cologne and the already alluded Strasbourg cathedrals. The former was not finished until the XX Century because of architectural difficulties impossible to surmount in the Middle Ages, and the latter was ultimately 'crowned' with the famous octagonal tower which made it one of the tallest structures in Europe.

Rib vaulting was considerably elaborated in Germany and Bohemia toward the end of the Middle Ages with much experimentation in detached ribs, rib grid patterns and undulating designs, like in the striking shape of Vladislav Hall in Prague. In Spain, French and English Gothic forms were, understandably, the most important early influences, but, again, a style of its own ultimately evolved with the abolishment of the intricate tracery of the High Gothic; a situation similar to that found in Italy. In this regard it should be mention the blending of architectural models that took place in Spain between the lingering pervading Moorish influence after the re-conquest (Mudejar Art) and Gothic motives. This could be clearly appreciated, among many others contemporary examples, in the elaborated designs and ornaments in the star vaults of the cathedral of Salamanca, a clear case of cultural syncretism.

If architectonically Gothic was innovative and original in sculpture it realized a final departure from the stylized conventions of the past, as could be appreciated in the rendition of the Margrave Ekkehard of Meissen and his consort Uta, attributed to the 'master of Naumburg', where the personality of the subjects is conveyed with a poignancy difficult to surpass.

Therefore, although in painting Gothic was plagued by the same lack of perspective, the flatness and disproportions of previous schools, their sculpture strove to realistically render human emotions, in a sense holiness in stone, not necessarily an accurate corporeal reproduction but, instead, moods of the Soul. In such strivings they fully succeeded, as shown in the smiling angels of Reims. Gothic rapidly replaced the Romanesque, and in fact essentially all the preceding Middle Ages styles. In substituting the masterpieces of mosaic and frescos of the Romanesque by cleverly utilizing the sun light filtering through the stained glass windows in polychromatic compositions, they achieved striking effects, drenching the inner spaces with an enchanting other worldly atmosphere.

Medieval thought, like every other human activity during this period, was dominated by the religious revolution brought about by Christianity. Yet biblical cosmological speculations had to be reconciled with the legacy of classic Greek thought, which could not be ignored and in fact remained a source of inspiration during the Dark Ages in no less of a proportion than the abundant ruins of the Roman Empire served in architecture. To this effect peripatetic conceptions were intertwined with biblical dogma thus providing the framework for medieval scholasticism, spiced here and there with a taste for Plato mostly by way of the Neo-Platonic version. The final product was amazingly synthetic, as outstanding as it was surprising, so durable indeed that even XVII Century philosophers had to battle with the self defeating attempt of providing 'rational proves' for the existence of God, something with no parallel in any other culture. The intellectual and spiritual repercussions of Thomas Aquinas 'Summa Theologica' were long lasting indeed, typifying the eclectic talents of the Gothic Soul, also manifested in the works of St Anselm and his efforts in the 'Ontological Argument'.

In literature the Middle Ages was a time of scarcity. Religious stories, liturgy and translations of ancient texts, mostly directly from Greek sources but also by way of Muslim compilations, occupied a prominent part of literary activities. This was, as we have seen, an age of gestation and the European languages were slowly evolving into their own. It is precisely in the Eurasia land mass that human descent has been better correlated and traced to linguistic characteristics. The above mentioned Indo-European languages, for instance, include besides the European group, also the Hittite, Armenian and Phrygian in Asia Minor, as well as the Indo-Iranian group including Sanskrit, which allow tracing the migration of these human groups from populations originating in Central Asia beyond the Caucasian massif. Most of these tongues appeared to have common Indo-European roots. Their main branches in the continent were Italic, Celtic, Germanic and Balto-Slavonic, from where derived the multiplicity of modern European languages. Another minor but nevertheless important group was the Finno-Ugrid family giving rise to modern Finnish, Hungarian and Estonian derivations.

Needless to say, the process of evolution of languages is slow and a continuous unrelenting process, despite efforts in some modern European countries to control and contain, by means of special institutions, its organic development by requiring from the government the "official seal" of approval (like the Royal Academy of the Language in Spain); a notion with no parallel in history. Language evolution by its nature is a continuous ongoing process, an expression of the soul of a human group, and therefore unyielding to regulation by any assumed superseding "Authority".

By the XI Century a distinct literary genre, the Chanson de Geste became popular, first in France and later on in the rest of Europe. Under the sponsorship of the feudal nobility this genre matured into a characteristic lyric verse in the XII and the XIII centuries: The Epic Poetry. (See also Appendix II)

Middle Age secular music seemed to have originated in folk songs evolving into the tradition of minstrels and troubadours. The ecclesiastical type, on the other hand, was a derivation from the Gregorian chant. Music notations at the beginning consisted of lines marks and a sign above the words to connote a rise or fall in the voices in the choruses. It was not before the XII Century that parallel horizontal lines were introduced to indicate voice pitch. By then the songs had acquired a complicated counterpoint, and by the XIV Century , also, an elaborated polyphony.

Music from being originally mainly vocal slowly began to incorporate an array of instruments, like the organ, introduced around the VIII Century and later on the harp or 'English zither', as well as an array of other instruments like flutes, shawms, trumpets, bagpipes, drums, and later on lutes, psalteries, metal stringed zithers etc. This imposing array of instruments, whose origin frequently is lost in the mist of time, permitted by the high Middle Ages the creation of musical groups with the means to deliver elaborated courtly performances, and also effected a reconciliation of southern monophonic with the northern polyphonic music types.

In the field of medicine the medieval period was a time of stagnation. The Hippocratic dictum, the emphasis in observation as a way of learning the source of ailing, was forgotten and in general replaced by the practices of the barbarians with the superstitious beliefs in magic, the healing power of faith, theurgist therapy and saintly invocations. Nonetheless, hidden in the recesses of the monasteries and perhaps by way of Arabian sources, enough was preserved of Galenic Medicine to perpetuate his dogma and therapeutic practices. Perhaps based in his influence medieval medicine effected a divorce of traditional medicine from surgery, a practice which was then relegated to barbers, bath keepers and other menial occupations who, besides minor surgery, like suture of wounds, opening of abscesses, treatment of fractures and couching of cataracts, among other procedures, also extracted teeth and performed blood-letting, with obvious adverse consequences to the advance of this science.

But not all was negative. In the XI Century took shape the School of Salerno which, as the historian Neuburger said, 'aroused the healing art from the decrepitude of half a millennium'. Its origin is obscure but it seemed to be the result of cross fertilizations of cultural influences radiating from Southern Italy, Byzantium and Toledo that helped to revive the ancient Hippocratic Greek practices. According to him surgical practice in Salerno was original, and the fields of obstetrics and nursery were 'cultivated by talented women'. It is claimed that the surgeons Roger of Palermo, who wrote the standard textbook in the subject, knew of cancer, device sutures for the intestines, used ashes of sponges and seaweed to treat goiters and mercury for dermal and parasitic infections. Unfortunately this school toward the end of the Dark Ages soon faded away, and after the sacking of Salerno by Henry VI in 1194 it began to decline irreversibly.

During the late Middle Ages the hospitals, usually under the purview of religious orders, increased in size and became better organized. Physicians formed guilds to protect their rights and the practice of medicine became a laic profession per excellence. Therapeutics, besides the above mentioned surgical procedures, consisted mainly of special diets and herbal remedies as purgatives, emetics, diuretics, diaphoretics, etc.

If the invention in Italy of eye glasses for near-sightedness in 1280 is excluded, in general medieval medicine did not substantially advanced technically over that of their predecessor Greco-Roman and Hellenistic Medicine, whose teachings, ironically enough, were frequently reintroduced into Europe by way of their Arabs and Byzantine neighbors.

But the invention of eye glasses was not the only technological feat of the Middle Ages. After the barbarian invasions ceased and a more peaceful and stable environment was secured, progress in many fields was achieved. The economy, of course, continued to be fundamentally agrarian, but after the incorporation movement began the size and economic importance of the towns roused. The new heavy wheeled plow pulled by horses, and the novel way to alternate the planting of the fields, brought substantial increase in agricultural yields.

The use of iron increased considerably during the Middle Ages in comparison to the Roman Empire which preferred bronze. Not only agricultural implements, but the manufacture of weapons and household implements, depended heavily on this metal, which was still produced in rather primitive smelters. Likewise, the building of wind and water mills grew exponentially from the times of the Romans. Accurate clocks and the compass also were invented during this time, which permitted not only a better structuring of daily activities but also contributed enormously to navigational expertise, essential for the voyages of discovery in the years to follow.

The High Middle Ages was certainly not a period of stagnation but rather of slow technological and social improvements in the life of Man after the commotions of the fall of the Roman Empire, the barbarians invasions, wars and epidemics. The preservation of the works of the ancients in the depths of monasteries permitted, in time, the rekindling of culture in what we historically call the 'Renaissance', helped by the likes of Roger Bacon, Adelard of Bath, Conches and Grossteste. Slowly, and as a result of all the progressive cultural changes taking place in

Western Europe during what we call the 'Middle Ages', a new supra-conscience was born: Western Christian Civilization.

It has been said of the Renaissance that it was the time when Western Europe experienced a renewed interest and, in many ways, a return to classicism as a source of inspiration in all cultural endeavors. To say the least, this view is an oversimplification and a distortion of the historic record. As we have seen even in Northern Europe, since the Carolingian times, Man was searching into the Roman past for enlightenment, although often only to be bogged down in the Byzantine quagmire. Already the High Gothic Art, primarily in sculpture, had been enliven by an expressionist outlook which torn away the conventional, stylized, impersonal and highly symbolic forms of its predecessors. Surely there was, as represented in their works, a measure of rigidity and, like in the previous styles, we perceive some semblance of societal stratification, but large doses of originality could be appreciated also in the great architectural masterpieces, an indication of a newly acquired freedom of inspiration.

The Renaissance only accelerated the process already in ferment with a more systematic study of classic methods and ideas. To this effect ancient texts were deliberately sought after and not only art and architecture, but the human body and mathematics, were avidly studied to provide for the desirable 'naturalism'. The 'turn to the past' was not to represent another artistic 'fad' but something more profound and all encompassing: the crystallization of a new supra-cultural organism. Virtually every area of cultural activity experienced similar longings; the general mood, we might say, converged in the same direction. Nature became, more than at any other time since classic times, a subject of thorough observation. The physical world was carefully analyzed to provide for a better understanding of its properties, or with the intention to reproduce it more faithfully in artistic works. Soon an exuberant output in every branch of art, science, literature, and music took place at a dizzying pace. Dante, Boccaccio, Petrarch and Machiavelli in literature; Ghiberti, Donatello, Pollaiuolo, Verrocchio and Michelangelo in Sculpture; Fray Angelico, Uccello, Lippi, Pollaiuolo, Botticelli and

Leonardo in painting; Duray, Ockeghem, Isaac and Obrecht in music, and Brunelleschi, Michelozzo and Battista Alberti in architecture, were trail blazers in the intellectual awakening.

In medicine Vesalius, the artificer of the new anatomy and destroyer of the Galenic-Aristotelian dogma which had dominated Hellenistic and medieval Medicine, Servetus, Falloppio, Eustachio, Fabricius and his pupil Harvey the discoverer of blood circulation, among others, also led the way each in his own area of expertise to give vivid interpretation to the new 'humanistic' ideal fermenting in the Western Mind, which was certainly helped by the development of the European printing press based in movable metal types which allowed wide cultural dissemination of the new discoveries and advances.

The subtle stirrings of this new soul were first manifested in the works of Giotto (there is some perspective of depth even in some frescos found at Herculaneum dated from the I Century AD) and went at the beginning almost unnoticed. They spread slowly and not before the 'Black Death' decimated the population of Europe. The revival of classicism and the new outlook began to gain momentum early in the XIV Century with the literary works of Dante and Boccaccio, who eulogized and appreciated the radical departure from conventional molds the paintings of Giotto represented and what they meant for the future. The new 'mood' soon spread to other arts and architecture. The buildings of Brunelleschi exhibited a most harmonious balance and discrete elegance with proportions reduced to 'human dimensions' intended to comfort and not, as the late Gothic cathedrals and churches had done before, to overwhelm the visitors.

If Brunelleschi masterpieces were inspired by architectural models from the old Roman Empire, Donatello, who also visited Rome, was largely influenced by what remained of the sculptural legacy of the ancients, which he imbued with a highly individualistic fire and masterly control of technique evoking a very realistic effect. But the Renaissance, of course, went beyond the mere copying of the ancients; it constituted something more than the sudden phenotypic expression of recessive cultural traits. The changes actually were true mutations, in essence a creation of something new. The fresh outlook focused on Nature in a more accurate and deliberate manner than even classicism ever did. This was going to be manifested above all in the representational arts. The paintings, but also sculptures, became realistic replicas of the physical world, and the artists commenced to study 'scientifically' human anatomy and rules of perspective which were further elaborated by Masaccio in his clever use of light and shadows, an effect perfected later on to a remarkable degree by the Netherland masters.

Yet, the break with the Gothic was not instantaneous or immediately obvious. Like is the case with biological evolution the transformations were rather subtle but unfolded rapidly. Many works of art actually were transitional forms, like some of the paintings by Veneziano, Lippo Lippi and Uccello. In sculpture after the magnificent efforts by Donatello and Bhiberti there was a period of quiescence until the times of Michelangelo. Likewise architecture, although already revealing under the influence of Michelozzo and Brunelleschi considerable departure from the Gothic mold, still included many remaining evidences of it. Once under way, however, the transformations initiated in Western Culture by a group of Florentines in the XV Century stamped irreversibly its future shape.

Music, of course, was not left behind in the transformation of art effected by the Renaissance. Ockeghem was the first to lead the way, but it was the task of Josquin des Prez to realize a revival which has been compared, by many, with the creative marvels of Michelangelo in the pictorial arts. Josquin is reputed to have rescued sacral music from the empty intervals of Gothic polyphonic style by introducing mathematical analysis of proportions and elaborated contrapuntal techniques, again searching for the harmonious taste so typical of the Renaissance. He excelled in the writing of motets, psalms and choir music, which he mastered to a degree of perfection difficult to surpass, and his new conceptions disseminated quickly to the rest of Western Europe.

The revival of classic studies in art, architecture and music definitely had an influence in the cultural efflorescence of the Italian Renaissance, but it was not unique. As the cultural shock waves spread throughout Northwestern Europe the process progressively changed itself reaching the dimensions of a complete transformation, the revelation of the independent ethos of a new communal soul. In all its creative accomplishments the new culture was very different to the Classics and extremely heterogeneous ethnically and linguistically. However, all its denominations shared common roots and from them, in time, ultimately sprung the European 'countries' with defined political frontiers. Besides the common cultural descent these nations also shared in the amazing scientific and technological advances of the age, propitiated by the rise of the bourgeoisie. The European cultural trait pool was large on account of the numerous evolutionary radiations of the original prototype, but frequent cross-fertilizations gave rise to considerable homogenization of the final product.

While literature, pictorial arts and music were experiencing a colossal transformation, in the realm of ideas it took Realism, the affirmation of the relevance and importance of the 'existing world', another century to finally be triumphantly wrestled from the asphyxiating embrace of medieval dogma and mores. The recapture by philosophy of classic REASON from the morass of scholastic bondage was a heroic enterprise indeed. The puzzle becomes understandable under careful scrutiny of historic facts.

Firstly, any attempt in this direction had to contend with the high Gothic synthesis mentioned above, the fact that Reason was relegated to a subordinated, subservient role in the fabric of theological defenses, that is to say, it was one of the weapons used by the Church to fight their adversaries and detractors; it had lost stature and independence. To illustrate this contention we only have to mention the already alluded case of the Ontological Argument of St. Anselm, which he used in an attempt to demonstrate the existence of God by introducing a circular logic in claiming that 'existence' is an attribute of perfection, and therefore a part of the 'Divine Essence'. It took 600 years and a more tolerant 'atmosphere' for Kant to discover that 'existence is not a predicate'.

This brings us to the second factor for the delay in the reassertion of Reason to the pedestal of the classics: Fear and religious fanaticism epitomized by one of the most infamous of all Christian institutions, the notorious Inquisition Tribunals. It was not until the XVI Century that Francis Bacon pointed to the way the inquire into Nature was to take, thus initiating the great epistemological debates of the Enlightenment. Terror, dogmatism and sophistry kept the conscience of the nascent Western Culture from realizing all its potentialities, but not even the recanting of Galileo could abort the blazing course it was to pursue from there on. The works of Copernicus, with his heliocentric view, helped to overcome the Aristotelian Dogma, therefore demoting the

Earth from the privilege position held by the ancients. Kepler theory of sidereal motions allowed it to escape the Ptolemaic tyranny of hemicycles, and Newton discovery of the law of universal Gravitation helped by the invention of mathematical Calculus, honor he shared with his contemporary Leibniz, effected a synthesis so powerful that revolutionized astronomy and physics.

The modern history of our culture has been explosive, with remarkable achievements in practically all recesses of human endeavors. In the representational arts the Renaissance lead the way to the Baroque, in its multifarious versions, followed in successive order by the Neoclassical, Rococo, Romantic, and the Modern World, heralded by the Industrial Revolution of the XVIII Century and the socio-political commotions of the last two centuries, and in the process creating and amassing an enormous wealth never imagined by their predecessors. In little more than a century and in rapid succession the inventions of steam power, telegraphy, electric light, telephone, the internal combustion engines, airplanes, radio, television, computers and rocket science revolutionized transportation and communication. Suffice is to say that Western Christian Civilization has undergone, perhaps more than any of its contemporaries, notable transformations throughout the ages but without losing its dynamism and dazzling creativity, even less its identity. Today, as we had said, Western fashion in the arts, literature, architecture and lesser crafts had inherited the world, in essence impinging in the standards of everybody else.

Once freed from the asphyxiating hold of Greek Geometry and with the appropriation of Indian-Arabic numerals mathematics, in the following centuries, exploded in a burst of creativity, helped by the rigorous formulations of the concepts of the derivative and the integral by Cauchy, Weierstrass and others, after the final acceptance of the notion of 'limit' in the XIX Century, which helped to exorcise this discipline once and for all, from the curse and embarrassment of Zeno's paradoxes, and so permitting the emancipation of calculus from obscure concepts about 'infinitesimals' and 'indivisibles', which had plagued this science since the pre-Socratics Atomists and Pythagoreans. Enormous strides in fields like theory of number, non-Euclidian geometries and group theory, to mention only some, has allowed spectacular advances in the fields of science and technology, including the theories of Relativity and Quantum Mechanics which took by storm the world of physics, initiating a radical re-interpretation of long held views on celestial mechanics and microcosmic events of far reaching consequences for mankind; as nuclear power and space exploration sufficiently prove.

The field of medicine was one of the mayor beneficiaries of the explosive technological progress of the last two centuries, both in the areas of diagnosis and treatment. The invention of the microscope by van Leeuwenhoek in the XVII Century lead in time to the Cell Theory in Biology and the discovery of bacterias, allowing in the XIX Century the seminal works of trailblazers like Pasteur, Koch and others in infection diseases and immunizations, ultimately leading to the discovery of penicillin in the XX Century by Alexander Fleming, which initiated the revolution of the modern Antibiotic Era. Also in the XIX Century the works of Karl Rokitansky and Rudolf Virchow (who laid the basis of cellular pathology also made possible by the use of the microscope) were majorly instrumental in elevating this discipline to the importance it enjoys at the present. The discovery of radioactivity by Madame Curie and X Rays by Roentgen permitted the enormous strides in diagnostic and therapeutic medicine we are today the beneficiaries. At the opposite end of the medical spectrum, during late XIX and early XX centuries, Sigmund Freud and collaborators after postulating the existence of the subconscious and libidinous drives, inaugurated the Psychoanalytical School in medicine, a portentous event with far reaching consequences, not only for medicine itself, but with repercussions in fields like literature, law, philosophy, sociology and even in the way that Man look at himself. In the field of Surgery the marvel of modern advances evolving from the medieval 'barber-surgeon' were possible, in great measure, as a result of the development of antiseptic techniques since the works of Joseph Lister in the XIX Century. Finally modern anesthesia has come a long way ever since the first usage of ether by Thomas Green Morton for removal of a neck tumor in 1846.

In the realm of ideas Western Culture had been very productive. Once freed from the medieval fetters of the scholastics it radiated and proliferated widely in Europe, giving rise subsequently to schools of great importance to the development of Science by searching, again taking their inspiration from ancient Greek themes, into the origin and nature of the intellect and of what is knowledge. British Empiricism, German Idealism, the American Pragmatics and Centro-European Existentialism, among others, struggled in the following centuries to find answers to these questions, and to define the place of Man in the World. Like the Hellenic and Chinese Schools before, Western Philosophy also has attempted to give norms of conduct for Man in society and provide for ethical and moral advice, in this regard encountering at times points of friction with Christianity. (See also the Appendix II)

It would not serve any further purpose to indulge in a careful perusal of historical events in the evolution of our culture; that will go beyond the scope and intention of this assay. The details are common knowledge and the content totally irrelevant to our goals.

Today the skyscrapers, automobiles, TV sets and other products of Western Modern Technology, as well as Western Music, Art and costumes had disseminated widely, flooding any conceivable corner of the World no matter how remote; a clear prove of the resounding success implied in that ubiquity. It will be a mistake, however, to claim that ours and Greco-Roman culture ARE THE SAME THING. Ours, from every angle was, in the beginnings, primarily RELIGION CENTERED, (in a sense a child of Christianity) and although in its strivings became later on emancipated from this influence we cannot deny Western Civilization pious origin.

Yet, many in the Western Nations hold a completely different view of themselves and history. They believe that their culture began with the classicism of Greece and Rome, that the 'Dark Ages' was a period of 'decline' succeeded by a 'revival', thence explaining the term we apply to this epoch of feverish productivity: The Renaissance. This name by itself implies an opinion in socio-cultural dynamics, essentially betraying the belief that we BELONG to the same historical process as Classic Antiquity, that is to say, to the same socio-cultural supra-organism.

This confused interpretation of historical evidence results from the fact that, as it was said before, the Roman Empire in the West did not disappeared in a natural or man-made catastrophic commotion like happened to other civilizations. After all, China and India , as we has seen, also went through periods of obvious cultural disarray and religious changes, but still we consider these civilizations alive today although a cultural decadence has set in both cases.

What is different in Western Civilization is that the SUM TOTAL of cultural expressivity completely changed from its predecessors. Not only in religion, but in architecture, language, music, literature and the arts there had been such a departure from the Greco-Roman cultural conventions as to render the Western World a new cultural supra-organism, the end result of an evolutionary line that can be traced back to early Mediterranean and Indo-European ancestors.

It is true that the Renaissance looked at the Roman past for guidance and inspiration in a more methodic and deliberate manner than previous generations of Europeans did, and that in the pictorial arts and architecture there was an impressive resemblance to classic forms, but this in itself is not unusual or surprising. When a new culture arises in the shadow of another such phenomena had been repeatedly observed. Early Greek Sculpture had a strong Egyptian influence represented, to some extent, in the solidity and rigidity of the human figure. Early Persian Art, as we had seen, betrays a strong Mesopotamian flavor. Yet nobody will ever remotely think of considering Greek a revival of Egyptian civilization or the abode of the Achaemenian Kings a resurgence of Mesopotamian culture. The early similarities soon were absorbed and diluted in the creative vigor of the new identity, which soon generated its own peculiar idiosyncratic style. All these similarities establish is A LINE OF DESCEND, as can also be observed in biological creatures.

Western Culture, we had already said, was in its inception RELIGION CENTERED, as also was its 'sister' Islam. Contrary to the paganism of the classics it reveled in themes contracted by its major sponsor: The Church. The iconography of Christianity, however, allowed for developments in the pictorial arts forbidden to the disciples of Mohamed, but in general, and for the first several centuries, these two cultures unfolded parallel evolutionary trends. Nevertheless, Islamic fanatical zeal as well as the patronage of the arts and music by enlighten rulers, coupled with the freedom of communication provided by the political stability then existing throughout the conquered lands (which extended in the hinterlands of Asia up to the frontiers with China, in the West to North Africa, including the Maghreb, and farther north even to the Iberic Peninsula), gave the Arabs an early advantage. Certainly helped by the active commerce permitted by the securing of the traditional trade routes and the despoiling of their victims (particularly the Sassanid Empire with its legendary material and cultural wealth), Mohammedanism was able to integrate the resources of a vast territory and establish neighboring relations with all remaining major cultural centers existing at that time. No wonder that the historical evolution of Arabic people, during the early formative period, seems to us almost 'explosive'.

By contrast, as we have seen, Western Christian Culture had very unpretentious childhood indeed, poor and humble when compared to its splendorous cousin. The slow disintegration of Rome in the V Century created a power vacuum difficult to fill with the nomadic communities roaming throughout Europe. Fear and mutual distrust were the order of the day and it was not until the times of Charlemagne in the IX Century that a precarious and fleeting unity was temporarily effected. The ruins of the Romans inspired some emulative attempts, empty gestures which aborted soon for lack of support from a disconcerted Church impotent to do anything about restituting their crumbling Universe and the relative poverty of non-clerical groups.

Western Europe, because of the diversity of its nomadic roots and the lack in the early stages of sufficiently strong secular powers, developed slowly under the guidance and tutelage of the Christian Church. It was not until the rising bourgeoisie had mustered enough wealth to rival the religious orders and landed aristocracy that the cultural outpour of the already described 'Renaissance' was possible. It is difficult to imagine a Florence without the patronage of the Medici.

It was precisely the new 'mood' transpiring from the increasing power of this nascent social class what catalyzed the emancipation of Western Art from the conventional, flat and stylized gothic-byzantine perspective and stifling molds. The social transformation that took place in Europe in the High Middle Ages was what energized the explosive cultural evolution that took place, a phenomenon only perhaps comparable in history to the changes in Iona preceding the Greek Golden Age. People were imbued by a 'new sense' of being 'masters of their own fate' divorced from religious prejudices and the control of royal and priestly classes. In no other place revolutionary and far reaching social changes similar to those taking place in Western Europe in the XV, XVI and XVII centuries, ever materialize or found equal repercussions. In fact, nothing like an organized and politicized 'middle class' ever arouse in Islam, India or China. The experience of the West in this respect is unique and self-contained.

In this regard it should be remembered the strong impact that Protestantism, with their work ethic and a freer intellectual environment, had in the Enlightenment and the rise of capitalism in Western European lands. The Reformation by extricating Man from the suffocating grip of bigotry and inquisitional terror had a commanding role in the further evolution of Western Culture.

Eventually the clash that provoked the canonical chasm of the Reformation and the final secession of the Anglican Church, further weakened the power of the religious institutions and concomitantly strengthened the scientific and technical advances that propitiated and fostered the Industrial Revolution, bringing to a fructiferous maturity the 'child' born in the Middle Ages. The Renaissance, on this light, could be equated to a 'crisis of passage'; something similar to a prolonged 'adolescence' of the socio-cultural entity we call 'Western Culture'.

As we have pointed out above, no other culture in the history of our planet has ever been known to have undergone both, such a spectacular and in many ways 'radical' change in its fundamental mettle. Invariably those efforts had been aborted before any further consequence had accrued. Societal paralysis had translated into lost of vitality, eventually precipitating a more or less slow demise. It will be interesting to postulate that EVERY CULTURE THAT EVER EXISTED, EXCEPT OUR OWN, HAD 'EXPIRED' IN A PREPUBERAL STAGE OF HISTORIC DEVELOPMENT. Their decadence had taken place prematurely, before the internal social evolution necessary to bring about the cultural changes had occurred, that is, before the rise of an independent and dynamic class would serve as a counterpoise to their established ruling circles. It is precisely this premature decadence of the others what had permitted ours to become pre-eminent facilitating the dissemination and imposition of our values and concepts throughout the civilized world. Again, we have to warn against the confusion of mistakenly assuming that these impositions of

Western values and culture represent a 'revival' of an underlining native culture in the lands where it has taken place. (See also Chapter XIV)

After 5000 years of radiating from the Neolithic proto-culture and undoubtedly based on its technology, Western Culture, like the placental mammals did after millions of years of evolution in the Cenozoic Era, has taken possession of the Earth. But not only in technology has Western Man shown prowess and dynamism; in art, music, literature etc., He has been enormously prolific and is in the process of imposing his standards upon practically every other human group.

CHAPTER XIII

Branching off from the veritable corpse of the defunct Roman Empire, in the Eastern Mediterranean, rose a prolific civilization destined to endure for a millennium: Byzantium. In reality the byzantine claim of belonging to the same socio-cultural supra-organism that its illustrious predecessor, if anything, was even stronger than that of their Western counterpart overturned by barbarians. In fact they, up to the end, considered themselves the true "Roman Empire". Of course Constantinople in the IV Century became the new proud capital of the Empire, the new seat of the government and all its branches. Latin was the official language and a new religious head, the Patriarch was created by Constantine; but he remained the final arbiter of governmental and church affairs.

In fact the Roman Empire in its new site slowly evolved in the following years, unencumbered by its enormous size and the need to maintain a huge army, before finally splitting into Eastern and Western sections after the death of Theodosius the Great at the end of the IV Century. Nevertheless, and despite the pounding of the barbarians, the "Eastern Romans" never lost hope of recovering the Western lands, until the final attempt by Justinian in the VI Century. In fact, shortly after the conclusion of the expensive and destructive Gothic wars most of Italy was overran by the Lombards, except for the small enclaves of Ravenna, Rome (which was literally gutted by the fratricidal war) and several communities to the South.

In following years the 'Eastern Romans' turned their vision to the East, toward Asia Manor and the Sassanid threat which was looming large. To the North also a new set of barbarians, the Bulgars, were pressing in the Danube frontier. Slowly, unnoticed to its population, the Eastern Roman Empire was experiencing a transformation into a new socio-cultural supra-organism, where the autochthonous Greek traditions (Indeed Greek became the official language in the VII Century AD) became mixed with Asiatic influences and what remained of Roman heritage. New characteristic cultural expressions began to appear, like the dome ceilings, the profuse use of mosaics, and the Greek cruciform pattern of their churches. In sculpture the carved sarcophagus became popular (we can trace the stylistic evolution of this art form in the works at Ravenna). Eventually sculpture developed the formalized schematic style of the VI Century for which the Byzantine taste is well known. The pictorial arts, likewise, developed about this time the frontal, solemn representation of saintly figures that appear to indicate an urge for spiritual communication. It has been claimed that for the worshiper the holy images were not merely aids to worship but living representations of the depicted deity.

Leo the Isaurian initiated in the VIII Century the iconoclastic interlude in the Orthodox Church, a movement which revealed a strong oriental influence in religion believes and tastes. When after seventy years of bickering and confusion images were restituted to their old venerable religious importance a great revival took place under the Macedonian Dynasty. From this time dates the IX Century Homilies manuscript of Saint Gregory Nazianzus. A deliberate attempt to revive the Roman style issued under a patronage of Constantine Porphyrogenitus, but again in the following centuries took place the reversal to the rigid highly formalized pictorial conventions that we had learned to identify with Byzantium. Could this represent a rebellion of the Byzantine spirit to the conventions of its predecessor Hellenistic Art?

Nowhere can we perceive the difference between this civilization and the traditional Roman and with the nascent Western Civilization that in the architectural plan of the church interiors. The figure of Christ as the bearded Pantocrator (instead of the youthful shepherd carrying in his shoulder a sheep as in contemporary depictions in the West) occupied the highest place in the cupola. Below in the half domes was the Virgin, farther down were scenes from the life of Christ and finally at the lowest level were figures of the saints, the whole rendering giving the worshiper a reproduction of the heavenly realms. This stratification of revered religious motives could only be an indication of a conceptual organizational pattern of the heavens of which human society was merely a poor reflex, helping to create an owe and fascination enhanced by the magnificent mosaics that, when present, tended to evoke in the observer an otherworldly feeling.

In the field of medicine this was, like in the West, a period of stagnation. Although recipients of the Greco-Roman tradition this was a time dominated by religious dogma, superstition, even magic beliefs and the perpetuation of old empiric practices. There were, however, several great writers whose compilations shed light about the state of the art during this epoch. Alexander of Trelles enjoyed great reputation and wrote twelve books about internal medicine, and Aetius of Amida also wrote extensively about the practice of surgery in the VI Century. Also worth of mention is Paul of Egina, whose seven books "On Medicine" is a tour de force about the practice of this discipline in the VII Century. Among other subjects his descriptions of the surgical procedures in vogue at that time are very revealing. Paul's very detailed accounting of many of them, like hernias, treatment of fractures, hemorrhoids, condylomata and fistulas, according to some authorities, seem to indicate some improvements in this discipline when compare to the times of Celsus. Like in the West also, the compassionate religious orders built numerous hospitals, hospices and leprosariums; a social role that alleviated the burden of the tragedies that befell upon the country particularly at the time of Justinian, when an epidemic, probably bubonic plague, decimated the population and almost threw the Empire into chaos.

Only slow progress mainly in surgical procedures and techniques, but no substantial advance in medicine, could be ascertain during the long egis of this venerated civilization; something entirely comparable to small mutations in biological creatures. Yet, Byzantium was a repository of the old tradition of Greek Medicine and its intercourse with Arabian culture was majorly instrumental in the rise of the School of Salerno which, as we saw, was of great importance in the genesis of the Health Sciences in the West.

Byzantine civilization, an evolutionary radiation from its Greco-Roman counterpart and also highly influenced by Western Asiatic cultures, fertilized the Eastern Mediterranean for a thousand years and was instrumental in the preservation and transmission of classic works in science, literature and philosophy to the nascent Western Civilization, mostly during the IX Century cultural revival of the Macedonian dynasties under the auspices of Bardas and Photius. Yet, this vital culture, despite of all outward indicators, never considered itself nothing else but the TRUE Roman Empire, the standard-bear-er of what in actuality was, after the IV Century, a veritable cultural corpse overran by barbarians.

Miguel Ochoa

It was the fate of the Byzantines to witness not only the demise of its counterpart in the West but also, in its own old age, the birth and rise of that civilization to which it so unintentionally contributed: Western Christian Civilization.

CHAPTER XIV

It is on the light of the facts we had been analyzing that the strange, even ominous 'homogenization' of contemporary cultural expressions should be understood. Modern Western Technology has become the great eraser of cultural variation by giving rise to a universal acceptance of its values and tastes, an amalgam of forms valid for humans no matter where their geographic locus. The symbols of the modern world like cars, planes, computers etc., are everywhere to be seen. But things are getting even more puzzling: the articles manufactured by this technology are becoming more stereotyped, losing their 'personalities' (Car 'models', for example, look more like each other now than half a century ago regardless of the brand name). This 'streamlining' of the products is a novel phenomena NOT FORCED BY DESIGN, ENGINEERING CONSTRAINS OR ANY OTHER NECESSITY, in other words, not demanded by the production process.

Parallel with this development there is a rising new type of human: THE MODERN CONSUMER whose destiny is to engross the profits of the corporate system and in the process create a new perverse inter-dependency of which hinges the survival of the system. Massive propaganda and advertisement pounded in the human mind since birth has created this new socio-political animal, a zombie-like creature whose main role in society is precisely to consume compulsively. This phenomena couple with the increase social role of government, as well as the amassing of large fortunes in few hands, has provoked a new kind of threat to society, the increasing indebtedness of the human community, a kind of economic entropy eating at its fabric.

What is the meaning of this new situation? What are the possible repercussions of this 'homogenization' of the human product? The immediate consequence will be that CULTURE WILL CEASE TO BE THE LOCUS OF SOCIETAL EVOLUTION because the erasing of cultural idiosyncrasies will impede the competition for survival of opposing traits. The ultimate results of this situation are predictable: culture if not submitted to radiation pressures will become stagnant and progressively decline. But what about if the phenomena we are witnessing represents the creation of another hierarchy of being, the level of a super-community? In such a case THE LOCUS OF EVOLUTION WILL TRANSFER TO THE HUMAN SOCIETY AS A WHOLE. No longer will the individual nations and civilizations be subject to independent survival challenges; instead the entire population of the World AS A UNIT would be experiencing these changes. But from where will come then a healthy competition for survival?

At this point it would be proper to ask what the overt signs of such a monumental attainment would be, what 'hints' should we be looking for in this regard. Are there any objective criteria we can go by in order to clarify this point? I think in this we are restricted by the limited perspective of our type of consciousness which forces us to judge from insufficient local clues the goals of organisms at higher stages of integration. We are, like in the case of Plato's cave, condemned to judge what occurs at loftier realms by the shadows projected in ours. From this limited vantage point what appears obvious is that if human society, despite of the absence of internal struggles and competition, continues to DEVELOP ITS TECHNOLOGY, it will be an indication that the new hierarchical level has been reached, that is, that the global super-community HAS BECOME THE NEW NUCLEUS OF EVOLUTIONARY CHANGE. If that is not the case, if decadence sets in, it will be an indication that the opposite is true.

A comparison with the biological world will help to clarify what has been said. In multi-cellular organisms the unit or 'nucleus' of evolutionary change is no longer the individual constitutive cell. A liver cell is not in competition with another of its own kind or with any other of the animal to which it belongs. The new evolutionary unit is now THE WHOLE animal. There has been a shift from protozoa to metazoan in the targeting of evolution along the scale of increasing complexity. In both, the Zoological and Botanic Kingdoms this would mean that the integrative process has transcend the old boundaries and reached a new hierarchical level, the dawning of a new feeling and awareness and a new set of needs and urges; in short, the attainment of a new conscience.

Now, animals compete for their survival and perpetuation not only with members of other species but frequently with those of their own. Likewise, nations and civilizations not only compete with those of different 'cultural species' but also with their own. Suffice is to remember the innumerable European wars to document this point. Only with the integration of hitherto independent biological or cultural organisms is that evolutionary relevance switch focus to a new higher organizational entity. In the socio-cultural sphere this means that this shift of evolutionary importance ONLY OCCUR AFTER POLITICAL INTEGRATION TAKES PLACE. In Germany, Prussia and Bavaria; in England, Scotland and Wales; in Spain, Cataluña and Biscay do not any longer evolve independently from the 'nations' they now belong to.

A pre-requisite for this world process of political integration is the creation of a common cultural background, the kind of historical phenomena we have been describing as taking place in association with the surprising dissemination of Western Culture. After this, there will need to be a world economic integration and abolishment of tariff barriers (something already happening in Western Europe). Finally, the abolition of political territorial divides will have to take place and the creation of a common government to rule the entire world.

To be sure the human community, as a whole, has not quite yet reached this goal, which still seems to lie far into the future. One of the reasons is the diversity of races and cultures which will need to be unified in a new universal socio-political corpus if this integration is to take place. Another big obstacle is the present wide gap of economic development among the different regions of the Earth, which will need to be reconciled before this unification could be contemplated; a formidable challenge indeed. Yet, the cultural uniformity in tastes and values presently taking place in the World led by Western Civilization might be indicative of a first step in this direction, a presage of things to come. Perhaps this paramount homogenization of products and tastes presently taking place, represents the early phase in the attainment of a higher stage of hierarchical integration of conscience, and the explanation for the continuous unprecedented technological progress which, many assume, to be the consequence of the 'arms race' and the competition of opposite economic systems. But the spin-offs of research in weapon systems cannot be credited for many of the present advances, particularly in the biological and medical fields as well as in space science.

I believe, therefore, that this progressive amalgamation of the 'cultural corpus' of the human society probably represents an indication of the historic trend toward world socio-political and economic unification. I am not claiming that this process will take place in the near future. There are enormous hurdles that need to be overcome before the eventual fulfillment of this presumptive pan-global socio-cultural supra-organic consciousness of which the present relentless technological 'progress' could be one of its identifiable manifestations. On the other hand the danger still remains that this amalgamation instead is a harbinger of impending decadence, but if that is the case, as it was said before, ultimately there will be technological and cultural stagnation.

What about Man himself? Is Man, the biological species, destined to immortalize his FORM by overpowering the 'forces' of Nature and subjugating the World, including His own self-destructiveness? If we are going to believe the laws of biology and the evidence afforded so far by history, we have to accept the transiency and ephemeral quality of everything that exist, whether animal, plant, cell or human community. As we mentioned before nothing so far has subverted mankind's mortality and it is difficult to see how it could. True that modern technology has bestowed upon us powers not even dreamt at several decades ago, and the possibility of genetic control of human evolution appears well within our reach. Yet, by mastering his own 'biologism' Man will be introducing a 'utilitarian' view of his destiny, something which can only accelerate his departure from this planet.

Why would that be so? Stated very simply, because He will be surrendering his spirituality and re-emphasizing the concept of humans as 'machines'. On the other hand humans could, in principle, have the power to design and manufacture even better machines, non-biological ones, which would be in a much better position to compete with us at our own game with the advantage of freedom from organic and spiritual human needs (a necessity if intelligent beings are to explore and colonize sidereal systems remote from our own and unencumbered by the limitations imposed on us by biological constrains).

If a utilitarian view of mankind eventually prevails there is no reason why it would not be decided, at one point in the future, to replace humans with the more efficient and docile robotic creatures. If this thought appears far-fetched it is, nevertheless, based on a perspective of societal dynamics which has pervaded Western nations ever since the Renaissance, becoming, despite of heated claims to the contrary, only aggravated in recent times. Man, it has been repeatedly documented by history, is his own worst enemy, capable of devouring himself like the mythical Uroborus. In so doing He will be unleashing the age of the auto programmable robot, a second generation of intelligent beings ushered into this world by the first, that is, by those that evolved 'spontaneously' from biological forms and who, unwittingly, would have then signed their own death sentence.

The eventual union of the entire Earth, whether by biological or 'artificial' beings, into a single socio-cultural supra-organism is a distinct possibility. Furthermore, a similar situation could take place in other planets of our galaxy creating the potentiality for still higher hierarchical levels of integration and, correspondingly, of even more complex consciousness. These new planetary cultural centers potentially could intercommunicate by means of methods hard to imagine today, or those that at present are the subject of science fiction(such as quantum "tunneling"), establishing the groundwork for still higher stages of socio-cultural complexity. The 'Struggle for Survival' would then have attained a new 'cosmic' dimension, and would be carried on in unimaginable ways by then far removed from our present experiences, perhaps at higher spatial dimensions.

Ultimately a final level will be reached which, per force, comprises all others: That of the Universe Itself, the one including 'everything else'. This level will be 'exhausted' by the totality of what exist. Nothing by definition would be located 'outside' of It. Motion would be impossible to this 'thing' which also would lack 'shape' because It will include all hierarchical dimensions and therefore be beyond space itself.

But an all-encompassing supra-conscience including entirely WHAT EXIST would not be subject to evolutionary pressures of any kind either, actually it would not be a part of evolution AT ALL simply because It would not have any other entity to compete with. Blessed in its serene solitude this truly Ultra-Conscience would lie beyond the laws of inheritance, incapable of learning anything new by the mere fact of in itself superseding every other hierarchical plane and any other type of improvable unit. Quite understandably, the idea of ultimate reality constituting the Ultra-Conscience of a Universe which IS the final integration of all that 'exist' will be repulsive to many. Our Christian conception of the 'divine' is more akin to that of a good shepherd looking after his flock of children here on Earth and encouraging them to behave well. An ethically ordained Universe, however, implies the primacy and absolute validity of our moral principles, as well as, the tacit acceptance of the possibility of communication between different spheres or levels of discourse.

A universal Ultra-Conscience, it has to be emphasized, an all pervading principle, does not need to be aware of other consciences at lower hierarchical locations or of what is happening to the components of these lower orders at any time. As we said before this situation is similar to the case of Man, who is not aware of the vicissitudes of the life of any constitutive cell of his body, although he profits from their collective labors and would not be what He is except for the orchestrated and aggregated product of their daily 'toil'. As it was said before, a person is ignorant as to how the individual cell 'feel' and is not sorrow or happy in regard to the birth, death or life history of each of them. That person certainly would be cognizant of major upheavals, like disease states in which large numbers of these cells will join forces to combat an enemy, but otherwise would be oblivious and unconcerned with the fate of anyone of them. Yet in the case of a putative Ultra-Conscience the situation will be even more bizarre. Because of the lack of a time dimension it could not be cognizant of stirrings among its formative units. In fact because of this exhaustion of possibilities IT would not be able to have any 'feelings' as we know them, and therefore would lack the capacity to worry or interest itself with the fate of its constitutive units from lower hierarchical stages. In fact this ultra-conscience would be incapable of 'worrying' or 'thinking' in the traditional sense either, because for that it would be needed a temporal dimension also.

The universal Ultra-Conscience would then be PURE SPACE AND EXIST BY NECESSITY, in itself incorporating every lower order of 'reality'. It can be said that this existence results from the universal design or building plan: IT THEN FOLLOWS FROM IT RATHER THAN CREATE IT. The cosmic Ultra-Conscience would thus be a final necessary terminus beyond anything which IS or can be; quite properly speaking the unavoidable consequence of the world structural order, A RESULT RATHER THAN A CAUSE, a product and ultimate expression of the progressive integration of matter and consciousness. Even more, the 'life' of such a conscience would lack intelligible meaning BY BEING OUTSIDE ANY FRAME OF REFERENCE. The latter is an attribute of matter and intrinsic to the Cosmo. Its individual parts have a beginning and an end BUT NOT THE WHOLE which, by definition, incorporates every single event that ever existed including their coordinate system: what we call 'Space-Time' itself. To claim, like many do, that the Universe 'began' at an specific 'instant' 15 billion years ago in a 'singularity' is irrational and lack perspective by forgetting that space-time is inextricably associated with matter, and events therefore could not have 'presided' over its birth. SO-CALLED SPACE-TIME IS INTERPENETRATED WITH THE FABRIC OF THE COSMO WHICH COULD NOT, THEN, BE FRAMED ON IT. Again, The Universe AS A WHOLE has to be devoid of any discernible 'purpose' or 'meaning', for which a TEMPORALIZED FIELD OF ACTIVITY is necessary.

Is there a place in this stratified Universe for immortality at the sub-ultra-conscience level? To answer this question we will first need to know if there is a possibility for 'Conscience' to exist REMOVED from matter, that is, if there is such a thing as PURE SPIRIT. Different types of consciousness, we had claimed, are characteristic of every cosmic hierarchical level. Ours, we had already said, is the metazoan, which we share with other animals but probably, as we said before, differ from theirs by being reflective, that is, self-conscious. For any Being in our own hierarchical spatio-temporal level to be eternal implies to SPAN our entire time dimension, because as it was said before, it will constitute space at a higher level of integration; an obvious impossibility. We have to remember that consciousness, being associated to organizational peculiarities in the clustering of what we call 'matter'(when giving rise to living forms), IS precisely the manifestation of its 'activity', and therefore PART of it. To believe in the possibility of thinking 'souls' detached from their material substratum (the bodies) is unsupported by any available evidence.

To speak, therefore, of an eternal non all-inclusive conscience is as sense-less as to believe its material substratum eternal. Matter AS A WHOLE might have those attributes, but not the specific condensations subject to evolution, whether it be a molecule of DNA, a cell or metazoan(including MAN) , and as illogical as to contend that they are infinitely big. Only the Universe itself, by definition the totality of everything that IS, does encompass the entire realm of what exist. IT is an age-less entity, hence devoid of MEANING as we know it.

There is a way to understand agelessness in material things. This is the theory that conceives the life of a living organism as eliciting in a spatial, not in a temporal, dimension. In our immediately higher hierarchical level our time will be perceived as ANOTHER SPATIAL DIMENSION, in other words, statically rather than dynamically. Motions will be shapes and destinies nothing but morphologies. For instance, goals and meaning, for a five dimensional creature, could only be found in its time frame, that is, in the fifth dimension (its forth spatial dimension would be our time). Because of this 'simultaneity' of every single event of our world (as judged from a higher hierarchy), for an hypothetical five dimensional being to talk about past, present and future in OUR lives would be sense-less because for him they are ALL SIMULTANEOUSLY PRESENT; that is, behold entirely in one single instant of HIS time. WE WILL REPRESENT ACTUALITY FOR HIM.

It follows from what we have been saying that our time truly constitute, in this hypothesis, THE RHYTHM OF ACTUALIZATION OF OUR CONSCIENCE AT A HIGHER SPATIAL DIMENSION. By traveling upon this magnitude with certain direction we do obtain the feeling of temporal passage, which is something fundamental to create the 'illusion' of motion, happening and causality (corner-stones to the interpretation of life as continuous change and free will as a logical consequence of a causally structured Universe).

That is why, time being a meaningless expression, the individual is truly AGE-LESS. Furthermore, motion and causality are illusions brought about by the way our conscience perceives the fourth dimension: literally 'climbing' through it and becoming aware of CONSECUTUVE CROSS-SECTION OF THIS FOURTH DIMENSION, each one being an 'instant' in a life which, in its totality then, would be defined AS THE SUM TOTAL OF ALL THESE CROSS-SECTIONS. Viewed with this perspective we, and our lives, become A UNITARY TETRADIMENSIONAL TOTO AND MAN THEN REPRESENT AN STACK OF INSTANCES.

Very far reaching in consequences would indeed be this hypothesis. According to it free will, causality and motion do represent nothing but false conceptions, distorted conclusions originating in the mysterious way our conscience senses the Cosmo: in successive "instants" instead that ALL AT ONCE, akin to the manner we perceive the static frames of a movie film as a DYNAMIC CONTINUUM when projected sequentially in the cinematographic screen. Now, if the Universe as a whole IS ACTUALITY it implies a strict DETERMINISM. We will perceive no more than a small fraction of those events because of our perceptive limitations, but they are factual and capable of being detectable ALL AT ONCE at a higher order of integration by an assumed creature with the capability to apprehend them.

Such strict determinism appears to contradict the microcosmic indeterminism expounded by Quantum Mechanics, or does it? The Copenhagen interpretation of the experimental facts has fallen in disfavor. Presently physicists believe that the impossibility to determine simultaneously the position and momentum of a subatomic particle is an incertitude INGRAINED in the events themselves and not related to the act of measuring them. Be as it may, numerous studies performed in the last several decades seem to support this quantum mechanical interpretation of events, instead of the traditional physical views of reality. What transpire from these experiments is a radically different conception of this 'reality', one in which phenomena are not independent from each other but actually 'interpenetrated' or 'entangled'; that means not individually separated but strangely interdependent and BOUND to the 'act' of observation AT OUR COSMIC LEVEL OF EXISTENCE. This inter-dependence will explain the 'incertitude' above alluded when we try to ascribe tangible attributes to something 'out there' detached from the perceiving event itself. Could this "entanglement" be a manifestation of the union of these events at a higher hierarchical level, perhaps a new dimension of space incapable to be phantom by our consciences?

How is to be understood a Universe where the separation of 'objective' and 'subjective', the distinction between a natural phenomena and the 'registering' act in our conscience, is fallacious? The answer lies in the 'artificiality' of the cognitive conventions resorted by Man to make 'sense' out of his Life in our cosmic level of existence. We said before that Conscience pervades everything and is inseparable from the events it records, a gelstad of a sort. That's why these events become sense-less entities in isolation. Microcosmic incertitude might be a mirage resulting from cognitive restrictions of our tetra- dimensional mind stemming from the need we have to categorize events, and PROPERTIES of them, in isolation when truly they form inextricable tangles. PREDICTIONS BECOME IMPOSSIBLE.

Regardless of which hypothesis we accept, the fact of the matter is that the different hierarchical levels are incapable of communicating with each other. Their existences might be indirectly surmised but we are unable to reach their consciences. It is like if a barrier would make impossible any relation with the other levels. As it was said before, we don't know what is like to 'feel' as a cell and a cell does not know what is like to feel like a molecule of DNA, although each hierarchy is totally dependent on the activities of its lower integrating units. Essentially, each developmental stage IS the building block for its immediate higher hierarchical neighbor in a line of ascending complexity, and each unit sub-sums the constitutive elements from the immediately lower level. Yet, again, the consciences of the contiguous domains are totally separated and mysteriously unable to inter-communicate among themselves. It follows that a 'Conscience' is more than the sum total of its lower hierarchical components; in fact it represents something new: A CRYSTALIZATION OF A NOVEL AWARENESS MATERIALIZING OUT OF THE CONCERTED ACTIVITY OF ITS CONSTITUTIVE PARTS.

It is difficult to understand how a conscience could include its lower hierarchical components and still be independent of the whims and desires of each one of them. The answer has to be found in the conception of organizational patterns, that is, in the way the building blocks or units are organized or 'laid out'. In the same manner that a house is more than the sum of its bricks, a human, or an animal, is more than the sum of his forming cells. The clue is the way those elements are brought together; that is what makes the difference.

Could then be that what we call consciousness is an expression of the way the elemental parts of a creature are conformed and organized? I think this point should be analyzed very carefully to avoid falling in inconsistencies. The general morphologic 'blue-print' of an animal, for instance, very closely resembles that of another representative of its own species; in other words, anatomically they all will display the same general 'body plan' and therefore are structurally similar, even identical to us. However, at the ultrastructural level (the one of molecules and chemistry) significant differences among these elements will be found. For one thing, their corresponding components, like for instance cellular membranes, can undergo subtle constitutive changes of a complex chemical nature that makes quite a difference as far as the rapidity and effectiveness of cellular intercommunication which, when concerning the Nervous System, translates, at least in higher mammals, into substantial behavioral diversity among individuals of the same species and, consequently, in variations in the quality of their souls because behavior is what defines personality. Even in normal individuals there are considerable difference in intelligence, behavior and what is generically defined as 'personality' which ultimately resides in variations at the molecular level. In fact, the so-called retro-transposons or 'jumping genes' by making copies of themselves and reinserting back at different points of the genome of nerve cells, are capable of eliciting profound differences in the behavior of a person, even among identical twins.

On the other hand there are cases when molecular derangements give rise to profound morphologic and/or functional changes in the affected individuals, even at times incompatible with life itself. In the case of Man suffice is to mention the case of Mongolism, a congenital disease resulting from a duplication of a chromosome resulting from genetic, and therefore molecular (DNA), derangements of their constitutive elements. The cluster of morbid signs of this condition in facial characteristics, heart abnormalities and the mental retardation, therefore, originate at a molecular locus; that is, two steps removed from the metazoan hierarchical level of the human suffering the disease. The medical literature is filled with similar examples of congenital 'molecular diseases arising in defects of the human genome, including among the better known, Hemophilia, Sickle Cell Anemia and the panoply of muscular dystrophies.

A METAZOAN THEREFORE COULD IN MANY CASES OWN PECULIARITIES OF HIS CONSCIENCE TO A HIERARCHICAL LEVEL REMOVED TWO ORDERS OF MAGNITUD FROM HIS OWN INSTEAD OF TO THAT OF HIS INMEDIATELY LOWER ONE. This remarkable fact attests to the profound interdependence of different hierarchies among themselves despite their apparent lack of evident intercommunication. This is an intriguing and apparently paradoxical fact. As was said before, living units at different planes of integration interdependent but do not intercommunicate. Here we find the roots of 'blind fate', the conception and meaning of the belief in 'what is going to happens will happen'. Our fate is frequently pre-ordained by events in a remote and strange world, the habitat of chemical compounds. Our individual conscience do not 'feel' what the molecules do but their functional peculiarities have far reaching consequences in our lives and behavior. Conversely we might also be 'dragged' by events at a higher hierarchical level of integration, 'felt' by our reflective consciousness but devoid of intelligible meaning for us.

This peculiarity of the structure of the Cosmo, this interpenetration of events at different orders of complexity is what instills the quality of predestination to the phenomena in our world. If what 'exist' is view not as 'things' accessible to our senses and understanding but as 'events' framed in our Space-Time this interpenetration maybe could be better understood. Constellations of these events at each cosmic strata 'shape' those at higher hierarchical realms (each event having a specific locus in its Space-Time) which, in their turn and for reasons unknown to us, influence also our behavior in ways we cannot understand and frequently believe irrational.

A pre-ordained Universe without motion, causality or 'purpose', a Universe where our mysterious conscience lives with the illusion of Free-Will in a 'time' dimension depending on, or representing, the rhythm of actualization of this same conscience, results from this perspective. We do not perceive INDIVIDUALLY the micro-events forming the macro-event which our physical bodies in every 'instant' constitute. The successive unfolding of these 'instances' bridged by our memory is what produces in us the notion of what we call Time. A cinematographic film is only meaningful to us when it is projected at a given speed in sync with our capacity to perceive an stream of frames as an intelligible sequence, but as we said before, when all the frames are actualized simultaneously it only represent for us a roll of celluloid. The true shape of the cosmic totality is denied to us because of our incapacity to apprehend higher dimensions of reality.

But then, what is conscience itself? What this strange sense of awareness at the root of life? Here is where the great mystery resides.

It is something clearly related to what we call 'matter' and 'energy', and therefore, to the integrating events that constitute the Self. But, again, it is more than they, more than the sum total of its components. IT IS SOMETHING THAT PERCEIVES ITS COSMIC HIERARCHY OF ACTIVITY THROUGH ITS SPATIAL DIMENSIONS EXCEPT ONE: THE TIME DIMENSION WHICH IS CAPTURED IN SUCCESSIVE FRAMES RATHER THAN IN ITS TOTALITY. This sequential awareness, the source of many perceptive and cognitive illusions, is, nevertheless, perennially associated with the events to which it also belongs, but on the other hand transcend them BY BRIDGING THE INDIVIDUAL FRAMES WITH MEMORY which is the unifying element of our conscience. Without memory phenomena will carry an isolated, secluded, remote existence, an incoherent meaningless succession of events. But if meaning can only be attained by this linking process of memory and there is a World Conscience encompassing ALL dimensions, then, the mere fact that this conscience would have to INCLUDE SIMULTANEOUSLY ALL AND EVERY POSSIBLE DIMENSION WOULD RENDER IT DEVOID OF ANY INTELLIGABLE MEANING FOR US, BECAUSE TIME WONT EXIST FOR SUCH A SUPERBEING; IT WOULD HAVE EXHAUSTED ALL TEMPORAL DIMENSIONS AND ENCOMPASS EXISTENCE IN ITS SPATIAL TOTALLITY. The putative World Conscience, then, would not 'climb any temporal ladder', only finite creatures and their consciences do. It otherwise will be subject TO COME TO AN END, something unthinkable in an all inclusive THING which, therefore, is beyond any destiny.

But an achieved complete entity in pure spatial dimensions would also be incapable of THINKNG (which is a dynamic process), some might adduce. We should, however, avoid mistakenly confuse thought with the act of thinking. THOUGHT IS A FINAL PRODUCT, NOT A PROCESS LIKE THINKING. Thought, therefore, is possible for the Ultra-Conscience as a 'complete construction'.

Does that mean that the Ultra-Conscience is omniscient? As is the case in the other hierarchical levels It will know ITSELF, but would not be cognizant of events at lower cosmic layers in the same way that we are not aware of the 'feelings' and 'urges' of a body cell. However, as also is the case in other levels, It would be strictly shaped by events at the lower hierarchical locations, and being THE HIGHEST of them, then, by the sum total of universal events. The Ultra-Conscience, therefore, IS PURE ACTUALIZED THOUGHT, which could only be 'thought' about the underlining substratum of its SELF inasmuch as, by definition, there is NOTHING beyond this Universal Self.

It follows, then, that the Universal Self has to represent COMPLETE AND FULFILLED DESTINY in view of the fact that it HAS TO INCLUDE every single universal event which had ever existed at any cosmic realm. In addition It could be neither in an inert or dynamic state, because such notions apply only within the scope of space-time frames which by definition are transcended by the Ultra-Conscience. In fact, the nature and psychological texture of this 'Actualized Thought' could not be phantom, it is ineffable, and impossible to be described or explained by being entirely removed from our perceptive experience: akin to the nature of the 'Infinite'. It also has to be beyond ethical conceptions valid for us in our cosmic level, and will lack the power to 'ordain' human 'affairs'.

This Ultra-Conscience, then, would have to be something very different to religious conceptions of a powerful GOD. In fact, it might be the antithesis of our beloved, omnipotent, omniscient, benevolent Father, the one who created the HEAVENS AND EARTH. Instead of 'creating', the Ultra-Conscience IS THE TOTALITY (although It was never 'created' either) of all its integrating events, and, inasmuch as every one of them IS A FINAL FORM, they are incapable of change or accessible to manipulation: ONLY A TRASCENDING POWER COULD. This appears paradoxical but is a logical consequence of what we had claimed to be the attributes of the Ultra-Conscience. On the other hand, this conscience would be aware only of events IN ITS COSMIC PLANE, and considering the fact that it is only inhabited by Itself, will follows, as it was already said, that IT WONT BE AWARE OF ANYTHING ELSE BUT ITSELF, in spite of being made up by all universal events which ever had existed and 'will' exist.

It hardly can be conceived that anything lacking in temporal dimension could be 'alive' when the dynamic nature of Life itself is taken into consideration, but the Ultra-Conscience IS THE CONSUMMATION OF ANY AND EVERY DESTINY; IN FACT IS DESTINY ITSELF by representing the sum total of all universal phenomena. Past, present and future, in reference to IT lack any meaning. The 'final' unique

FORM of every single creature or process that ever existed is included in the Universe by being a constitutive part of IT and reflects in ITS EXISTENCE, in other words, in ITS FATE (which is shape) that the Ultra-Conscience cannot escape. The Ultra-Conscience is a PRISIONER OF ITSELF BY NOT BEING ABLE TO BE DIFFERENT, in a sense a peculiar result of its COMPLETENESS, an exhaustion of possibilities, a sublime actualization of potentialities.

Judged from our point of view such a universal being, an all encompassing and omnipresent Ultra-Conscience, would be a power-less and help-less 'thing', the final product in an ascending series of hierarchical arranged phenomena; an strange stratification appearing to be 'the grand design', the general blue-print of existence. However, any hard judgment passed on the Ultra-Conscience from the narrow vantage point of the Human Race, living and carrying out our activities in the restricted range of a limited cosmic level, runs the risk of being tarnished with prejudice.

Anybody who is helpless and powerless on account of being unable to 'control' events of fundamental importance to his or her 'life' is certainly, to us, a sorrowful figure. That is because we believe in 'free will' and the helplessness implies meekness, lack of determination and strength of character, or perhaps, bad luck. What about in the case of the Ultra-Conscience? In a temporalized field of activity, in a life 'as we know it', this impotence to control events means that for one reason or another they are 'out of our power' to do so. However, in the case of the Ultra-Conscience THE EVENTS ARE NOT JUST 'HAPPENING', BUT INSTEAD THEY ARE, BY DEFINITION, ALREADY INTEGRAL PARTS OF IT. A being cannot be a 'play thing' of Fate when FATE ITSELF IS A CONSTITUTIVE PART OF THAT BEING. Nothing is external and beyond the Ultra-Conscience, its existence does not take place in any time frame. Nothing could be 'happening' to IT and, consequently, helplessness is not a term applicable in this case. Likewise, 'powerlessness' is not appropriately used in this context either, because in the case of the Ultra-Conscience ALL DESTINIES HAD ALREADY BEEN FULFILLED. A FUTURE DOES NOT EXIST, IT BECOMES A MENINGLESS TERM.

The Ultra-Conscience, then, truly cannot be a helpless and powerless entity. By transcending all dimensions it 'places itself' in a unique 'position' of its own, beyond and above anything known; by being TOTAL ACTUALITY IT CAN NEITHER WISH NOR WILL ANYTHING WHICH THERE IS NOT, BECAUSE IT IS ALL-INCLUSIVE, IN ESSENCE A CULMINATION OF ALL DESTINIES. What then is the purpose and significance of such an existence? This, of course, is the wrong question to formulate. Ulterior meaning can only be had in relation to a time dimension and for the Ultra Conscience there is none.

But if the substratum of life everywhere is self-awareness, and conscience is defined precisely as THIS sense of awareness, then the Ultra-Conscience would have to be assumed alive, living in a peculiar non-temporalized condition because it is ALL ACTUALITY AND THOUGHT ABOUT ITSELF: PURE, FINAL AND UNCHANGEABLE. These are strange but logical properties of the highest, all inclusive, hierarchical plane of WHAT EXIST. IT is eternal, imperturbable, strictly deterministic and complete in every respect; no need has been left unsatisfied or potentiality without realization. The Ultra-Conscience 'animating' what exists permeates the Cosmo with its pervading sense-awareness, with a definite and irreversible 'here and now' where will and accomplishment are the same thing.

Obviously such a Universe could not be ethically ordained. Any universal event that did or will exist in our perceptive cognitive frame of awareness, like those at different hierarchical levels of existence, is ACTUAL FACT HERE AND NOW and none, of course, could be reversed. It is a world of fulfilled potentiality the one inhabited by the Ultra-Conscience in an undisturbed solitude of content and insurmountable attainment; an idyllic state of beatific peace and harmony devoid of unsatisfied desires, strife or sterile passions.

APPENDIX I

Mutations, genetic segregations and recombinations are the basis for phenotypic variation in biological evolution, in the same manner that cultural trait transformation, with subsequent divergences or convergences, serves as a basis for the heterogeneity of cultural expressions which evolutionary unit is the civilization, nation or country. Like with living organisms, where the vicissitudes of a single or group of genes occasionally could be followed through a population (color of eyes or skin etc.), it is also possible to trace the fate of cultural traits by their evolution in time through different supra-organismic cultural entities. A couple of examples might help to clarify this point.

The use of mosaics in ornamentation, for instance, was firstly utilized by the Sumerians and later on taken, not only by other Mesopotamian 'people', but also used by the Minoans and Classic Greeks who seemed to have used them strictly as pebbles for floor coverings. It was not until the Hellenistic times, however, that the tesserae were firstly employed with pictorial intentions, mostly to depict scenes borrowed from contemporary paintings. Also during this period wall mosaics began to be used, although it was not until the full impact of Christian Art that a pinnacle of unsurpassed opulence and mastering of technique was achieved by the already mentioned Byzantine Empire, which utilized them extensively in their renderings of religious motifs, exploiting exhaustively its expressive potential to convey the richness of its symbolic content. (The sectile mosaics of Islam appeared to have been an independent elaboration from the Mesopotamian glazed tile, which we saw adorning the Babylonian and Achaemenian palaces and temples). This fashion became dormant and subservient to painting after the fall of Byzantium, until a new revival of a sort took place in the XX Century with the so-called representational arts.

The art of the mosaic, therefore, from humble beginnings as decorative designs on baked clay in Mesopotamia, 'mutated' to pebbles of stone and glass during the classic period of Greece and Rome before transmuting into the tesserae, literally 'climbing up the walls', in the Hellenistic interlude to become, finally, a very effective pictorial representational vehicle in Late Antiquity. The mosaic 'gene' later on became dormant, and in the early part of the XX Century underwent a minor mutation, but its importance in the overall 'cultural genome' had clearly declined to a secondary, subservient role again.

Another cultural trait which evolution could be traced with relative ease today is that of the architectural arch. False arches are known to exist at least since the Second Millennia BC, as proved by archeological findings at several Hittite sites, including the capital Hattusa and neighboring Mediterranean territories. True arches, however, those making use of voussoirs or wedge-shaped blocks, are only known since the IX Century BC; like those in Tell Halaf in Northern Syria. Although they did not make extensive use of this form the Greeks knew the technique and used it occasionally in the gates of cities. The Etruscans also frequently used them, and could be considered the group which properly introduced their utilization in Europe. The know-how was then appropriated by Republican Rome and there it bloomed into full maturity in the spectacular aqueducts, triumphal arches, and public buildings we all know.

It was in the early imperial years when the first examples of non-semicircular arches (a stylistic evolution which was to come into its own in the palaces and monuments of their Asiatic enemies the Sassanid Persians) first appeared, becoming, later on, highly favored by Rome's cousins the Byzantines; as could be still appreciated in the splendid renderings supporting the dome of Hagia Sofia and Hagia Irene. Whether the pointed arch in Asia was originally a further elaboration from the Romans, or represents an independent version in the Middle East is difficult to establish. In any case what should be noted is that this style transcended cultural barriers to reappear in a different socio-cultural supra-organism, like Islam, which appropriated the technique from their contemporaries the Byzantine and Persians, and in whose hands it evolved into the peculiar shapes we have learned to identify with this culture.

During the Middle Ages in Western Europe the pointed arch trait, whether derived from Moslem or earlier Roman sources, proceeded to evolve in a substantially different fashion than in the Islamic lands. We only have to mention the Gothic style and its ramifications to understand the intense cultural radiation that took place there. With the Renaissance the rounded arch shape, which was in a 'recessive' conformation since the fall of Rome, was reintroduced into Europe, although soon became confined to churches until the XIX Century when new architectonic devices and materials made it popular again in public works: Like bridges, viaducts, buildings etc.

Specific techniques and art forms, therefore, undergo traceable modification in different cultures, sometimes, like in the case of genes, becoming clearly and explicitly expressed, while in other occasions they 'hide' in a latent conformation as a 'recessive trait', an undercurrent at any moment capable of turning into a new explosion of creativity.

But not only in art and architecture can we study transformational patterns of cultural characteristics. Very enlightening is the evolution of alphabetic writing. It first appeared, as far as is known, in the Phoenician city of Byblos in the XVII Century B.C. It consisted of 22 abstract characters (letters) totally devoid of any graphic association. The versatility and adaptability of such method over the preceding hieroglyphic or cuneiform writing, used then in Egypt and the Levant, was such that this form of scripture rapidly became popular among the populations in the Eastern Mediterranean.

But it did not irrupt in fully developed form out from nowhere. In Ras Shamra a sort of alphabetic script of 30 signs, but devoid of vowel sounds, written in cuneiform characters in clay tablets dating approximately to the XX Century B.C. was found, suggesting it could have been an early evolutionary ancestor of alphabetic writing, an indication that this notation did not rose from a vacuum but that it truly represented a cultural mutation whose survival depended of its usefulness to the human civilized groups that adopted it. This new type of scripture was fairly rapidly selected by the Hebrews and Greeks, and progressively obliterated early forms of scripture used in Egypt and civilized communities in the Levant and Europe.

Analyses of cultural traits, therefore, not only permits to determine affinities and differences among cultural supra-organisms, but also their evolution in time could be traced in the same manner that genetic evolution and descend could be determine in biological organisms.

APPENDIX II

Very revealing indeed is the analysis of the vicissitudes and further evolution of the nations emerging from the collapsed remnants of the Roman Empire. We have claimed that the modern nation, with defined frontiers and form of government, actually represent supra-cultural organisms in their own right belonging to the species Western European civilization; the successor to the illustrious defunct Roman ancestor. A cultural analysis of the historical evolution of Germany and France, at one time constitutive parts of the Carolingian Empire, will be helpful in the clarification of this point.

After the death of Louis the Child in 911 AD these lands, which were united under the empire of Charlemagne, began to follow separate political courses when the nobles of East Frankland refused the accept Charles the Simple from West Frankland as their emperor. No great differences were apparent at that time between these two states. Submerged in the depth of the Dark Ages, subjected to invasions and periodic harassments by barbarians and having to struggle with powerful feudal lords, the Capetians and Ottonians tried to hold to power with the help of the Church, which they attempted to wrestle from the control of the nobles. It appears that in the Germanic lands Otto I followed the lead of his father Henry but he was more successful than his predecessor, ultimately reasserting his control in the appointment of bishops and other prelates, even using the royal chapel as training ground for the applicants to ecclesiastic roles. As a result of his efforts, and the help of the Church, the strengthen Otto became the most powerful monarch of his time.

But ambition did not ended there, and soon he tried to procure for himself the title of Roman Emperor (held before by the Carolingians) after marrying the heiress to the throne of Italy. Once crowned by Pope John XII he became deeply enmeshed in the politics of Italy, whose wealth he intended to harness to enrich his extended empire. Otto's successors remained embroiled in the politics of Italy while the popes, with the help of the German nobles, also tried to stir problems for the emperors in their homeland. Under the Hohenstaufen's a protracted struggle with the popes ensued (to the point that Pope Innocent IV organized a crusade against Frederick II) and after many years and the death of Frederick II, with the help of Charles of Anjou brother of Louis IX of France, the Germanic domains in Italy and Sicily were finally conquered. On account of these ambitions and draining struggles away from the homeland, imperial power in the Germanic territories was considerably weaken, and the land became fractioned in several independent principalities with common tradition and language.

The case of France is different. Although originally confronting the same problems than their Germanic counterparts with the powerful barons, the feudal lords, and the need to turn back the onslaught of the barbarians invasions, the notion of belonging to one community sharing the same historical objectives began to take form slowly in people's mind, certainly helped by the enlighten reigns of Phillip Augustus and Louis IX, although the struggle with the barons continued under Phillip the Fair. Ironically, the protracted struggles against England in the XIII and XIV centuries, contrary to the contemporary disarray prevailing in their geographic neighbors, helped to kindle the flame of nationalism in France which emerged from the Hundred Years War as a united state.

While the Germanic Emperors tried with futile attempts to impose their will in Italy and the Papacy, in the process neglecting their own lands which they ultimately lost, the French, more conveniently after the death of Boniface VIII, brought temporarily a subservient and pliable Pope Clement V and his successors to a 'reprieve' in Avignon, where they adopted a general policy more in line with their 'hosts' wishes. Granted that this sojourn in France was only temporary, but the mere fact that it was possible indicate the political clout of the French kings at that time. This was clearly a quite different approach to the confrontational policy of the German emperors in dealing with the papacy, a struggle that lasted more than 300 years.

Can we detect, historically and culturally, any difference between these two engenders from the collapse of the Roman Empire to justify the thesis that they represent two different socio-cultural supra-organisms belonging to the species Western Christian Civilization? A search into history and a cultural comparative analysis might help.

The first thing to stand out is language. French is a well known Romance Language which was evolving for many years in the territory of what is today France corresponding to the Roman province of Gaul, which was in late antiquity occupied by the Franks, who did become thoroughly Romanized. German, on the other hand, evolved primarily from the dialects of the barbarians North of the Danube and Rhine rivers, which were the frontiers of the Roman Empire and whose lands were incorporated by Charlemagne to the Carolingian Empire in the IX Century. In fact as early as 842 AD, in a written oath taken for an alliance, both Louis the German and Charles the Bald sworn in the language of the other, which were already at that time early versions of French and German.

As far as religion is concern these two countries inherited the common religion of the Late Empire, but the subsequent evolution of Church institutions in these lands is quite different. Monastic life flourished in France as early as 910 with the Cluniacs and in 1098 with the Cistercians orders which soon founded houses all over Western Europe. The Germans however became enmeshed in the investiture controversy and the protracted debilitating struggle with the popes which they finally lost, leaving behind, as we have seen, a divided and embittered 'country' resentful and suspicious of both laity and ecclesiastic authority.

The Reformation impacted these French and Germanic lands very differently. It is conceivable that the 'ugly mood' prevailing in the latter has to do with the fact that a professor of the Bible in Wittenberg, rather than another similar accredited academician in some other of the splendid universities of Western Europe, initiated the momentous changes that forever transformed the face of the continent. Granted that will be reformers had appeared before in different parts of Europe. Attackers of the Church, particularly after the disgraceful 'exile in Avignon', took place throughout Western Europe during the XIV and XV Centuries: Like Marsilius of Padua, John Wycliffe in England and the luckless John Huss in Bohemia. Yet, their struggles came to nothing.

A completely different story was with Martin Luther whose ideas spread like wildfire, but at the beginning mostly in the Germanic lands and Low Countries. It is no coincidence that the most important reform centers at the time were Zurich, Basel, Strasbourg and Geneva, lead by men like Martin Bucer and Ulrich Zwingli. John Calvin is no exemption because, although born in France, he developed his reform program also in Switzerland (It has to be remembered that at that time Switzerland still was included in the Germanic territories). The case of the Anglican Church and its derivations is different because it was not created by a process within the Church itself, but rather by direct command from the King.

Protestantism spread widely in Western Europe provoking fratricidal struggles in XVI-XVII Century France followed by an impasse, until the nullification of the edict of Nantes in the XVII Century, during the reign of Louis XIV, put an end to the Huguenot threat. France emerged as the most powerful nation of Europe in a great measure thanks to the 'good office' of Cardinal Richelieu, while the Germanic lands suffered the catastrophe and devastation of the Thirty Years War, when according to some estimates it lost 1/3 of its population. The territory remained divided in principalities, some Protestants, like Saxony and Swabia and others catholic like Bavaria and also Austria, whose emperor inherited, since the early Renaissance, the empty title of 'Holly Roman Emperor'. It took Germany close to another two centuries to achieve political unity after excluding the Austro-Hungarian Empire from its fold.

In religion, therefore, there was also a clear divergence between France and Germany. While France emerged ultimately as a solid Catholic country, Germany became a mottle of Catholic and Protestant lands.

When it comes to art and architecture I find great difficulty in identifying clear cut differences between these two countries. There is so much cross insemination among them that the analysis is plagued with uncertainties. In architecture, for instance, we cannot speak of characteristic Germanic or French Romanesque and Gothic Schools, although the latter, as we saw, was born in France. This doesn't mean that there were not individual differences in style which did not survive their creators and, therefore, failed to leave permanent cultural imprints.

French Painting during the Romanesque Period had no significant departure from Carolingian models, but the effect is more decorative. That was not the case in sculpture which revived after the Carolingian interlude, first in Southern France where it was used profusely in the exterior of churches, like the impressive collection of carved figures in the cloister of Saint Pierre in Moissac, which include, mainly in the capitals of the supporting piers, diabolic and fantastic animals besides foliage designs and scenes from the Bible.

In the Germanic lands Ottonian Art was stiff and solemn, a mood that can be better appreciated in the illuminated manuscripts which evoke a mood of sobriety and grandeur to the observer. In the XIV Century there was some originality in painting, as could be appreciated in 'The Nativity' of the Grabower Altar in Kunsthalle, by Master Bertram, whose realistic and emotionally forceful style depart from the conventions of the prevailing International Gothic perhaps, according to some authorities, because of Bohemian influence after the visit to Prague of the Italian painter Tommaso da Modena.

French Gothic painting was mainly decorative and, like with its predecessor the Romanesque, the works display a flat perspective. It seemed to have originated in the illuminated manuscripts and gave rise to a prolific school of miniature compositions mainly of decorative intent, like those in the 'Book of Hours' of Queen Anne of Brittany. In the XIV and XV Centuries this style was heavily influenced by Italy, as could be seen in the ' Hours of Etienne Chevalier' and the 'Josephus' at the Bibliotheque Nationale of Paris, a work of Jean Fouquet who was known to have visited Rome in 1445.

French Gothic Sculpture was solid but, as it was said before, graceful and detached, the figures conveying a personal look as if representing true individuals. Many of the original works, mainly in churches, are anonymous. A well known sculptor was Claus Sluter who worked in Burgundy where he completed his 'Well of Moses', a work that exhibited all the attributes of this art.

As was the case in France, Romanesque and Gothic influences in Germany were strong and dictated the course of its art in the high Middle Ages. A typical example is the English Pilgrimage Altar from Master Francke in Kunsthalle, which display an International Gothic style with strong French influence. Interestingly, in Germany a curious

Romanesque sculpture, 'The shrine of the three Kings' in the cathedral of Cologne already disclosed classicist and naturalist features that foreshadow French masterpieces by more than half a century. Likewise in the apogee of the High Gothic, a group of statues in the cathedral of Naumburg display a realism presaging the forthcoming International Model.

During the Renaissance French Art was, like in the case of architecture, heavily influenced by Italian artists which also introduced into France the Mannerist Style (See below). Il Rosso Florentino and Francesco Primaticcio inaugurated the first school of Fontainebleau about 1532, which was followed less than a century later, by the second with the works of Jacques Bellange. In portraiture Jean Clouet produced realistic renderings, as could be appreciated in his 'Unknown Man' at Chantilly.

One of the factors in this early impact of Italian Art in France was the invasion of Italy by Henry VIII and Luis XII. Hybrid forms of Gothic buildings with Italian models became common in the late XV Century and, curiously enough, became more obvious in the French castles; the Chateaux casted away their forbidding façade and interiors proper of feudal castles, for the pleasant airy elegancy of Classicism. Italian influence was also seen in church designs, like in Saint Eustache in Paris. This was the time when the delicate elongated figures of Mannerism were introduced in France thanks to the auspices of Francis I, who continued the struggles of his predecessors for Italian territories against Charles V of Spain. Mannerism flourished in France for about a century. Its rejection of classic canons of taste and beauty could be appreciated in the ugliness and grotesque figures in the works of Bellange and Callot.

Such a momentous historical event as the Renaissance, however, could not fail ultimately to inspire Germanic artists. In architecture predominated decoration motives rather than a major stylistic form. Typical examples are the ceremonial entrance to the castle at Brieg by Jacob Bahr and the Ottheinrichsbau of the castle of Heidelberg. In painting, as in other places of Europe, German masters became preoccupied with the challenge of creating a feeling of space. Men like Multscher, Konrad Witz and Michael Pacher, among others, created vigorous, firm and in many ways realistic renderings, conveying an underlining mood of strong emotions that contrasted with the delicacy and almost poetic feeling of other contemporaneous work.

But it was during the XV and XVI centuries that a crop of highly talented painters 'saw the light' in the Germanic territories. It is hardly necessary to mention them. Holbein the Younger, Albrecht Durer and Lucas Cranach, among others, wanted to represent life as they thought it was: brutal, unforgiving, even vicious, like could be appreciated in the Isenheim Altarpiece painted by Matthias Grunewald, whose central panel reveal a torn body of Christ expressing all the horrors of the crucifixion, a far cry from the repose and serenity of other contemporary works. Some of the paintings of Cranach are considered intermediate forms between International Gothic and Mannerism, and the prolific genius of Durer rendered everlasting masterpieces not only in painting but also in woodcut, engraving, and decorative design . As so often happens this generation of genius left no worthy descendants, and painting in the Germanic lands declined in quality as well as in importance after these artists passed away. This situation has intriguing similarities to what is observed in the biological field, where characteristics acquired by a living organism may fail to be transmitted to their descendants, that is, they failed to be preserved in the genome of the species as mutations.

If there was something characteristic in this group of German artists was the clever use of Mannerism for the brutal frankness of their work helped by the proclivity for fantasy, the introduction in their paintings of demonic figures or otherworldly imaginary creatures. This tendency could be clearly appreciated in some of the works of Lucas Cranach the elder, like 'Saint George and the Princess' in the Uffizi Museum, Florence.

German sculpture was not as outstanding as painting was. Still in the XVI Century they were working in a late Gothic style. The most original sculptor was Veit Stoss who spent most of his working life in Poland. He was very proficient in carving wood, achieving superb results by giving the renderings a feeling of classical realism. Yet this art form was hung in the past and never prospered enough to achieved independence from traditional molds.

During the 'Le Grand Siècle' France grew to cultural preeminence and in fact replaced Italy in setting the pace in style and taste. Classicism and the Baroque struggled to impose their standards of beauty and excellence. In architecture this was the age when Francois Mansart built the Orleans wing of the Chateau of Blois and, of course, when the epitome of Classic taste, the Versailles Palace, was erected at a great human and financial cost by Le Vau and Hardouin-Mansart. In painting and sculpture Classicism was revived, revered, and its standards of excellence became almost 'sacred'. Charles Lebrun was pompously placed by 'The Sun King Louis XIV ' in charge of the reorganization of the Academie Royale de Peinture et de Sculpture, which set standards for painting and sculpture. Nicolas Poussin was the prototype of excellence for the Academy despite of the fact that he spent most of his life in Italy where he became inspired by the Venetian masters. Poussin painted placid bucolic settings based in mythological themes, like 'Cephalus and Aurora'. Some of his pictures had a strange statuesque quality resulting from his admiration of Classic Sculpture. Also representatives of this school were Claude Gelle and Phillipe de Champaigne. Toward the end of the century the influence of Anthony Van Dyck became strong, which served to soften the severe neo-classicism of the 'Grand Siècle'. Sculpture, during this period, was not too outstanding and followed a classical inspiration under the egis of the controlling Academy. Toward the end of the XVII Century Pierre Puget produced some statues with more expression and life in them.

Classicism and the Baroque were late to arrive in the Germanic lands because of the chaos created by the Thirty Year War and its aftermath. In architecture there were superb examples of this school but they were highly imitative of French creations, particularly of the Versailles Palace, which the European royalties, mostly in the Germanic lands strove to imitate. The Belvedere Palace in Vienna built by Johann Lucas, and the Schloss Castle of Berlin by Andreas Schluter are clear examples of this frenzy. Although late in arrival Baroque also clutched the land in its prolonged agony, and still was turning out outstanding examples well into the XVIII Century, like the Karlskirche Church of Vienna.

The XVIII Century in France began with a rebellion against the imposition of Classicism and a new taste for color. Rococo born in France stormed its native land also in the XVIII Century, soon influencing not only architecture but its elegance and delicacy spread to interior decoration, the arts, furniture and utensils. Chief exponents of this school were Aurele Meissonier and Gilles Marie Oppenordt. Antoine Watteau was one of the first to adopt this new technique which he applied to his 'fetes galantes'. The Age of the Rococo pervaded also representative art forms with its elaborated ornamentation and fancifully curved forms. In fact official taste was changing and the Academy under Boucher adopted the new standards. The works of Honore Fragonard and Simeon Chardin, whose still lives had a strong Dutch influence, belonged to this period. But toward the middle of the century there was a revival of Classicism. From this time dated the landscapes of Joseph Vien and the dramatic renderings of Louis David, like 'Death of Marat'. His disciple Dominique Ingres was a master of drawing and achieved fame with his portraiture, like the one of Madame Moitessier, and in fact became the typical representative of the Classical Style.

Like in France, in Germany Rococo soon became quite popular. The Abbey Church of Banz built by Johann Dientzenhofer was one of the first works in this style, and factories to manufacture the products to adorn the houses of the wealthy, like the porcelain factories in Meissen and Nymphenburg, became very prosperous. A master decorator was Francois Cuvillies who learn his trait in France, and whose unsurpassed achievement was the Nymphenburg Palace of Munich.

The following Romantic Movement in art again stressed color over form and movement over static balance. The 'Raft of the Medusa' is a typical representation of this style and a masterpiece of Theodore Gericault. His successor as leading exponents of this school was Eugene Delacroix. Not surprising, in view of the social turmoil of the times, his early paintings depicted violent scenes like his famous 'Liberty Leading the People', which was inspired in the Paris uprising of 1830.

From this time also dates the Barbizon School which believed that the painter should meet nature working outdoor rather than from his or her studio. Among its early representatives were Theodore Rousseau, Charles Daubigny and Camille Corot. Many in this school emphasized everyday people in their labors, like Jean Millet who portrayed working peasants scenes, and the caricaturist Honore Daumier who painted the workers of Paris. Gustave Courbet painted realistic pictures like the 'Funeral at Ornans' and the 'Painter's Studio'. The style of these artists was vigorous and above all unconventional, certainly not to the taste of the artistic establishment.

Later in the XIX Century there was a revolt against the rigid impositions of the stultifying Academy which was bound sooner or later to explode, particularly in the post-revolutionary ferment afflicting France after the downfall of Napoleon. Eventually disgruntled painters, like Edouard Manet and others, founded the notorious 'Salon de Refuses', in essence initiating a revolution in art by rejecting the asphyxiating pedantry of the 'academicians'. Soon followed the Impressionistic School which focused in the 'fleeting impressions of Nature', a revolution in painting, a dawning of a new taste with no comparison in modern history, at first bitterly opposed by traditions but ultimately embraced with passion by throngs of admirers in the Western World. The name and examples of painters of this school are too numerous and well known to need repetition. Claude Monet, Camille Pissarro, Paul Cezanne, Georges Seurat, among many others, are today almost household names. As so frequently happens in human affairs a reaction of a sort took effect, and again a group of painters searched for 'form'. Paul Cezanne was a pioneer of this group and his search for solidity, durability and balance made him to paint many times over the Mont Sainte-Victoire of his native land.

Paul Gauguin and Vincent Van Gogh were predecessors of what is call XX Century Non-naturalistic Art. To this latter group belonged Expressionism, Cubism and the Abstract schools. Henri Matisse and others with their violent, shocking colors, Georges Braque and Pablo Picasso, also working in France, with their distorted forms to stress their 'fundamental' components, and modern Abstract painters dealing in colors and lines divorced from any reality, are the representatives of these modern schools.

Ever since the Renaissance there has been a fundamental debate, not limited to France, as to what is the most important esthetic principle in painting: whether form and line as proposed by Raphael and Poussin, or color as affirmed by Titian and Rubens. The struggle of these opposing schools ultimately gave rise to the color apotheosis of the Impressionists and the final divorce of line and shape from reality in abstract painting.

German artists participated in the neo-classic and romantic

movements of the XVIII and XIX Centuries, but yet no significant departures from themes in other European lands took place. But in the XX Century German painters were very active in the expressionistic movements, founding in Dresden the group entitled Die Brucke to which belonged men of the caliber of Ludwig Kirchner, Max Pechstein and Erich Heckel among others. Also world famous in this school were Oskar Kokoschka and the sculptor Ernst Barlach. Worth of mention also is the Die Blaue Reiter group of Munich, to which belonged men of the stature of Paul Klee and Wassily Kandinsky.

Even before the split of the Carolingian Empire there was a genuine French literary genre in the Chansons de Geste. The works, written in the formative period of the French Language, consist of contemporaneous stories and deeds about Charlemagne and other personages of the times. The best known, of course, is the famous Chanson de Roland. Other narratives and styles followed, like the so-called Romances and the Fabliaux which described situations in human life, frequently of a comic flavor about individuals of any social status whether nobles or villain characters. In fact, it is claim that, many of the Canterbury Tales were taken by Chaucer from the Fabliaux. French Poetry, Prose and Drama all had their origin during the high Middle Ages. Closely related to the Fabliaux was the Roman de Renart, a collection of satirical stories from Northern France, and the Roman de la Rose, a love poem written in a satiric spirit by two different authors, Guillaume de Lorris and Jean de Meun. From this time also dates a remarkable historical chronicle, the 'Conquete de Constantinople' by Geoffroy de Villehardouin, which was called 'a Chanson de Geste in prose'. In the Early Renaissance (XIV Century) Froissart wrote his witty 'Chroniques' also about an historical event, and Francois Villon, reputed to be the best author of the XV Century, wrote his masterpiece 'L'Epitaphe Villon' and the 'Testament'. Villon was also a prolific author of Ballads, Rondeau and wrote realist poems about the Paris underworld.

The best known prose writer of the times is reputed to be Philippe de Commynes, who wrote among other compositions, his 'Memoires' in a personal clear style suitable to his purpose. Intriguingly, the best prose of this period is said to be anonymous stories about romances, like the 'Quinze Joyes de mariage'. These works are inspired in the medieval Fabliaux and the style is eloquent and engaging, prove of the maturity French Language was achieving at the time.

The first written records in a Germanic language appeared in the VIII Century. They mostly consisted of clerical writings about biblical stories and liturgical matters, many of them translations from the Latin. There was also an oral tradition similar to other places of Europe consisting of songs in vernacular (the Heldenlieder) extolling the deeds of heroes, mourning the dead, lamentations, hymns, etc.

In the next two centuries, as feudalism took shape in Western Europe, not only the German Language continued to evolve, but the vernacular grew into the then traditional forms of Epics and Love Lyrics sang by the wandering minstrels. Many of the works were inspired in French Epics, but some were original. This was the time when the Epic 'Nibelungenlied', the story of the hero Siegfried and the rout of the Burgandians, became enormously popular. This was also the times when Wolfram von Eschenbach wrote his masterpiece 'Parzival'. Lyric verses, the Minnesang, Prose and Drama were also heavily influenced by French standards.

During the Renaissance Francois Rabelais was a transitional figure in France. Some of his early stories recalled the Fabliaux. His biting sarcasm in the 'Gargantua et Pantagruel' stories not only amuse and entertain but are serious criticisms against the Church and some professions (In this some of his stories are reputed to be somewhat reminiscences of episodes of the Quixote). During the XVI Century the French Language reached maturity and its achievements surpassed those of contemporary European countries. In Drama there were many translations of Italian works and Etienne Jodelle wrote the first modern tragedy 'Cleopatre captive' and the comedy 'Eugene'. Robert Garnier also wrote lyrical plays and Pierre Larivey or Guinta was known for his comedies. Poetry, like in other countries, was very popular in this period. Among the best known poets were Clement Mariot, who excelled in mythological themes, Le Maire de Belges, the court poet Mellin de Saint Gelais and Victor Brodeau.

However, the most prominent poet of this period was Pierre de Ronsard who, together with other colleagues, formed a group called

'Pleiade' whose purpose was to polish the French Language to a level which will permit the writing of literary masterpieces comparable to the works of the classics. Ronsard himself was very prolific, writing in many poetic styles including Sonnets, Odes and Elegies. Other poets from the 'Pleiade' group also achieved renown with their works, including Joachim du Bellay and Remy Belleau.

The second part of the XVI Century was the period of fratricidal religious war in France which reflected in the literary works of the period. Theodore Agrippa d'Aubigne wrote Les Tragiques and Guillaume du Bartas wrote his epic of creation 'La Semaine'. In Prose there were also numerous storytellers including, besides the famous Rabelais, names like Nicolas de Troyes, Bonaventure des Periers and Noel du Fail, who wrote collections of short stories. As an essayist Michel de Montaigne reigned supreme.

The Renaissance in Germany, contrary to France, was not a time of intellectual ferment in literature. A courtly Renaissance in places like Rottenburg and Innsbruck, instead, revived interest in medieval chivalry. Humanism failed to produce any great original figures in the Germanic lands. Largely the movement became entrenched in the universities, and their works, mostly written in Latin, failed to reach the common people; even Drama was also plagued by the same defect. Satirical and sarcastic works were common, reflecting the deep displeasure of the people with church institutions and morality in general. In his 'Narrenschiff' Sebastian Brant delved into these problems, which appeared then far from resolution.

It could be that the commotion of the Reformation in the Germanic lands has something to do with the dearth of originality during this period, but the point is hard to establish. Political and social life was highly destabilized by the consequences of Luther rebellion for quite a long time. However it is claimed that his translation of the Bible from Hebrew and Greek sources enriched and enlivened the German Language which, despite of all the problems, had been maturing over the centuries as a literary vehicle, both for popular and scholarly works. Stylistically the language was been perfected and became important, as could be documented, in the works of Johann Fischer.

The XVII Century in France was a period of recovery from the religious wars of the previous century. Works in prose and poetry were numerous. This was an interlude of peace which reflected in the urge for placid and smooth cadence afforded by verses, like those of Francois de Malherbe and others. Fiction was also very popular. Typical representative of the age was Honore d'Urfe whose 'Astree' appealed to a wide variety of tastes. One of the reasons for this upsurge of interest in literary themes and of cultural endeavors in general, was the foundation during the reign of Louis XIII of the 'Academies', where diverse themes were discussed and standards of excellence established, including the perfection of the literary language. Certainly very influential in this period were the ideas of Rene Descartes, the versatile genius of the age.

The second part of the XVII was one of the most prolific periods of French literature. The public disturbances caused by the 'Fronde' strengthen the power of the Monarchy against the lesser nobility and the raising Middle Classes. There was a measure of disenchantment associated with a new realism and even cynicism pervading society. This was called the Classical Period, the age of authors like La Rochefoucauld, Bossuet, M Jourdain and others.

This also was the golden age of the Theatre in France. The country was already setting the pace in culture, manners and taste to the rest of Europe, but French Drama, after very humble beginnings, grew to world prominence in less than a century. Pierre Corneille and Jean Racine were revolutionizing Theatre with their realistic portrays of human passions and emotions, as well as, a quest for perfection, while the satirist Moliere amused and entertained the audiences with his representation of real human types. Poetry was also alive during this time. The works of Boileau in the burlesque genre and La Fontaine's 'Fables', with amusing details of the common and ordinary in life, are outstanding works in poetry.

The XVII Century which saw France converting into the epitome of culture and good taste was, as we have already seen, one of devastation and despair for the Germanic lands that saw their population decimated, their fields wasted and their country divided by the fratricidal Thirty Years War. No wonder that there was a general mood that stressed the transiency of everything human and the importance of the here and now. Stoicism, the urge to persevere regardless of the flickering fortune of the transient, became a popular attitude, and this general frame of mind, not surprisingly, pervaded literature also.

It was in Poetry that the soul of the German nation better expressed these feelings, greatly helped by the technical advances propitiated by Martin Opitz, who was instrumental in 'polishing' the verse and color the composition. There was an exuberance of religious and secular inspirations. Men like Paul Fleming and Paul Gerhardt, whose hymns are still played today, as well as, the works of Andreas Gryphius are but few examples from this period. But Prose also saw an upsurge of activity greatly helped by the maturing of the German Language which allowed a polishing of the style. Among the best were the works of Johann Beer and H J C von Grimmelshausen, who wrote with poignant realism about the Germany he knew.

As so often happens in human history, after the burst of talent in XVII Century France, there was a pause in the following one. Works in French, in all genres of literature, were numerous but they pale by comparison with their predecessors. Louis XIV has died and the Rococo age arrived. There was an air of frivolity and some relaxation of the fastidious standards of the previous century. Yet, there was considerable literary activity in all categories, including theater, prose and poetry. Pierre Bayle and Bernard le Bovier de Fontenelle, in their writings, attacked the social prejudice and intolerance prevailing in their times and so presaging at things to come. The works of Diderot, better known for being the editor of the famous Encyclopedia, and a few novels by the ubiquitous genius of Voltaire, like 'Candide', also dated from this period. This historic age also witnessed the growth of the autobiographical memoirs, like the one of the duc of Saint-Simon about his life in the court of Louis XIV, and the 'Confessions' of Jacques Rousseau, also renowned for his 'Social Contract'.

During the Enlightenment and helped by the new optimism, the belief in progress, the betterment of the human condition, and the emphasis in the primacy of Reason, the German lands began to recover from the disasters of the previous century. Literature became heavily influenced by English works and, somewhat belatedly, there was also a move, mainly in Leipzig, to introduce literary reforms according to French Classic principles. This soon led to resistance and criticism about the rigidities these norms imposed in exposition and in the free run of imagination. During this period F G Klopstock wrote in hexameters his 'Der Messias'.

The lure of Classicism, however, did not dissipated and in the Germanic lands it found its highest exponent in Gotthold Ephraim Lessing who, more than anybody else, was instrumental in the attempt to free Drama from the influence of French conventions and to recover what he considered the authentic classicism of the original Greek standards. Thanks to his influence German Literature gained a new stature and matured as an intellectual vehicle. His dramas, which he admitted were influenced by English Theatre, emphasized personal themes. Among his best are 'Emilia Galotti' and 'Nathan der Weise'.

The ferment of the Enlightenment with the outpouring of rationalistic ideas provoked a repulsion of conventional religion, both in France and the Germanic lands, and the socio-political upheaval impacted heavily in literature. In Germany it took shape a movement, the 'Sturm und Drang', rejecting Rationalism and French classic standards. This movement was imbued with the popular new religious conceptions of Pietism and the revolutionary ideas of Rousseau and Edward Young among others. Johann Gottfried von Herder, a disciple of Kant, expounded his concepts about the uniqueness of nations, and the repudiation of any notion that will contradict that idea, in the name of universal standards applicable to all men. The Soul of the German nation was clearly taking shape and defining its 'individuality'.

This was also the age of Goethe, who during his youth was also strongly impacted by the intellectual revolt of the age, and in time came to symbolize the new Ethos of the nascent nation, outshining and inspiring with his genius the works of his illustrious contemporaries. The literary exploits of Goethe are too familiar and popular to need recount: Dramas, novels and satire spun from his fertile imagination. Contemporary of Goethe, and also belonging to the 'Sturm und Drang', was Friedrich von Schiller, whose inspiring works, like 'Kabale' and 'Liebe', were examples of mastery of the language and more adaptable to the requirement of Theatre than those of his compatriots.

The youthful idealism of the 'Sturm und Drang' eventually burned itself in the political reality of the age. 'Literary Classicism' was then embraced. Freedom became freedom within the law after the disappointments of the French Revolution. This was, however, a mature age of literature in the Germanic lands, the time when Schiller wrote his masterpieces in Drama and Goethe his world renowned 'Faust'.

In France the chaos of the French Revolution and its aftermath was not propitious to intellectual activity, and literature in all its manifestations declined. It was after the fall of Napoleon and the 1830 uprising that the so-call Romantic Movement in art and literature took shape. There was less fear to think and to act and many people felt repelled by traditional ways of thinking. There was a backlash against Reason and outmoded standards, which many blamed for the national debacle suffered by France. Representatives of this new school of thought and action are many. In the Theatre Alexander Dumas, Victor Hugo and Musset do not need introduction. Novels, once the shackles of Classicism were thrown away, became intimate portraits of people, ideas and sentiments. Autobiography, historical, and psychological genres also became popular. Honore de Balzac, Benjamin Constant and George Sand, besides Dumas and Victor Hugo, are only few of those deserving mention.

The uprisings of 1848 and the censorship of Napoleon III were very detrimental to the Romantic Movement, which saw itself also attacked by the new mood of positivism embraced by the middle class, in a sense a longing for the lost world of the Enlightenment, an urge for 'objectivity' and 'analysis' proposed by men like Fustel de Coulanges and Ernest Renan. This new literary mood coalesced around the so-called Parnassian School, which wanted to 'save' poetry from the verbal and literary excesses of the romantics. Leconte de Lisle 'Poemes antiques' and 'Poemes barbares' are essentially longings for a lost world that seemed better by comparison to their present 'wretch reality'. Gautier, Baudelaire, Sully Prudhommme and Jose Maria Heredia were prominent contributors to the new school.

The new drive to maximize objectivity soon led to the belief that fiction should nevertheless embrace a canon of 'Realism', in other words that fiction should be based in the reality of everyday life. Gustave Flaubert 'Madame Bovary' and Jules de Goncourt novels about personages of real life are few typical examples of this school. Theater did not escape this urge. Victor Hugo 'Les Burgraves' and the famous 'La Dame Aux camelias' of Alexandre Dumas also belonged to this genre. The epitome of this literary undercurrent came with the so-called Naturalist School, which considered that novel and drama should serve ultimately a scientific end by studying the modifications of human temperament and behavior according to environmental changes. Besides Zola to this movement belonged the works of Guy de Maupassant, who achieved world fame with his numerous short stories and few novels portraying episodes in the life of common human characters, and what their behavior, in response to different challenges revealed about their personalities.

This infatuation with 'scientification' was going sooner or later to provoke a response. To this reaction belonged Karl Huysmans 'A rebours' which is a critic of esthetic taste, and Anatole France 'Histoire contemporaine'. Finally during this XIX Century rose in France the so-called Symbolic Movement in Poetry which stressed individual inner experiences, the unity behind apparent multiplicity of form which constitute outside reality. Many poets of this period could be classified as symbolist by their themes and sensitivities, even if they officially didn't subscribe to that school. Arthur Rimbaud was trying to find himself in his poems, like 'Une Saison en enfer', but unfortunately ultimately failed, which prompted him to abandon forever poetry. Stephane Mallarme was one of the major exponents of this school. His verses are reputed to have a melodic almost musical character.

The mainstream of thought in Europe saw no barriers and Germany was no exception. In the XIX Century A W Schlegel , an admired and translator of Shakespeare, argued that modern literature should deal with contemporary challenges and problems. His critical essays were normative to the new literary school. Not bound by the thematic restrictions imposed by classicism the romantic poets climbed an esthetic ladder that gave free ride to the imagination. Among its more ardent representatives were J L Tieck, who wrote comedies, novels and short stories, and J P Richter, who wrote novels emphasizing the problems accruing in daily life. Some of his novels, like the 'Hesperus', 'Titan' and 'Flegeljahre' became very popular. Romanticism in Germany was heavily impacted by the Napoleonic invasion and its emphasis shifted to historical matters and in a sense to patriotic themes. The works of E M Arndt and M von Schenkendorf belonged to this period. Heinrich von Kleist of Prussia, who was a leading voice in the patriotic movement against Napoleon, wrote plays, drama and short stories stressing the leading importance of the inner voice and feelings in human life. Other authors of repute were Zacharias Werner and T W Hoffmann among others. In following years the Romantic Movement in Germany, perhaps because of the exigencies of a new age, decline in importance, but a remnant of followers took intellectual refuge in Swabia, of which the leading figure was E Morike.

After the collapse of Napoleon and for the sake of avoiding another destabilization of the European 'balance' there was a reaction against many of the revolutionary ideals throughout Europe. In the Germanic lands the censorship imposed to many literary works proved tragic. This was a period of pessimism and disenchantment to many. To stray off the restricted orbit where a person conducts his life was to invite calamity. This is clearly reflected in Franz Grillparzer dramas of which his trilogy Das goldene Vliess is typical.

Lyric poetry in the Germanic lands found difficulties in plowing away from classical and romantic molds. So is the case with Heinrich Heine who became highly critic precisely of German patriotic romanticism. His masterpiece Buch der Lieder evidenced the conflict between dream and reality. Belonging to the same group of poets were Friedrich Ruckert and the already mentioned Eduard Morike. Many critics of the existing order and the clamping of liberties which were going eventually to lead to the revolts of 1848, saw their writings prohibited, including Heine himself, Karl Gutzkow and Theodor Mundt among others.

The social and political realities of the times, such as technological advances and urbanization, led many authors in Germany to embrace a realistic view of life. They extolled above everything else the 'here and now', in other words, to see the positive side of life, while others became highly critical of the social changes and labor conditions prevailing at that time. A school of literary history was then inaugurated. Friedrich Hebbel is one of the best known exponents of this school. His plays expressed the clash of the individual drives and urges with the conventions and restrictions of outside reality. His dramas, like 'Judith' and 'Herodes' are poignant and mastery in composition.

The close of the XIX Century saw in Germany, paralleled to France, the rise of the Naturalistic School which proclaimed 'scientific objectivity' as a fundamental principle, and in an unconventional way came to consider every angle of life, no matter how small and apparently inconsequential, a valid subject of literary attention. Typical exponent of this school was Arno Holz who in his 'Buch der Zeit' followed the lead of Emile Zola. The play writer Gerhart Hauptmann in his Vor Sonnenaufgang divested himself of any semblance of traditional compositional standards by creating a work with no plot, heralding the proliferation of styles and casting of conventions typical of XX Century art and literature. Not surprisingly, about this time and perhaps inspired in the Impressionist school in painting, rose a paralleled movement in Literature. It was a desire to bring up moods by lyrical contrivances.

At the turn of the XX Century in Germany, like in France, many authors also embraced Symbolism. Its center was in Prague and its main theme was a search for the Self in a rapidly changing world where traditional social standards were not valid anymore. By metaphor and imagination they tried to convey inner urges and moods incapable of easy verbalization. Rainer Maria Rilke melodious verses, Franz Kafka nightmarish and anguished novels and the works of others, like Max Brod, and Gustav Meyrink also belong to this group. Thomas Mann too used Symbolism for his literary ends. Among his masterpieces are the Buddenbrooks and the Der Zauberberg, a critical piece about the modern intellect.

France was in the winning side of the two devastating world wars. Like happens in other branches of art, XX Century literature in France, perhaps because of the advances in communication and publication, did become an amalgam of forms and styles that defy any classification and certainly are not specific of any given society. In general the convergence of tastes and intercourse of styles and ideas makes impossible to identify specific characteristics to a given country that will evolve independently of foreign influences. There is no predominant genre or conception but a profusion of novels, dramas and poetry.

The aftermath of the First World War in Germany witnessed the rise of a new literary school called Social Realism, characterized by sweeping indictments of the war. The works of Arnold Zweig and Erich Maria Remarque belong to this time. Subsequently, the rise of Nazism and the persecutions were not propitious to cultural endeavors, but after the Second World War there has been an outpour of literary works. German Literature was, understandably, buffeted by and trying to adapt to the catastrophe of two world wars and the need to find solace and a firm ground to serve as a basis of inspiration in a collapsing world of promises. The mood which already has turn inward tried to find permanent values in evocation of 'states of mind' to serve as refuge to the soul from the transiency of the here and now. This move was called, again parallel to a similar mood in painting, Expressionism. The plays of Johannes Sorge and Georg Kaiser are characteristic of this school. But, as is the case in France and essentially in the rest of what we consider 'The Civilized World', in Germany also there has been recently a proliferation of styles and works that defy the imagination, where everything is simultaneously transient and eternal.

The origin of French Music can be dated to the X Century with the Ecclesiastic School of Notre Dame. There was, as in other places of Europe, a Troubadour tradition of love lyrics and chivalry exploits to entertain the feudal lords. In the XII Century a type of song called the Motet performed by musicians called Jongleurs became popular. During the Early Renaissance Burgundy, which then included the Low Countries, became an important musical center. Chansons, Motets an Ecclesiastic Music were composed in profusion. This was the time of Guillaume Dufay who composed music in aqll, the popular form of the time. Also Guilles Binchois and Antoine Busnois wrote Rondeaux and other vernacular genres. With the arrival of Calvinism in the XVI Century French music suffered a period of stagnation and in the Protestant lands only translations of the Psalms were permitted.

French Opera had a beginning during the flowering or the arts in the XVII Century when France was ruled by Louis XIV. Italians operas had become popular and Jean Baptiste Lully produced operas in Italian style, a type of tragedy, to the taste of the 'Sun King'. The most popular French Opera of all times 'Carmen' of Georges Bizet was composed in the following century. Harpsichord compositions flourished with names like Jacques Champion and Louis Couperin. Jean Philippe Rameau, who published a book in music theory, also during this period, enriched orchestral music with the introduction of the clarinet. Also during this period a genre of secular vocal music, the 'air de cour', became very popular.

The XIX Century was also the Romantic Era of French Literature and the time when French Music reached its pinnacle of excellence with renowned names like Maurice Ravel, Claude Debussy, Jules Massenet and one of the most creative genius of the Age: Hector Berlioz.

In the XX Century, like in literature and other arts, there has been a proliferation of styles. Early in the century neo-Classicism was very fertile ground. Albert Roussel, who introduced Asiatic themes, and Pierre Boulez were prominent examples of this school. A new type of waltz, the so-called 'valse musette' became popular during this period. Technical innovations couldn't have failed in such a century, and a group of musicians composed computer assisted lyrics which they called 'Spectral Music'.

In the Germanic lands the equivalents of the French troubadours of the XII Century were the minnesingers. They were wandering people, mainly musicians pricing the deeds of heroes or narrating romantic stories. During the Renaissance German Music was enriched by styles, techniques, and instrumentation from neighboring lands, mainly Italy and France. In the XVI Century polyphony was introduced in the land and was used in chorales, mostly of protestant authorship. Interestingly Martin Luther himself was one of the leading composers of this style.

The XVIII Century witnessed in the Germanic lands an outpour of genius with no equal. This was the age of Johann Sebastian Bach and George Frederick Handel, who revolutionized music with his innovations for Choral Music, chamber groups and keyboard instruments. The rapidly expanded role of the orchestra, and the introduction of piano in place of the harpsichord, allowed for the elaboration of immortal masterpieces. Joseph Haydn, permitted by the rapidly expanding role of instrumentation, was then the originator of the musical genres called sonatas and symphonies. The prolific genius of Wolfgang Amadeus Mozart culminated, and in a sense capped, this incomparable Baroque Period in Germany. Mozart fertile mind spin-off a never ended series of compositions in all existing classical musical genres including concertos, masses, string quartets, operas and symphonies.

But the outpour of genius was not over. During the so-called Romantic Era of the XIX Century Ludwig van Beethoven and Franz Schubert were active. The former wrote unforgettable piano and violin concerts, symphonies and quartets, while Schubert created cycles of romantic poetry and music called 'Lied'. This was the age of Johann Strauss Waltzes and the compositions of Johannes Brahms, Robert Schumann, Richard Strauss and Felix Mendelssohn among others. In this century also Richard Wagner, who rejected traditionalistic styles in music, created the recurrent thematic recourses called 'leitmotivs' in his operatic masterpieces.

In the XX Century there was a 'parting of ways' between Austrian Music, which led by Arnold Schoenberg and others followed an avant-garde atonal path, and Berlin with a cabaret-like atmosphere exemplified by Kurt Weill. After the Nazi era and its aftermath modern German Music embraced unabashed the atonal avant-garde technique and 'modernism' in all its dimensions.

––––––––––––––––

It is in philosophy, I believe, that significant difference between German and French cultural manifestations becomes more clearly defined, perhaps because 'ideas' are fundamental constitutive parts of individual and communal character, therefore beyond the transiency and flickering nature of fashion, fads and ease to be adopted by different human groups, inherent in other cultural manifestations whether or not they belong to the same civilizational group. Because of this importance it will be necessary to make a brief outline, in those areas pertinent to our purpose, of the philosophical thought, and their exponents, both in Germany and France.

As we had seen, philosophy during the Middle Ages and early Renaissance was largely under the control of the Catholic Church and religious believes dictated all speculative theorizing. Because of the ecclesiastic sway over most of Europe there was no difference in philosophical positions among the different regions pertinent to our inquire. The Scholastic Dogma reigned supreme. However, in the Germanic lands proliferated a kind of Christian Mysticism whose more representative figures were Meister Eckhart and Jacob Boehme. Their beliefs were influenced by the conceptions of Theophrastus Bombastus von Hohenheim, better known as Paracelsus (a pseudome he used to indicate that he was better than the famous Roman physician Celsus), an alchemist and physician who thought everything in Nature was instilled with life, and who was also the founder of the Iatrochemical School. He subscribed, like the mystics, to the idea of Man as an 'autonomous microcosm'. Now, Paracelsus was not small town apothecary. He, like Luther, taught at the University of Basle, and also like him decided to set a bonfire with the books of traditional authorities in his profession (in this case Celsus and Avicenna) . The German mystics also believed that all beings in Nature were independent entities, rejecting the notion of hierarchical controls by superseding authorities. In medicine Paracelsus was the originator of the idea that diseases were vital entities or 'seeds'. That is, he gave the morbid processes nosological status.

We will begin our brief comparative analysis of philosophical concepts with the XVII Century Rationalists, who led the first attempts to free human thought from the impositions of scholastic religious dogma and the terrors of the inquisition. Born in France Rene Descartes had an accidental life. Besides his invention of Analytical Geometry his works in philosophy, as exposed in his 'Discourse of Method' among other publications, consisted in a reaffirmation of the existing world by resorting to his 'cogito', which he used to recover the reality of the world of sense experience after affirming that 'thought' has to have a substratum: 'The Mind'. Then and by a reasoning of scholastic flavor he concluded that if a mind conceives of God, then God should exist. From there to recover the material world of the senses it was an easy road.

Another French scientist-philosopher contemporary to Descartes was Blaise Pascal. In his short life he conceived his well known mathematical works in probability theory and the invention of the first calculating machine. In religion his work consisted of a series of notes written at different times of his life and published posthumously under the title 'Pensees'. As he originally intended, the writings are an apology for Christianity. Pascal conceded the impossibility of proving the existence of God by Reason alone, but urged the readers to bet on the existence of a supreme deity, indicating that if the believer was right that will translate in eternal bliss and if he was wrong he will experience only a finite loss.

Gottfried Wilhelm von Leibniz was the most eloquent and well known representative of the rationalistic move in philosophy of the Germanic lands. Born in 1648 he witnessed the violence and religious wars then devastating the country. His versatile genius encompassed many field of intellectual endeavor, including law, religion and politics among others, but he is more popularly known today for his works in mathematics, although his philosophical pieces are of seminal importance. As a good XVII Century rationalist Leibniz used Reason to 'prove' the existence of God utilizing in his Theodicy an argument which, again, resembles the Scholastics. He was widely traveled and spent time in France and England. His most popular philosophical work is a compilation written in French and published posthumously under the title 'Monadology', where he argues that the essence of all things were indivisible 'monads', created all at once but different among themselves, indestructible, isolated yet functioning and perceiving according to God pre-established harmony. These monads also were 'mirrors of the Universe' and 'windowless' which was supposed to mean that they lacked communication with the external world, that is, with other monads; but that universal harmony is kept by the intersection of God's grace. It is tempting to speculate that his notion of mathematical 'infinitesimals' was inspired in his conception of the monads.

Leibniz Epistemology is based in his classification of what is true as 'truths of reason' and 'truths of facts'. The truths of Reasons were those whose denial implied contradiction, while the truths of facts were those that, although true, their denial did not implied a contradiction. Propositions according to him were analytic, when the predicate is included in the subject, like 'all normal horses have four legs' and those when it is not, like 'John is a diabetic'.

The philosophical work of Leibniz is extensive. He strongly believed, like the Calvinist affirmed, that Man destiny was predetermined, but yet that somehow He should be held responsible for his acts. Leibniz also was in difficulty to account for the source of evil in a world created by a 'Perfect Being'. His invocation of a 'divine explanation' for whatever could not be accounted for otherwise is fairly common among other contemporary rationalist philosophers. It could be stated with confidence that Leibniz was a 'child of his age', but the concept of indivisible monads which were 'mirrors of the Universe' have a flavor that resembles the conceptions of the German Mystics and Nature-Philosophers.

The French Philosophers of the XVIII Century were not so preoccupied with the need to invoke God in their arguments. These were the philosophers of the Enlightenment that flowered mostly in

France after the death of Louis XIV, the generation that believed in 'human progress and perfectibility', those who subscribed to reason, liberty, happiness and progress. The names are many to mention all. The raising bourgeoisie embarked in an attack to the establish institutions of the Old Regime including the Nobility, the King, and the Church. 'Reason' was to discover the 'hidden law of society' in the same way that Newton and Kepler had discovered the laws of celestial motion and gravitation. The works of Voltaire, whose prolific genius and biting sarcasm set the tone for the Enlightenment, those of Montesquieu who tried in his 'The Spirit of the Laws' to apply the method of Natural Science to the study of society, the naïve hopes of Condorcet who believed in a future utopia when all men will be equals and lived together in peace and harmony, and the publishing of the enormous 'Encyclopedia' in 35 volumes by Denis Diderot against the will of the Church and Nobility, all expressed the belief in the power of Reason to search for solution to human and societal problems. The 'Encyclopedia' was supposed to be a compilation of XVIII Century human knowledge as seen through the eyes of the 'enlightened authors', with emphasis in the new advances and expectations of the Age.

But Diderot was not a pure rationalist. In his treatise 'Thoughts in the interpretation of Nature' he outlined what he believed was a way to true knowledge. Reason alone was not going by itself to accomplish that. For him the fundamental ingredient was 'experimentation'. He postulated that there were three stages in 'experimental reasoning': First the observation of Nature, what we might define as the empiric component, second 'reflection' by the mind, what could more properly be call the act of reasoning, and finally 'experimentation', when tests are design to prove or disprove the inferences drawn by the act of reflection and give rise to the interpretation of facts and true knowledge. The influence of Francis Bacon 'Novum Organum' is clear. The departure from the premises of the pure rationalists is obvious, but he, like all rationalists, accepted in his conceptions the existence of an outside reality unaltered by intervention of the human mind.

Jean Jacques Rousseau was actually a native of Geneva who appeared in Paris in 1742. He originally agreed with the ideas of the philosophes and knew Diderot, but ultimately disagreed with them. He hated the impositions of the then existing order of aristocrats, kings and

Church. Rousseau believed in the potential for 'goodness' of Man, but held that in a 'primitive isolation' Man was a savage dominated by the need to survive and care for himself, an amoral being but not necessarily vicious; what he referred as 'the noble savage'. Only in association with others humans Man acquired a sense of responsibility, and rational behavior replaces instinctual tendencies; in other words, there was need to associate for the common good. In this opinion he deferred with Locke, who believed that essentially Man was good and rational even before the formation of civilized society. Rousseau conception of an ideal society, as it was explained in his 'Social Contract', was that of a direct kind of democracy where men will meet face to face and decide what was best for all. There was no need for impositions from above invoking divine rights or any other ultra-terrestrial justification. Those in the minority, after a decision is reached, will then gracefully acquiesce as part of the 'contract'. Rousseau also, in his 'Emile', wrote about the nature of education. Some of the ideas outlined in this book were later incorporated into the national educational system of France.

Julien de La Mettrie was by profession a physician and an extreme representative of those materialistic philosophers who cropped during the Enlightenment and endorsed a 'mechanistic conception of Nature and the World'. He agreed with the notion that all world phenomena can be explained by the work of material components no important how small, but disagreed with the idea that the soul of Man was an immaterial principle that vitalized the body giving humans options and 'free will'. For him what we call the soul was not an intangible principle but the manifestation of the activity of material components, what we might refer as cells today.

La Mettrie in his work 'Man a Machine' eloquently mentioned how an intelligent Man can be turned into an idiot by disease, indicating that the soul is not a separate entity from the body but subjected to all the vicissitudes of living. He also pointed out how in the zoological scale intelligence and size of the brain are roughly correlated. Knowledge for him consisted of a comparison of sensory ideas in the brain, what he called 'imagination', mediated by language which was an invention of Man. Therefore for him, what we consider today psychological activity has an underlining material substratum. The necessity for an immaterial intangible soul dissipated in thin air. Because of his conceptions La

Mettrie was forced to leave France and by way of Holland he reached Prussia, where he was given asylum thanks to the 'magnanimity' of Frederick the Great.

Ettienne Bonnot de Condillac also was an admirer of Locke. He, like the English pace-setter, subscribed to the idea that all mental processes could be reduced to units of sensation from which interplay could be derived the normal behavior and intellectual life of Man. He accounted for the higher processes of the human mind, like comparing, classifying, analyzing etc., by what he called 'attention' which he considered a form of sensation, a term he uses ambiguously probably to signify the capability of the high association centers to focus in a given task. He therefore promoted 'sensation' to the highest throne of the intellect.

Auguste Compte was born in the chaotic aftermath of the French revolution, in a country torn by a passionate diversity of points of view as to the political direction the nation should take. His main purpose was to make sense about what was happening to society and what could be expected in the future. In his youth he was strongly influenced by the notions of his teacher Claude Saint-Simon and the inspirations of John Stuart Mill.

Compte conceived a societal evolution of three phases. The theological phase, when society is governed by a priestly class and Man 'invent' gods to explain Nature and his place in the World in a progressive animist, polytheist and finally monotheist phase. Man draws purpose and restrain from such an order. The next phase he called metaphysical, when Man turn against his divine creations and disembody them, converting his beliefs into abstract principles and eternal essences following the dictates of 'Truth' and 'Reason'. At this stage Man turn against the creatures he had created and the institutions that support them. When Man then revolt against the establish order and demand equality and public sovereignty, the community is threaten by disintegration and disorder. Traditional society is shaken in its foundation.

Western Man, according to him, has found a way out of this disastrous condition in science and technology, which, he thought, will give rise to a new 'positive' phase based in stable and permanent beliefs that will provide for a solid basis to society. Compte, curiously, thought that Man then will morally regenerate under a managerial class and the spiritual guidance of the 'positive philosophers'. Human behavior, he digressed, will also change, becoming more cooperative, less ambition and people will see the need to associate with others for the 'common good'.

Compte extended his classification of societal evolution to the stages in the progression of the intellect of Man, which, according to him, evolves through similar stages of theological, metaphysical and positive thinking. Man therefore is a reflection of society or viseversa. Facts, he claims with other contemporary positivists, need theories to make a sense of them. But theories need to be about facts, a quandary that is solved through theorizing, the ingredient provided by the intellect, a frame to make sense of the 'facts'. It is this theorizing what underwent the evolutionary phases of the mind.

Likewise the sciences evolve by way of similar transitional stages, each category being simpler but broader than the one that follows. According to him astronomy became a science before physics, physics before chemistry, chemistry before biology and biology before sociology, which he promoted to the category of a science and credited to show that 'the natural sciences are branches from a single trunk, thereby giving a character of unity to the variety of special studies that are now scattered abroad in a fatal dispersion'. These stages are based on the premise that the extension of a scientific discipline (how broad it is) is inversely proportional to the 'intension'.

Compte claimed that his purpose was to promote the unity of Man intellectual pursues. He hoped for the creation of a new type of scientific worker who would discover the general ordering principles of his field of expertise and relate them to the new discoveries.

Enlighten ideas, of course, were not exclusive of France during this period. Locke has written his 'Essay Concerning Human Understanding' in 1690 and Francis Bacon has extolled the importance of inductive reasoning. Their vision slowly did percolate the continent. No longer Man could be oblivious of what he perceived through his senses which they adduced was an important source of knowledge. Blind faith was demoted to the rank of belief and therefore considered unscientific.

Contributory causes to the 'Enlightenment', and the looming social political changes in France, were also the early stirrings of the Industrial Age with the demographic changes it gave rise to, the dismal condition of French Government and society after the draining wars of the

'Sun King', the widespread use of the printing press, and the cultural gatherings in the aristocratic salons which helped to disseminate the new ideas. The Enlightenment also had political consequences. The 'Enlightened Absolutism', inaugurated in Europe after the end of the seven years war was in many ways, the direct consequence of the ideas of the philosophes. Catherine the Great of Russia, Frederick the Great of Prussia, Charles III of Spain, Pombal of Portugal, Josephus II of Austria, and Gustavus III of Sweden were those who attempted reforms in agreement with the notions of the social thinkers, although in most cases they were half-hearted efforts that collided with the political realities of their societies. One other unintended consequence of the Enlightment was the abolishment (which lasted 41 years), of the Jesuits Order by Pope Clement XIV on 1773.

In the XVIII Century, in Germany, Immanuel Kant rebuttal to British Empiricism was a heroic and successful attempt to salvage Reason from the threat of irrelevancy resulting from the assault of the Empiricists, mainly David Hume, who famously proclaimed that 'There could not be a final prove of causality'. Much has been said about the meticulous compulsive professor who literally set the clocks of his native Koenigsberg. In his book 'Critique of Pure Reason' he attempted, by his own words, to make a 'Copernican Revolution in Philosophy'.

Kant began by agreeing with the existence of 'analytic' truths, those when predicates are included in the subject (like in 'birds have wings') and when its negation will lead to a contradiction. Synthetic truths were those when predicates are not included in the subject and can only be known to be so by sense experience. But Kant created in addition a new category, which he called 'A Priori Synthetic' knowledge, represented by truths that despite of being so (that is, when their negation did not implied a contradiction), nevertheless could be apprehended through the intellectual power of the mind without the intervention of sense perceptions. In this category he included mathematical and physical truths, which he hoped to have saved for posterity.

But to be able to apprehend these truths the mind needed what he called 'categories of understanding'. Events had to be perceived according to a frame of reference that included what we called 'Space' and 'Time', which he referred to as 'Forms of Intuition'. Kant fertile mind created many more categories, among which were 'Substance' and 'Causality', whose existence was denied by the empiricists.(It is intriguing to speculate that, after all, causality is implied in the internal organization of the nervous system, even in its most simple functional unit: THE REFLEX ARCH. The response to extreme heat applied to a hand or feet will lead to an instantaneous jerky motion away from the source BEFORE A CENTRAL CONSCIOUS COMMAND FROM THE BRAIN, as if nature realizes the deleterious consequences of a severe burn.)

Kant other works were less seminal, although still ethically important. In his 'Critique of Practical Reason' he endorsed the freedom of Man, the immortality of the soul and, not surprising, the existence of God. He also wrote about aesthetics and metaphysics.

It is quite obvious that Kant's epistemology was a valiant callisthenic attempt to save Reason from the attacks threatening to reduce the Western epistemological tradition to cruel insignificance.

The XIX Century saw in philosophy a reaction to the 'Rationalism' and 'Materialism' pervading human thought in the previous century and France was not an exception. Henri Bergson, with his concept of 'Elan Vital', the idea of life as a cosmic undivided movement underlining the apparent multiplicity of what we conceived as 'Reality', and the notion of 'Duration' as a true expression of time, which he viewed as an interpenetrated web of events giving rise to 'Creative Evolution', was the principal exponent of these conceptions in his country. His 'Elan' was not a mechanical material concept, but an impetus originating in life itself. Time for him was not a passive thing either but a real active entity 'biting into things'. Bergson falls in the group of thinkers who detested the mechanic and deterministic view of Science. He expounded the primacy of 'Will' over 'Intellect', and made Time and Change central to his system.

Johann Gottlieb Fichte was a transitional figure between the realism of the Enlightenment and the idealism that was going to dominate German philosophy in the XIX Century. On him the mutating ethos of the German soul is clearly discernible. He was a disciple of Kant and was particularly enamored with his conception of the 'Freedom of the Will'. But, according to Fichte, this concept was in conflict with the rest of his epistemology and particularly with the notion of a 'Thing in Itself' which, according to Kant, is unknown but the source of knowledge after transformed by Man's intellect, that is, by the categories of our understanding.

In his book 'The Vocation of Man' Fichte claimed that the mind creates the reality a person accepts. He doesn't deny the existence of an external world but for him it was unassailable to the human mind. This opinion was central to his system because it freed Man from the rigid determinism that such a conception implies. For him an independent external reality accessible to the Self was repulsive because he believed that sensations were only 'Modifications of the Self'. The external world could only be apprehended by the principle of 'Causality', which he believes to be unproven. An 'Object' of knowledge was, therefore, something personal, divorce from external existence.

Once the odious principle of causality is cast away Man is freed from the rigid determinism it implies. Fichte needed a way to justify such rejection and then posited a 'Subjective Idealism' as a way to access the inner world, a way to empower the self to 'Construct Freely' one's inner reality. But the need for an 'External Reality', and the existence of other selves in order to exercise his ethical urges, forced Man to transcend the limitations of knowledge of a putative external world Fichte judged impossible and therefore irrelevant. He, not surprisingly perhaps for an idealistic mind, found in FAITH the agent. For him, strangely enough, 'Knowledge' does not reveal reality. If it only represents knowledge of oneself and nothing more, then Man needed a more powerful agent to access a putative outside reality. For Fichte this 'Faith' is the true agent that permits humans to accept the existence of others similar to them with whom they could not otherwise intercommunicate. This allowed men not only to know but also to DO, which for him implied to achieve, to strive and to carry on one's obligation.

During his life Fichte transformed from been a rationalist in the Kantian mold to a dogmatic idealist. From embracing the principles of the French Revolution when his homeland was invaded by Napoleon, he became hateful, fanatically xenophobic and extremely conservative, to the point of endorsing an strict control of society by the State, a conception that made him years after, together with his colleague Hegel, 'darlings' of the Nazi movement. In Fichte the anti-rationalistic line that German philosophy was going to take later in the century became clearly manifested.

In Georg Wilhelm Friedrich Hegel the idealist movement originating in Germany reached its epitome. He proceeded with the attack on Empiricism, but disagreed in some important points from the opinions and positions of his contemporaries. Admittedly his writings are difficult and dense, yet he, perhaps more than any other philosopher of his time, had a profound influence in XIX Century and first half of XX Century history, in part as a result of the 'Materialistic Dialectic' expounded by his disciple Karl Marx.

Hegel believed that the Kantian separation of the mind and the subject of enquire is false and that they form a unitarian entity where 'the rational is real and the real rational'. He believed that the creative process had three stages: abstract, dialectic and speculative. In the abstract stage every element or product of thought is view in isolation, that is, 'abstracted' from any context and having an existence of its own. In the dialectic stage it is realized that there is no existence in isolation, that in order for something to 'be' it has to be related to others. In the speculative stage the Mind finally realize that what appears as metaphysical opposites could somehow be reconciled. He rejects the notion of 'causation' because he believed that any cause has an effect and there is no such a thing as 'First Cause'. For him speculative reason only can effect reconciliation between these apparent contradictions. A similarity to some oriental beliefs is clearly present.

The 'Logic' of Hegel is complicated and obscure. It consists of three parts: the doctrines of Being, Essence and Idea or Notion. The doctrine of Being is an analysis of what is the basic stuff of Reality and is intimately related to the other doctrines. In the doctrine of Essence he concludes that when the immediate nature of Being is analyzed by the intellect to search for features satisfying to the Mind, we come to realize that this could not be done in isolation, but only by comparing its 'essential features' to others. But this Hegel find incomplete for the final categorization of Being. This he does with his doctrine of Notion or Idea, a conception very difficult to grasp. He considers this Notion a reconciliation of the other two doctrines. Being, he claims, should be known not only for itself but in-and-for itself. If Being is a qualitative condition, in other words what makes something different to others, Notion is a 'Quantified Quality' or measure. In his dialectic Hegel has gone from the universal to the particular and finally to the individual.

Hegel philosophy of History is based in a rhythmic dynamic that has been popularly known as the triadic 'Thesis, Antithesis and Synthesis' which refers to his categories of 'Idea or Reason', 'Nature' and 'Spirit'(a concept that has intriguing similarities to the 'Logos' of the Stoics).The Idea he describes as the 'powerful essence', the formative principle. The primary category of Nature is space and the primary category of Spirit is time. The working of the Spirit wrestles the Idea from Nature and become temporalized. The goal of history, he claims, is the actualization of Spirit as freedom, wresting itself from the trappings of Nature to seek reunion with itself as Idea, a self realization of his 'Ideal Being'. Obviously the Ideal Being is part of the Spirit, an alienated part of It, sequestered by Nature but in the process of self realization the Spirit frees the Idea from bondage, subordinates Nature to his Will and in joining the Idea attains self-consciousness. That explains the aim of History. It is a constant dynamic process, a cosmic battle that resembles the struggles of mythological heroes against the tectonic powers engendered by mother Earth.

For Hegel, the embodiment of universal freedom is The State, understood not as a political system but as the sum total of its cultural expression like art, religion, philosophy etc. It represented a totality that pursued its own aims. That was what freedom meant. Individuals exist for the sake of this State; they are means toward an end. In the dialectic of the development of historical consciousness Hegel makes a review of past and present cultures, and concludes that the German Spirit embodies the most cherish ideals, and it is where the individual can find genuine fulfillment of their passions and interests by unification of 'the objective idea of freedom with the particular subjective passions of mankind'. Subjective freedom, he claims, could not be realized until it finds its place within the State.

Karl Marx is too well known to need introduction. Some authorities do not count him among the philosophers but rather consider him a social critic. His works, however, included a coherent corpus of novel views about society and history, which unquestionably represent harmonious and original philosophical conceptions forming a powerful system to understand the problems afflicting the societies of the times, and afford potential cures. There is not any other philosopher whose ideas have had a similar impact in the industrialized societies of his time.

Marx was a disciple of Hegel from whom he inherited the idea that history was a dynamic progressive process toward a goal. While for Hegel the prime mover was the Spirit with his freedom extricating the Idea from the sequestration of Nature and effecting by this mean a synthesis that determined the course of history, for Marx it was the different modes of production throughout the ages what determines the course of human history by creating a new 'Mode of Consciousness'. He proposed that a material rectification of the ills of the industrial system was what will achieve the goal of advancing the course of history by correcting, by a process of class struggle, the social iniquities of the times. Contrary to Hegel's conception for him the socio-political and even religious evolution of society are a consequence rather than a cause of the way the material production process, including labor conditions, is organized.

According to Marx a system of production will reach a point of maximal efficiency before the 'internal contradictions' and problems which will threaten it are manifested. This systemic problem is what explains the 'growth and bust' dynamics of capitalistic societies. It is only by avoiding the excesses and improving the working conditions that a 'synthesis' of a sort is effected, a process that had been coined 'Dialectic Materialism' by other authors. (Marx never used this term).

The further course of Marx ideas is too well known to need any comments. It is only fair to say that he didn't have the faintness idea as to where his thematic conceptions were going to lead in the XX Century. There was one factor he failed to include in his equations: HUMAN NATURE.

Arthur Schopenhauer, a contemporary of Hegel and Fichte, had the temerity of scheduling his lectures in the University of Berlin at the same time that his illustrious compatriot Hegel, with disastrous consequences for him. He was highly critical of the philosophical systems and patriotic rambles of his two colleagues, which he considered politically motivated and in a sense self serving. In many ways he defended the Kantian philosophical postulates with some modifications. Schopenhauer agreed with the notion that raw sensations are processed by the mind using space, time and causation, which for him replaces all other 'Categories of the Understanding' proposed by Kant, and then transformed them into perceptions or 'Ideas'.

In his seminal work 'The World as Will and Idea' he claimed that the conscious mind, from sense effects related to his own body, infer the existence of other bodies. By this conceptualization the ideas are formed. The mind by way of the understanding can therefore create a world of ideas that will nevertheless remain dormant unless an external reality will intervene to make perceptions possible, giving rise to phenomena related to each other by the category of Causality. Therefore it is the human understanding what renders the world intelligible to the mind by way of the process of categorization. But human Reason permit Man to formulate abstract ideas and concepts that allow him to rise above the mere perceptual categorization and then to transcend this reality and achieve an state of contemplative attitude, an state of ecstasy removed from basic emotions that the passions of the 'Will' engenders.

When it comes to understand the reality behind the world of appearances Schopenhauer returned to the concept of the self view as an object, that is, knowledge of the external world based in the experience or knowledge of oneself. A person can perceive his body as an Idea subjected to the same laws as other bodies, that is, cause and effect, or as an act of Will which produces an autonomous ' movement of the body', an independent act removed from the change of causality which gives Man its freedom and responsibility.

Schopenhauer considers the body as 'Objectified Will' because an act of Will results in movement of the body which itself is an Idea. This Will is prescient in all things, a force that makes them what they are, not only in particular events but in immutable universals beyond causation. 'Noumena' the underlining primeval stuff of the world of ideas, we know is a world of Will, beyond the world of perceptions, yet very real.

The Will however has its demoniac character, it creates a world of desires and wants that can never be satiated and is the source of much suffering and frustration. Man can rise above this world of wanting by an 'inner disposition' that free him from this condition and elevate him to a realm free from the Will, a transcendent state of peaceful 'aesthetic contemplation' of things in themselves no longer subject to causation. The similarity of these beliefs to mysticism in any religious denomination is clear. The resemblance of the Will to the generative principle of the 'libido' in Freudian psychology is also very real.

Another contemporary of Fichte and Hegel was Friedrich Schelling who began by agreeing with the ethical conceptions of his colleagues, only to disagree later on and accept the existence of an outside reality which could only be apprehended by speculative and intellectual intuition. He did not accept that morality is the highest point of subjectivity. For him Mind and Nature both work in similar ways, but the Mind does it deliberately while Nature does it unintentionally.

In an attempt to reconcile the objective and the subjective worlds Schelling returned to the concept of Ideas, the only medium where this union could be effected, but only if these Ideas could be the source of the finite Self and the finite World. In a difficult metaphysical exercise he then claimed that considering that the Ideas have to be necessary and free they can drift away from its origin, because of their 'freedom' to transform into the objective phenomenal world, and therefore fell from the unity with God, the only solid anchor of the Ideas. In a final group of lectures Schelling delved into the nature of God and concluded that it could only be known through experience, something to which many mystics will agree on. Schelling together with Lorenz Oken was one of the originators of the Nature Philosophical School.

Friedrich Wilhelm Nietzsche works are hard to categorize. He is accepted as a philosopher but could be considered as well a moral and religious critic. Many of his contemporaries detested what they believed to be his rude and impolite manner of attacking the traditional and comfortable set of values and conventions of the XIX Century bourgeoisie society. He denied the claim that the ultimate end of society is material prosperity and comfort. Sarcastically he dubbed this belief 'shop-keeper mentality'. In fact he called utilitarian ethics 'pig philosophy'.

Like many other philosophers and political thinkers of the following century Nietzsche scorned at acts of collective action and social mobilization. He conceived the possibility of the perfectibility of Man, the need of a new kind of human who could realize his capacity by transcending his condition and rise above the herd-like mentality of society: what he called the superman. In his work 'Beyond Good and Evil' he claimed that concepts like 'Good', 'Bad' and 'Evil' arose 'by spiteful trans-valuation of classical values by the meek and lowly'. He blamed squarely Jewish and Christian theologians for considering as 'Evil' some biological functions 'fundamental to creation and strength'.

Nietzsche dug into the basic constitution of human behavior and discovered as a primary motivator of human actions 'the drive or will to power', the zest to live creatively and even dangerously; a principle that should shake in its foundations the set of values imposed by Christian Morality. The dynamic ever shifting nature of life required a continuous change in valuations. There are not absolutes. He claims that the intellectual pursue of pure knowledge could decrease the critical capacity to live and make decisions.

Nietzsche father was a Minister and the passion and fervor he displayed in his beliefs in many ways has a religious flavor. He is famously reputed for the assertion that 'God is death', killed by the age of Science and modern materialism. Not being able to find the needed solace and mental peace in traditional religion Nietzsche found solution for the urge to immortality in his theory of 'eternal recurrences'.

The attack to 'classical reason' continued unabated in the first part of the XX Century, strangely enough, this time by a mathematical student called Edmund Husserl, perhaps as a reaction to the advances in science and technology that were threatening to swept aside the relevance of the old and venerable discipline of philosophy.

Husserl preoccupation with the nature of what reality is and of how could we obtain true information about it led him, like to Descartes before, to a position of systematic doubt toward traditional conceptions about what is known and could be known, including the possibility of non-existence of an 'outside reality'. Phenomenology, as he defined it, was a presupposition-less science. It was the root of the 'existentialist' movement of the first half of the XX Century.

The sciences, according to him, are dogmatic because they do not examine the condition that make knowledge possible, in view of the fact that the categories used to analyze natural events are unsuited to take account of conscious events. The reason for this, he declared, is because consciousness itself could not be explained in term of natural causes in view of the fact that we ourselves, and the laws that regulate our behavior, are also part of our experience. Husserl claimed that we should suspend all preconceptions about the world that surround us, that is, to 'suspend judgment' because of the possibility that our perceptions of a real outside world could be deceptive hallucinations. He claimed that the only things 'real' for us are, from the phenomenological standpoint, 'a nexus of experiences of perception and the emotions such perceptions have in us'. In doing this we perform a 'phenomenological reduction', what the Greek philosophers used to call an 'epoche'. Having done this a second reduction should be done in order to discover their 'essence or absolute form and structure'; what he called 'Eidetic Reduction'.

But in any act of perceptions it is needed a 'perceiver' and the thing 'perceived'. The first he called 'Noesis' and what is perceived 'Noema'. Husserl then applies his method of reduction reflectively to the perceiver and discovered the deep eternal essence of the self.

Martin Heidegger was a disciple of Husserl, and originally adopted the phenomenological method of reduction of his illustrious predecessor in the University of Freiburg to describe human nature or 'presence', what he called 'Dasein'. He hoped by this to return to the basic constituents of 'immediate experience', the fundamental data as they 'show themselves'. Heidegger considered that the ontological content of philosophy was Being and by his phenomenological analysis of the essentials of the 'Dasein' it is discovered what he describes as the experience of 'Being in the World'. By World it is understood not a passive physical outside reality, a container of a sort, but a 'field' of activity where Man is engaged, a self-World of concern and participation that exist as long as there is that concern. Man need to be actively engaged in a profession or labor of any kind or even involved in a love affair, in other words engaged in the world in order to 'be in the World', what he called 'existential participation'. Heidegger claimed therefore that the World is constitutive of Man's being, in other words, that the Cartesian subject-object dichotomy is fallacious.

The World of 'Being in the World' is structured in various different 'existential modalities'. The 'Environment' is the region where the tools or objects Man uses in consecution of his purpose are, what he called the 'instrumental world'. Heidegger here makes a difference between been 'at hand' when an instrument or tool is view as a task related object and 'on hand' a term that refers in this case to the physical characteristics of the object in question.

The 'Communal Modality' refers to the gregarious nature of Man.

In general he claims that Man lives in an inauthentic state of communal mode: the anonymous one. In this state Man's self is depersonalized and reduced to the condition of a 'on hand' object, a tool for the benefit of others that deprives himself of his 'existential freedoms' which are absolute requirement to live an 'authentic life'. In this state Man becomes depersonalized, dragged by the boring habits and conventions of everyday existence, a condition of humble acceptance which could be summarized as a following of prescribed social codes. What is lacking in this mode, Heidegger claimed, is 'concern'.

A Man by his 'factuality' realizes that he has been thrown into this world without his consultation and that he has to accept this imposition as a fact. This is his destiny. By his 'existentiality' Man apprehend himself as a possibility. He is a free and responsible agent full of potentiality to redefine himself. If 'factuality' is rooted in the past, 'existentiality' is rooted in the future. 'Fallenness' is the dangerous tendency of Man to enmesh himself in his daily toils and divert himself from his future possibilities.

Heidegger claims that 'the ground determinant' of the human situation is 'anxiety', cause by the confrontation of Man with his finitude, that is, with 'nothingness'. He claimed that this concept could not be apprehended by 'theoretical intentionality' because pure thought is only related to specific objects, so consequently this nothingness is only conceivable at a 'pre-theoretical level' of understanding. Confronted by the fact that he cannot escape his finitude, that he has nowhere to hide, Man has to adopt an attitude of 'being into death' and 'reaffirm himself with the whole of his being at every decisive moment' instead of adopting an attitude of denial.

Heidegger held that there is a 'trans-moral concept of guilt' resulting from our necessity to choose among different alternatives and possibilities in our life. Man authenticity depends of the capacity for 'resolution'. Man has to behold himself in his existential time, accepts his past, appraise his future possibilities in light of his physical finitude and choose his path with his 'whole' being.

Karl Jasper was another German existential philosopher who was highly critical of the 'system builders' like Hegel. He considered that the way to truth was not to objectify reality but in essence an act of introspection, a self reflection. Reality was a 'penetration to the depth of the self'. Central to his conception was the idea of 'Existenz', which defied description because it did not refer to anything that could be apprehended in a final form by the human mind because it was constantly changing and becoming, always 'on the way'.

The basic substratum of our 'reality', that beyond determinate being or conceptualized reality is the Umgreifende, a German word that approach the English 'Encompassing', the unknowable presence behind identifiable Being and beyond any conceptualization. This encompassing has two modalities the 'Being-in-Itself' and the 'Being-which-we -are'. This last is what he took as starting point of his philosophical inquire.

This 'being-which-we-are' he divided into 'empirical existence', 'consciousnesses' and what he called the 'Spirit'. At the empirical level of existence Man view himself as an object among other objects and therefore as a 'datum', therefore accessible to analysis by any scientific discipline. Consciousness could refer to the particularized living consciousness and therefore still attached to empirical reality, or consciousness as such which open to Man the realm of 'Ideas' of eternal permanent validity, a conception that clearly goes back to Plato metaphysic. For Jasper 'Spirit' meant the principle of unification of the empiric component and consciousness. It is an integrating element of the self.

The 'Being-in-Itself' is not known directly but only through the 'Being-which-we-are' and has one of his roots in the 'World', understood as the realm of appearances that present themselves to inquire. This world can never be apprehended in its totality and its boundaries are always beyond our reach. The other root is 'transcendence', a component of the 'Being-in-Itself' which lies beyond any possibility of been known, an elusive indefinable reality.

'Existenz' incorporates all the modes of 'Encompassing' and reaches the depths of the Self. It can only be approached by what Jaspers calls 'concrete elucidations' which is beyond any definition because it is potentiality, the possibility of a decision for which Man is responsible because of its freedom. This is what Jasper calls the 'individual historicity', what makes a man unique.

According to Jasper Encompassing has its root in Reason, but a Reason that has not the conventional meaning we ascribe to this term. In his philosophical conception Reason includes not only the rational element of thought but also the irrational component; it is a revelation of the unity of Universal law but remains united with Existenz. These two elements of our Conscience are inextricably associated. Reason by itself becomes 'empty intellectualism' and Existenz by itself gives rise to irrational striving, the passions that unchecked could drive the individual to his own destruction.

Central to Jasper conceptions is the human need of communication with others. In fact for him to exist is to communicate because 'no man achieves his humanity in isolation'. For him truth and communication are inseparable. In our empirical existence, he claimed, truth is not absolute but a temporary thing constantly in a process of change, but in the communication of oneself with his Spirit there is a timeless dimension and the possibility to apprehend universally valid truths.

Jasper accepts that there are communications among different Spirits as long as there is a 'common agreement as concern the order which comprehend them'. Existenz also can intercommunicate with each other. They will retain their empirical mode but reach beyond in a 'loving struggle' to communicate the 'inner most meaning of its being'. According to him existential communication is communication among 'irreplaceable persons', and it is by means of this type of communication that the self comes to 'a full consciousness of itself as a being qualified by historicity, uniqueness, freedom and communality'. Reason, he claims, has an important role to play in existential communication as a bond between the modes of Encompassing. When empirical existence is absolutized the essence of Man is lost and he is reduced to simple animality. When conscience is absolutized it result in 'empty intellectualism', a 'wooden culture' of a sort, that is, intellection and creativity are sacrificed to a 'communal substance'.

In the XX Century France experienced in its own flesh the horror of two world wars and Existentialism, in its atheistic version, became fashionable, mostly during and after the Second World War. Its most popular exponent in France was Jean-Paul Sartre whose ontology has points of similarities with Heidegger conceptions. For him being is trans-phenomenal in character and 'overflow' any boundary Man want to attach to it, that is, escape any conceptualization by the human mind. The fundamental being, so expressed, has two components or modes: the 'Being-in-Itself' and the 'Being-for Itself'. The former is the given, amorphous, complete, impervious to change, roughly comparable to objectified reality. The latter is however incomplete, fluid and structure-less, akin to human consciousness. The Being-for-Itself depends for its existence in the Being-in-Itself and comes into being by an act of 'inhalation' of the former. According to his difficult ontology Sartre states that Being-for-Itself emerges as a nothing that 'lies like a coil in the heart of being, like a worm'. This act of separation, therefore, generates the concept of 'Nothingness' which is fundamental in his system. It is not an abstract idea but a real thing dependent on being for its existence and central to his philosophy. This nothingness brought into the world by Man he claims to be the source of freedom. In fact, as a good existentialist Sartre claims that this freedom is the nature of Man, a defining characteristic of him and inseparably couple with 'anxiety', the mode of being of freedom.

Sartre classifies consciousness as non-positional and positional. The former which he also called pre-reflective is that which the self 'experience as presence' or simple awareness, and the positional corresponds to the Cartesian reflective consciousness of intentional character, and its object of interest could be the external world, or the self; in a sense a discovery of the ego. Both the world and the ego are therefore bound by the 'projective activity' of the for-Itself. One cannot exist without the other. Like Heidegger Sartre believes that Man find himself thrown into the World. The way he put it is that because of his 'facticity' the for-Itself apprehend itself as 'a hole in the heart of being infected with nothingness abandoned into the world without justification but still animated by freedom.'

Central to Sartre metaphysical theorizing is his concept of 'The Other'. 'The Other' is a need of the for-Itself to realize and know itself. Any reaction of being with other putative beings reveals something about us. Pride, shame, compassion and human emotions in general cannot be understood in isolation, but only in reference to others etc. This 'Other' is instilled with meaning by 'situations'. Gestures and actions in isolation are devoid of meaning, which needs an appropriate context. A laugh can have many meanings in isolation: it could express happiness, nervousness, even sadness or mockery. Only a specific 'situation' will instill it with appropriate meaning.

According to Sartre, Man had no essence; what He Is is what he does with his life, that is, with his existence. Central to this notion is the predicate that Man is absolutely free to choose. Even if a man is subjected to torture it is his decision to cooperate with his captors or not. God is a fiction and Man is alone in the Universe, that is the source of his fears and anguished condition. According to this school the important thing in life is not material prosperity and the pursue of happiness, as the materialistic philosophies proposed, but to do what one thinks to be proper according to his or her conscience; in other words to live an 'authentic' life. Finally Sartre was the originator of what is called 'Existential Psychoanalysis', which differed from the widely known Freudian one in that the latter search for a libidinal basis to be found in the past history of the subject, while existential psychoanalysis broad their search to include not only the past but also the future projects of the individual. Sartre claimed that the irreducible minimum of man's strivings is the 'desire to be', that is, to attain identification with the in-itself to convert into a in-itself for-itself, a union that can be properly identify with God, which for him represents the fundamental striving of Man, one which is destine to fail because the self can only lose Itself as for-Itself.

Maurice Merleau-Ponty was another French philosopher of the first part of the XX Century whose theories were based in a phenomenological starting point. He however considered that perception was a fundamental epistemological data but not conceived as the Empiricists did as a 'bundle of sensations'. His position was also far from the Idealistic point of view. Merleau-Ponty contention was that what he called 'perceptual consciousness' are the primary structures, our avenue of access to the true reality that underlie all further elaborations of the mind, in other words, are the building blocks of what he called 'intellectual consciousness' . These 'primary structures' are for him the phenomenological basis of perception. Perceptions, on the other hand, were not a passive collection of data but 'a sensory-motor behavior ', the world of human consciousness before any reflective thought.

But Man lives in a cultural and social milieu and there are different levels of experience that are perceived in their 'irreducible specificity' of qualitative distinctive characteristics. Merleau-Ponty then believed that in all aspects of human endeavors there are these experiences which could be categorized as fundamental structures of perceptual consciousness, but 'enriched' and consequently irreducible to perceptions as 'such'.

Gabriel Marcel was another existential philosopher of the first half of the XX Century. As he explained in his voluminous work 'The Mystery of Being' he develop an approach where the fundamental entity of discourse is what he called the 'involved self', not an abstraction 'in a privileged Olympus of the Spirit', a global and all inclusive perspective or an objectified reality of a sort (as in other existential works), but rather something 'concrete' involved in world affairs, an itinerant being, a wanderer through life. He agreed with Sartre in the notion that there is no such a thing as an abstract essence of Man divested from the concrete which had any absolute validity. Man is a situational being, that is, inextricably associated to its situation. For him the philosophical task is to study Man in his situation.

Marcel shared with others XX Century thinkers the fear that modern Man is in peril of losing his humanity in the increasing regimentation of society, the fear to be reduced to an impersonal number, a replaceable object. He considers that the fundamental task in philosophy is the search for the true Self through 'reflection'. He defines two levels: one is the analytical primary reflection that 'dissolves the unity of experience' into its elemental components, an objectified realty capable of scientific analysis, and another is a recuperative secondary act of reflection when that unity is reestablished, what permits Man to know the 'depths of the Self' and recovers himself 'in act', instead of apprehended as a passive subject; what he called 'existential indubitable'. Body and Mind form an inextricable union. 'Body-he claimed- is not my possession but is part of me'.

Central to Marcel thought is the notion of 'participation'. In the same way that mind and body are inextricable parts of the Self, when a person submerges himself in a worldly task he and the material substratum of this task becomes parts of a whole. He offers the examples of a peasant and his land which reach a point they are part of each other. For him existence is participation. The ego-centric life diminishes existence. Closely related to this notion is what he call 'encounter' which for him meant to acknowledge other individuals as persons.

Finally Marcel defines what for him are a 'mystery' and a 'problem'. The former is something subjective, something that 'transcend any determinable technique', while a 'problem' is something amenable of being manipulated and fixed. When we try to reduce a mystery to a problem its significance disappears. When the mystery of evil is objectified and converted into a problem it is falsified. Finally Marcel as a good existentialist has to comment on the notion of freedom. For him it is an inward awareness of the self capability for commitment to action, whether conventionally or ethically, good or bad.

Albert Camus had a trouble and short life. His mother was half-mute and his father died in the First World War when he was still young. Struggling with poverty and disease he, nevertheless, was able to complete his education and became politically very active, joining for a while the Algiers Communist Party and subsequently becoming involved with the French Anarchist movement. He was also a prolific writer and became the second younger person to receive the Noble Price in Literature.

Camus rebellion never found a satisfactory resting place in any man made doctrine. He grew at the time of the Russian Revolution and the vogue of surrealism which he despised. The 'Absurd' had been made fashionable by the Existentialists with whom he socialized in the Parisian 'Cafe the Flore' after the end of the Second World War only to, later own, disavow any intellectual association with them.

Camus philosophical ideas are best expressed in his seminal work 'The Rebel' although they had been expressed in 'the Myth of Sisyphus', 'The Stranger' and 'The Plague'. The quest for meaning in an absurd world is to find it in rebellion, which is an instillation of purpose in one's life. It is clear that he became disenchanted with all the revolutionary ideas circulating in Europe since the second half of the XIX Century and tried to find a reason for it. In 'The Rebel' he is meticulous in his search, dividing his book in three parts: 'Metaphysical Rebellion', 'Historical Rebellion' and 'Rebellion in Art'. After denying that true rebellion could be achieved by embracing a nihilistic or utopian attitudes he concludes that the true rebel should combine a balance between recognition of the relativity of values and a commitment to action, in other words, a world affirming zest rather than a worthless denial, of moderation rather than radicalism.

What can we conclude in this comparative brief cultural analysis of France and Germany? Can we determine if they represent or not different socio-cultural supra-organisms?

We can categorically affirm that as far as language and religion is concern they differ considerably. German and French are completely different tongues with different roots. In religion the Germanic lands were the birth of the Reformation and, until very recently, it was a mottle of Catholic and Protestant regions while France, after the religious wars of the XVI Century and the defeat of the Huguenots, emerged a united country.

In what concern art and architecture these two nations, which shared the same cultural roots, had paralleled evolutions and considerable trans-cultural intercourse among themselves and with the rest of Europe. We have seen the early impact that the Italian Renaissance had in France thanks to the invasions of Italy by Edward VIII, Louis XII and Francis I. But the cultural upheavals of this period finally also reached the Germanic lands in the form of a crop of talented artists, like Durer, Holbein and Lucas Cranach, among others, who portrayed life with the brutal reality sometimes it offers.

The XVII Century saw France becoming culturally supreme, setting the pace in Classicism and the Baroque, while these styles were late to arrive in Germany because of the Thirty Years War and its aftermath. Their works also were mostly imitative of the French masters and, in fact, afterward France never lost the leadership of Europe. The Rococo, Romantic, Neoclassic, and Impressionist Schools followed during the XVIII and XIX centuries, despite the commotions of the French Revolution and the disastrous wars of Louis XIV and Napoleon. Even in the XX Century the schools of Cubism and Expressionism had their origin in France, while in Germany, although the latter had magnificent representatives, their work in general lacked originality. Only in the XX Century, with the groups Die Brucke in Dresden and the Blaue Reiter in Munich, Germany produced artists of great stature. (See Above).

We can conclude therefore that in what refers to art and architecture, after a short efflorescence in Germany during the Renaissance, France set the pace in taste, style and originality, although both countries shared in the same cultural specifications.

In literature the Germans also fell behind the French in the

Renaissance. Not only there were numerous French writers in poetry, prose etc., but the poet Ronsard form the group of the Pleiade for the purpose of polishing and improving the French language to allow the creation of masterpieces rivaling the works of the Classics. These were also the times of Rabelais, Nicolas de Troyes and Bonaventura des Periers.

On the other hand, in the Germanic lands, as we have seen, Renaissance ideas were entrenched in academic institutions and failed to reach the populace. The land, during and after the Reformation, was divided by religion and traveling was difficult, even dangerous.

In the XVII Century in France there was an outpour of literary work in all genders, following the foundation of the 'Academy' during the reign of Louis XIII. Standards of excellence were enacted and ways of perfecting the language were pursued, a preoccupation that, as we saw, had its historical origin with the Pleiade group of the Renaissance. The result of these efforts soon became apparent. This was the golden age of French Literature and also the Theatre, with the dramas of Racine and Corneille as well as the satires of Moliere.

Germany, on the contrary, during the XVII Century, as we saw, was suffering and later recuperating from the effect of the Thirty Years War. The language was slowly maturing and literary activity, although modest in reference to the glory of France during this period, was active, particularly in Poetry but also in Prose.

In the XVIII Century works in all branches of literature continued to be published in France. But these were the times of the Enlightenment and the 'philosophes' political and social ideas monopolized the intellectual ferment of the age.

Germany during this century began to recuperate from the horrors of the previous one and the ideas of the Enlightenment began slowly to percolate. There was an attempt to impose literary rules similar to the French Academy, but the move encountered stiff opposition. Lessing was instrumental in freeing drama from the strong influence of French convention and the 'Sturm und Drang' movement, in opposition to French rationalism, took shape. Finally during this century Germany produce two literary genius of international stature: Goethe and Schiller. The stirring of a new soul was becoming manifest.

In France the XIX began with the aftermath of the Napoleonic wars. This was the age of Romanticism and even in France there was a backlash to Rationalism. The novels became personal portraits of people and situations. Victor Hugo and Dumas wrote then their masterpieces, but the political disappointments of the second part of the century provoked an anti-romantic movement and a longing for the idealistic 'good old time' of the Enlightenment. This situation gave rise to the so-called 'Parnassian School' to which belonged Lecanto, Gautier and Baudelaire. The number of literary schools then proliferated according to new fads. Realism, Naturalism and Symbolism are few notorious examples. One wonders how much this new and flickering mood has to do with the Napoleon III dictatorship and the humiliation of the German invasion that followed.

Germany literary course, during the XIX century, was in many ways similar to the French. Romanticism penetrated the land but its emphasis, due to Napoleon I invasions in the early part of the century, was in patriotic themes. There was also an anti-rationalistic movement exemplified by Schegel who thought literature should treat contemporary themes. After the collapse of Napoleon the peace and censorship imposed in the Germanic lands proved very detrimental to literary activity, which had to endorse the restrictions imposed by the system. Many writers saw their works prohibited, including the great poet Heine.

The subsequent course of literary activity in both countries, predictably, was very much dependent on historical circumstances which conclusively favored the French, which had a golden age of a sort in the XIX Century. The beginning of the XX Century saw in Germany a flowering of the Symbolic school with the works of Rilke, Kafka and Mann, but later in the century the interpenetration of styles and literary subjects defy any classificatory attempt. Unquestionably though, the two world wars and their aftermath, until very recently, had a detrimental effect in German literary production.

Later in the century dizzying advances in communication, printing and technology gave rise to a proliferation of thematic contents and styles in both of these countries (and indeed in the entire civilized world), that defy any classification. In Germany, because it was in the losing side in both world wars, the mood, not surprisingly, for a while turned inward and the authors tried to find refuge and solace in permanent values by creating a style that, for lack of a better term, was called Expressionism.

In conclusion, therefore, France was also a pace-setter in literature with the foundation of groups intended to improve and preserve the French language. Germany lagged behind and reacted against the classicism of its neighbor, as well as, against the 'rigidities' of imposing literary standards, an idea which was foreign to them. It was only with the maturing of the German Language in the XVIII Century that great literary works began to be produced.

In music in the XVII Century, Lully and others were introducing the operatic genre, while the Germanic lands, in the following century, witnessed a true apotheosis with the flowering of talented musicians and composers that had no equals. These were the times of Mozart, Bach and Handel, and when Haydn introduced the sonatas and symphonies in the repertoire of musical genres. The XIX Century was the pinnacle of classic music in France under famous names like Ravel, Debussy and Berlioz, while in Germany Beethoven and Schubert composed their immortal masterpieces. In the XX Century, in both nations, the proliferations of styles and cultural convergences defy any categorization, but no musicians comparable to those of the XVIII and XIX centuries did appear in these lands.

Historically, therefore, the outburst of musical compositional masterpieces happened before in the Germanic lands, where sonatas and symphonies were firstly introduced to the musical repertoire, although ultimately these genres found their way to the rest of Europe.

In philosophy, as we has seen, France was the cradle of modern rationalistic thought in the XVII Century with the works of Descartes, and in the XVIII with the 'philosophes', while the Germanic lands saw the rise of the 'Nature Philosophers', the group inaugurated by Friedrich Schelling and Lorenz Oken, rooted in the repudiation that existed there for the mechanical Universe created by Newton and Descartes, and the conception that inert matter is activated by external forces. Instead they believed that material objects were permeated by an inner force similar to the activity of the mind, a sort of spiritual essence akin to the freedom of the Will. Predecessor of the Nature-Philosophers were the already mentioned mystic Jacob Boehme, with his lucubrations about Man being a self contained microcosm, and Leibniz himself who, as we had seen, expounded the idea of a Cosmos composed of 'windowless monads', individual units that reflected the Universe and were animated by an inner force. In the XIX Century the dialectic of reconciliation of opposites (probably with historical roots in oriental mysticism) so much favored by Germanic thought in the systems of Kant and Hegel was, subsequently, used by Schelling and Oken to outline their conception of the Universe as the end result of an historical development, with Man its final product. Man, therefore, was a complete microcosm because, being this final product, it summed up all the steps of the previous evolution of Nature and the World.

Also in XIX Century Germany rose the influential Idealist movement which was among other things anti-rational, although it had profound echoes from Plato. The different authors, Fichte, Hegel, Schopenhauer and Nietzsche, among others, lacked thematic agreement and in fact often were at odd with each other. What they all agreed upon is in the conception that 'reality' was not a given unelaborated outside entity, and that it had a lot to do with the mind. The political and social repercussions of this movement were enormous, mainly through the works of Karl Marx. In Germany also took shape during the XIX Century the Phenomenological School with Husserl, which begot the Existential movement of the XX Century that, above all, expounded the belief that the freedom and responsibility of Man provided the true meaning for human existence. In this school, for the first time in Central Europe, philosophical thought converged in the works of illustrious representatives both in Germany with Heidegger, Jasper and others and in France with Sartre, Marcel, Merleau-Ponty and Camus.

France and Germany, therefore, from being part of the same Carolingian Empire in the early Middle Ages, commenced to divert culturally when they became politically separated, and by the time of the Renaissance both possessed different languages. In religion Germany was the cradle of the Reformation, and a deeply rooted mystic thought culminated in the ruminations of the Nature-Philosophers. Culturally the French were pace-setters in art, architecture and in literature, while the Germanic lands witnessed the musical apotheosis of the XVIII and XIX Centuries.

Finally in philosophy the French embraced Rationalism while Germany originated the opposite Idealistic and Phenomenological schools of thought, the final indication that we are dealing with different ethos, a manifestation of the individuality of their souls.

But that was not all. In Germany the anti-rationalistic mood got, in the XIX Century, a patriotic overtone. Despite the eventual defeat of Napoleon the ideas of the French Revolution helped to form the conception of the 'nation', a human community joint by a general will and the idea of self-determination with ethnic-linguistic associations. This conceptualized entity was imbued with a sense of manifested destiny and even purpose. Perhaps this explains the Hegelian assertion in his Philosophy of History that Germany was the pinnacle of the historic evolution of a nation-state, or the admonishments of Johann Gottfried von Herder, a disciple of Kant and a participant in the XVIII Century 'Sturm und Drang', against the cultural domination by the French : 'Spew out the ugly slime of the Siene. Speak German' he vociferously implored to his compatriots. Fichte, on the other hand, lamented that a Germanic race, like the Franks, could have forgotten its native linguistic roots. For him and his followers the French had lost their way and betrayed their ethnic and linguistic identity. These Prussian conceptions, as we know all too well, were to bear heavily in subsequent World History, as the Franco-German war of 1870 and the two world wars of the XX Century proved to satiety.

Culturally, linguistically and in religion these two nations presently represent different socio-cultural supra-organisms stemming from the schism of the Carolingian Empire, one of the main branches of Western Christian Civilization. The French, particularly since the reign of the 'Sun King', are generally view to be debonair and worldly people, lovers of elegance, etiquette and the 'good life', while the Germans evolved into an stoic, regimented, militaristic and introspected nation (at least until very recently), evidence that at the present they possess different communal souls.

INDEX